Chez Maxim's

Chez Maxim's

Secrets and Recipes
from the World's Most Famous Restaurant

Presented by
the Countess of Toulouse-Lautrec

McGraw-Hill Book Company, Inc.

New York   Toronto   London

Library of Congress Catalog Card Number : 62-11944
printed in France
16245

Table of Contents

The great Maxim's

The first time I went to Maxim's, it was thanks to the French Navy. This was in 1933. My husband was a young officer aboard the "Jeanne d'Arc", the French naval training ship, and his captain had entrusted him with a mission of the utmost strategic importance: finding a good ship's cook. I had the idea of asking the owner of Maxim's if he might have an assistant cook ready to be called for military service and willing to go to sea. My idea worked perfectly. Maxim's quickly found an apprentice cook who was about to leave for the army. We had him transferred and assigned to the "Jeanne d'Arc" and he indeed proved worthy of Maxim's reputation. The captain was delighted and so was my husband. As for myself, I was overjoyed, because I had finally crossed the threshold of what was the world's most famous but most mysterious restaurant.

For Maxim's, up until about 1930—the year when one might say it underwent a moral face-lifting—was a place where women were seen, but *never* ladies. *Baedeker's Handbook for Paris*, in its 1900 edition, set the matter straight with admirable tact by mentioning Maxim's as "an elegantly fitted-up restaurant, frequented mainly at night, *for gentlemen only*". Of course, this ban only aroused the ladies' curiosity. People said so many things about Maxim's: that Champagne flowed like tap water, gold was flung about by the handful, dukes and princes (and occasionally kings) ruined themselves over beautiful but heartless "*grandes cocottes*". It was the shrine of high living at the turn of the century, the golden age that the French call *La Belle Epoque*. When men talked about it, they put on the conspiratorial faces and ultra-discreet tones which have the gift of driving women mad. I remember overhearing my father and grandfather chuckle heartily together as they whispered the story of an exploit by Maurice Bertrand, who once brought his evening's ration of Champagne to Maxim's in a coffin! We couldn't help being shocked but dying to hear more. Legend has it that before World War I, quite a few authentic society ladies sneaked into Maxim's by a secret staircase, their faces heavily veiled, for a late supper in a private room, "just to see what it was like".

Today, this mystery and intrigue is past and forgotten. Maxim's is no longer an out-of-bounds speak-easy for society women. They can enter the restaurant by the front door; their daughters' debuts are celebrated there. Maxim's is still one of the most sought-after restaurants in Paris, in fact, in the world, but it is now a very respectable place. To be admitted, it is no longer sufficient to possess a great name or fortune (or both, which is even more rare), but one's reputation must also be spotless and one's grooming immaculate. How did this amazing metamorphosis come about? What is the explanation for Maxim's success in these two totally different veins? Ever since that day in 1933, I have been a regular customer at Maxim's and, wanting to unveil this mystery, I have hunted for the secret of this success which seems to break all the rules. And I think I have found it.

tradition

presented by the Countess of Toulouse-Lautrec

It all began with a riot. At the end of the last century, an Italian ice-cream vendor named Imoda set up shop at 3, Rue Royale where the speciality of the house was meat essence ice cream. On July 14, 1890, Bastille Day in France, he had the strange idea of draping his shop with German flags. Indignant Parisians boycotted his business. Soon afterwards, Imoda was forced to sell out. His property was bought by a certain Maxime Gaillard who was working at Reynold's, a bar at 23, Rue Royale, and who was determined to go into business for himself. What does a man do when he has lots of ambition and very little money? He borrows. Maxime Gaillard was able to raise the necessary money with the help of the neighborhood butcher and wine dealer, and a Champagne salesman. On April 11, 1893, he signed a lease stipulating that he was to "live peacefully and cleanly, without causing any disturbance in the rented quarters!" On May 21 of the same year, after spending nearly $20,000 on redecoration, he opened the doors of Maxim's to the public.

But the public did not come running. Only hansom-cab drivers seemed to patronize his establishment. Business was so bad that on New Year's Day of 1894 his debts amounted to nearly $40,000. He was headed straight for bankruptcy when that desperately needed miracle suddenly occurred.

The miracle turned up in the form of Arnold de Contades, one of the better-known playboys of the day. With his close friend Irma de Montigny, a beautiful and celebrated gold digger, Contades walked into Maxim's one evening for a glass of beer. The place appealed to him, he promised to return with some of his friends, and he kept his promise. In a few weeks, by one of those unfathomable epidemics whose secret is sacred to snobdom, Maxim's had become the meeting-place for Paris's "gilded youth". Maxime Gaillard had succeeded. With barely the time to celebrate, he died on January 26, 1895, leaving his business to Cornuché, his loyal Maître d'Hôtel. The restaurant's accounts coldly record the phases of the illness which took his life: "January 4, 1 bathrobe, 25 francs; January 9, 1 rubber cushion, 22 francs; January 24, life insurance premium, 1,164.30 francs; January 29, funeral, 40 francs." Poor Maxime Gaillard.

But, as the French used to say under the Old Regime, "Maxime is dead, long live Maxim's". Under Cornuché's skillful management, the restaurant continued to enjoy an unbelievable popularity. All the celebrities of France, and soon of Europe and even America, became steady customers at Maxim's. The greatest names, the largest fortunes, the most famous figures in the arts, business, and sports congregated here to work off their excess zest for good living.

Among the steady customers of Maxim's from 1895 to 1914 were the Comte de Montesquiou, Prince Murat, Prince Henri d'Orléans, and Comte Boni de Castellane (who married Anna Gould); Max Lebaudy (known as "the little sugar bowl" because he made his tremendous fortune in sugar);

Gordon Bennett, the publisher of the "New York Herald Tribune"; Sem, the cartoonist; and even Marcel Proust. Not to mention those Russian Grand Dukes who landed at Maxim's around 1900 and whose lavishness, gaiety, and quenchless thirsts made them full-fledged customers immediately. Then too, there was a cohort of kings—Edward VII of England, Oscar of Sweden, George of Greece, and Alphonse XIII of Spain—who, every time they visited Paris, stretched the rules of protocol to go incognito to Maxim's where everyone pretended not to notice them. "It's marvellous", Edward VII remarked one day; "Here, everyone knows me but no one notices me".

What did they find in this magic spot? I've often asked myself this question. Seated at my table—which was formerly King Edward VII's—I have stared wonderingly at the decoration of Maxim's which has not

Entrance to the world's most famous restaurant.

changed since Cornuché had it done over in 1900 for the Paris World's Fair: the tall mirrors framed by mahogany whorls, the red velvet seats, the comfortable but discreet nudes on the walls, and the vari-colored ceiling of the main room. And, since I believe that places have a memory, I have tried to grasp what the revelers of *La Belle Epoque* found at Maxim's.

They did not come just for amusement—a word that no longer has much significance. No, they came to prove to everyone else—and most of all to themselves—that they were rich and powerful, and that the world was theirs for the asking. To nourish this ideal night after night, they invented every form of amusing and conspicuous gaiety within the range of their money and imaginations. For, admission to Maxim's was not enough; there was the additional consecration of being considered the most snobbish of the snobs.

In this respect, wealth—or the art of throwing it away—was a very powerful argument. One day, Grand Duke Serge offered beautiful Augustine a dozen oysters, each of which contained a pearl worth $2,000. Gordon Bennett was in the habit of paying 25 gold louis—the equivalent of $250 today—for a bouquet of violets. Another American, the wealthy Mr. Todd, amused himself one evening by showering some $80,000 worth of gold coins on the floor at Maxim's and watching the "little girls" scuttle to pick them up. In 1932, when the restaurant's seats were taken out and replaced, the stupefied workers discovered hundreds of gold louis which had slipped unnoticed from the pockets of merrymakers thirty years earlier.

A quick wit was another form of wealth greatly admired. Before World War I, Maxim's registered a startling turnover of smart quips, always funny, often cruel, and in most cases difficult to translate. Some of the steady customers were professionals at this game, wielding barbed remarks the way duelists once wielded swords. It was Boni de Castellane who proclaimed: "Society women are born shocked, but once emancipated they kick their heels higher than the rest". It was also he who declared: "Virtue is the mediocre attribute of women who have never had a favorable opportunity to lose it."

After midnight, once all were high on Champagne, there were no limits to the whims of a crowd at Maxim's. Maurice Bertrand, who was leaving the place one morning at dawn after a wild night, decided to hire a city bus. He put on a conductor's uniform and drove a load of first stupefied and then delighted Parisians from Passy to the heart of the city by a route no bus had ever taken before. Jules Ravaud once borrowed a vegetable cart from a peddler and, garbed in evening clothes and a high silk hat, got between

The Countess of Toulouse-Lautrec and Louis Vaudable.

the shafts and walked up the Champs-Elysées, selling carrots and cabbages to the passers-by. He then returned the cart to the old woman along with the proceeds of his sales. As for Gordon Bennett, he held a banquet for some friends at Maxim's where a luscious nude was served for dessert.

Women were the perfect foil to display the money and wit of Maxim's customers. And that was the function of the famous "*grandes cocottes*". Who were they? Today, their race has died out. They were neither "kept women" nor prostitutes. They were more like what we imagine *geishas* to be. On general principles, they had to be pretty, but wit was important as well. Their manners were good, they knew everything about the art of receiving, and they knew even more about the art of throwing money away. Being loved by one of these amazing creatures assured a man's place in society. Ruining himself for one of their smiles automatically meant glory... a fickle, precarious glory, but one which men fought for. Alas, men have always been fools!

Paulette : never a check; never a coat mislaid.

The most famous of these "*demi-mondaines*", as they were called, were queens in their own right and exerted absolute power over a court of admirers. They were naturally the fiercest of rivals. Extraordinary jewels and celebrated lovers were their status symbols. And Maxim's was the chosen place where they appeared nearly every night, to make sure that their stock market quotations did not drop.

"La Belle Otéro" was probably the most remarkable of these "institutions". She enjoyed the favors of the Prince of Wales—the future Edward VI—and Grand Duke Peter of Russia; in fact, at one time or another she was the mistress of nearly all the crowned heads of Europe. Even Wilhelm II of Germany was not immune to her charms. The terrible Kaiser who was to drench the world in fire and blood with World War I used to call Otéro "my little savage" and even wrote a pantomime for her! One day, however, she decided to settle down to a steady lover, the famous Baron Ollstreder. The reason for her choice? "He's the ugliest of them all", she replied. She neglected to mention that he was also the richest by far. Ollstreder's fabulous fortune had resisted all the fluctuations of international high finance, but his heart sank when he saw the rate at which Otéro could do away with his millions. After showering her with country estates, carriages, furs, and an astonishing collection of jewelry —including the diamond *rivière* once owned by Marie Antoinette—he saw to his dismay that she wanted still more and he gave up the cause. Otéro was in control of every situation. Once a noted explorer named Payen offered her $8,000 to spend one night with him. Disdainfully she refused. His only recourse was suicide.

Emilienne d'Alençon was the favorite of King Leopold of Belgium. Originally a vaudeville artist, she started out in her career by presenting a trained-rabbit act at a circus. She regularly brought her rabbits—dyed pink and wearing paper collars—to Maxim's, where she turned them over to Ursule, the lady in charge of the washrooms.

As for Liane de Pougy, Otéro's most formidable rival, she had her jeweler follow her everywhere so that the necessary would always be at the immediate disposal of an expansive admirer.

One evening, Otéro decided to settle the score with Liane de Pougy. She decked herself out in all the jewelry in her possession—and Heaven knows, it was almost unlimited!—and made her entrance at Maxim's literally dripping with diamonds, pearls, rubies, sapphires and emeralds. Eye-witnesses later attested that so dazzling was the glitter, no one could look at her for more than a few seconds! Otéro was triumphant... until her "victim" Liane de Pougy, secretly warned, sailed through the door. Dressed in a classically simple white dress with no ornamentation, not a jewel in sight, she was trailed by her maid wearing necklaces, pendants and *rivières*, cabochons, earrings and a diadem—Liane's full collection of jewelry!

Practically all of the "*grandes cocottes*" have vanished, as have the lesser "*cocottes*", who waited quietly every evening at Maxim's until they found a companion. In a way, these latter were part of the restaurant's menu. Steady customers used to call them the "*plats du jour*" (daily specials). Hugo, the Maître d'Hôtel at Maxim's in the 1900's, tells in his memoirs of how he used to inform a "*plat du jour*" that she had been "noticed" by discreetly touching a wart on his cheek with his index finger. Who knows how many tumultuous and ephemeral love affairs were launched by Hugo's wart!

But *this* Maxim's is a thing of the past.

The miracle is that another Maxim's, radically different, but just as brilliant, has risen from the ashes of this glorious past, like the phœnix, a bird of greater beauty at each rebirth. This resurrection took place in 1934 and is indissolubly linked to the arrival of the world's most famous Maître d'Hôtel: Albert.

What happened between the turn of the century and the appearance of Albert? Nothing but a long and painful intermission. World War I, in wiping out an entire society and its concept of the fine art of living, dealt a mortal blow to the old Maxim's. At the end of the war, new customers crossed the threshold at 3, Rue Royale and tried to enjoy life in the same old way. But gradually and inevitably the tone was changing, the atmosphere becoming heavier. Maxim's was on its way to becoming a caricature of Maxim's. This was naturally reflected in its receipts. Things became so bad that in 1930 the British company which owned the restaurant (having bought it from Cornuché in 1907) decided to get rid of their white elephant.

But Maxim's had fallen so low that for many long months not an offer was made. It was not until 1931 that a buyer appeared: Octave Vaudable, the father of the present owner of Maxim's, Louis Vaudable; and he dared to attempt what no other would dare: the resurrection of the ghost of Maxim's. True, he was already the owner of Larue, another great restaurant. He was therefore no novice. And to succeed in this seemingly hopeless venture, he was armed with two secret weapons: the unrivaled quality of his wines and the presence of Albert.

I knew Albert well. For years, I watched him preside over the entrance to the main room at Maxim's. Impassive and solemnly penguin-like, he turned his cold blue eyes upon newcomers and identified every face with a name drawn from the recesses of his infallible memory. I would not go so far as to say we were friends. Albert had no friends. All he had were connections, but he had them all, from the Aga Khan to the Duke of Windsor, not to mention the innumerable duchesses, film stars, and millionaires on his roster. In a few words, I would say that Albert's success in his career and in the comeback of Maxim's was based on his art of snobbing the snobs.

No, Albert was not the type of spineless Maître d'Hôtel with which we are all familiar. Imbued with the grandeur of his mission, he obliged his customers to submit to the terrifically strict laws of a tradition of which he knew himself to be one of the last ramparts. For Maxim's, Albert was far more than a Maître d'Hôtel; he was a court official of infallible judgement, instinctively assigning everyone to his proper place. All Paris society begged for the consecration of this man whose job was the service of others. A great lawyer once said: "I knew that I had succeeded in life the day that Albert called me by name".

When Albert accepted Vaudable's offer, it was on certain conditions. He had already had a brilliant career, having launched other nightclubs in Paris, Le Touquet, and Deauville. He told his new employer that he would give himself a year—not a day more—to pull Maxim's from its rut. It was not Maxim's giving Albert a trial but Albert condescending to give Maxim's a chance to be worthy of his own genius. One month later, Vaudable was turning people away at the door. By the end of the year, Maxim's was once more *the* place to be seen.

How did Albert work this miracle? By terror and austerity. Mercilessly ridding Maxim's of its clientele of the lean post-war years, he cut out all offshoots of a past he deemed dishonorable. Having dinner at Maxim's became a difficult undertaking reserved for an elite and select handful. Anyone unable to really justify his presence in the restaurant found himself up against Albert's cool, haughty courtesy, and once was enough. At the same time, Albert laid down some iron rules of discipline for the staff: flawless service, perfect courtesy, and discreet efficiency. Those unable to conform to his methods were fired without hesitation.

Until his retirement in 1959, which was followed almost at once by his death, Albert remained the symbol of Maxim's newly-regained prestige. He deserved all the more credit for this, for in the meantime a new war had been fought and a new upheaval in social values wrought. During the four-year German occupation of Paris, Maxim's was a shadow of its old self, with menus reduced to a rationed minimum. The restaurant was under the control of a German commissioner who fortunately was liberal and easy-going, and the officers of the Wehrmacht took a great liking to Maxim's atmosphere and especially to Maxim's wines. This reached such proportions that Louis Vaudable was beside himself, seeing his cellars thus pillaged by barbarians (who began their meals with dessert wines!). Night after night, he broke into his own cellar, loaded 30,000 of his most cherished bottles on four trucks, and transported them to a safe hiding-place in Burgundy. The commissioner was kind enough to feign ignorance of the whole affair.

Once the war was over, Maxim's had to start again from scratch. Albert, now over sixty, was devoted to his job to the point of participating as fully in this even more brilliant resurrection as he had in the first. Once again, one hundred people were convinced every night that they had the best table in the house and, once again, one hundred people were socially classed without error. I have never forgotten our joy upon returning to Maxim's in 1946 and finding Albert at his post, as haughty as ever.

Dear Albert! We really owe him a great deal. Reviving Maxim's was his way of reviving a certain form of civilization. As Marcel Proust said, "Great headwaiters are the only true preservers of social customs".

The other evening, over an appropriate dish, a *Sole Albert*, I was evoking these memories of a bygone Maxim's with the representative of the present Maxim's, Louis Vaudable. I like Louis Vaudable, first because he is quiet and, naturally talkative myself, I appreciate his eloquent silence. Then too, he never lacks that touch of fantasy without which life would be unbearable. Finally, he is both a gastronome and one of the best wine connoisseurs in France.

When I asked Louis Vaudable to define the style of Maxim's 1962 as compared to that of Maxim's 1900, his reply was the following: "The style has changed, it's true, but today, as in the past, Maxim's remains one of the few places in the world where generations of people have never stopped being happy and their happiness is in the walls, the mirrors which reflect your image, the very air and atmosphere of Maxim's.

"Maxim's is like a private mansion where an introduction is necessary before entering. Once introduced, you are a guest and you can expect the softest, the most personal, and if you so desire the most extravagant treatment.

"Because of the private character of Maxim's, the food and service should not be mentioned. Observations of this sort would be quite out of place. But, for this to be possible, everything must be beyond reproach. To achieve this perfection, several conditions must be observed. To begin with, the quality of the ingredients must be closely controlled." For years, Louis Vaudable got up at four in the morning to go to market himself at the *Halles* in Paris. Today it is the job of an assistant he trained himself. Says Vaudable: "Always create competition between suppliers. They are

The famous Albert.

all eager to serve Maxim's. It is like an appointment to a Royal Court. All that we can, we buy directly from the provinces—butter, cheese, poultry—so that there can be no doubt about their origins.

"Then comes the cooking. This is the responsibility of Alex Humbert and his 20 assistants. Humbert is not merely a great cook, he is an artist, a kind of Van Gogh, bursting with creativity and imagination. That is why Maxim's regularly organizes dinners for the *Club des Cent* and other gastronomic groups, where new dishes can be tested.

"From top to bottom", said Louis Vaudable, "you have to make the personnel conscious of their function and the part they play in the 'Managing Family'. When one of them leaves Maxim's it is to retire. New recruits either realize immediately that they can never fit into our style, or they spend their entire career with us. They feel they belong to the aristocracy in their field." This is especially true in the case of Roger, Albert's disciple and worthy successor. He already has the experience and knowledge that gives him that "sixth sense" when greeting a guest. This is also a fact with Edouard Pommier, the steward in charge of the 200,000 bottles of 842 different wines and vintages, from the year 1870 on up. "I must confess", adds Louis Vaudable, "that wine is my hobby. I know no greater pleasure than hunting for good wines among the producers."

It is true that Louis Vaudable selected a Maxim's Champagne which for the 1952 vintage won a third prize behind Moët and Bollinger in a blind taste test. Since then, Maxim's Champagne and Maxim's Wines are sold all over the world and especially in the United States.

Louis Vaudable graduated from a business college at the age of 21, spent three years as a trainee in different kitchens, and then two years at every level of the biggest hotels in Berlin, Saint Moritz, London, Prague and New York. He is not only an enthusiastic *restaurateur*, he is also a shrewd businessman. One result: in 1950 he convinced Pan American Airlines to serve Maxim's meals on their flights, and this is still going strong.

As our conversation was drawing to a close, the Duke and Duchess of Windsor entered the room and sat down at their table. Roger presented no menu, asked them nothing, and sent the order to Mr. Humbert. "How

Two of Humbert's twenty assistants.

Exchanging recipes with Alex Humbert.

could he guess so accurately?" I asked. "A question of practice; just looking at how the Duchess lowers her eyelids." Roger gave us the answer... a medium-rare woodcock, a spinach soufflé and Brie cheese on a straw-covered platter, accompanied by a bottle of Dom Perignon. In another corner, Liz Taylor was discreetly leaving her table with her escort but no one made any sign of having noticed her presence. A few tables away, Onassis, the famous Greek shipowner, and Paul Getty, the richest man in the world, were dining quietly together, perhaps discussing the best way to catch crawfish in the Scottish brooks. In another corner, Maurice Carrère was entertaining Bernard Buffet and Marlene Dietrich. In the background rang out young voices from the party given by Madame Vaudable to welcome the girls of L'Académie Maxim's, known today as L'Académie, a creation of Madame Vaudable's where girls from all corners of the globe—and particularly from the United States—are initiated into the subtleties of French culture and the art of being a perfect hostess. Madame Vaudable and Maurice Carrère devote themselves to the young at Maxim's, organizing special dinners and parties for them. Yes, all of this contributes to Maxim's popularity.

But I think there is another way of putting it, another word for the key to this mystery. It is a beautiful word that holds the secret to all perfection. My personal conviction is that Maxim's has a Soul.

The Art of Perfect

No act is more human or satisfying than an act of hospitality. To invite a friend into his home and to his table is one of civilized man's highest privileges; even an enmity, by tradition, is suspended at the threshold. And, it goes without saying that we assume entire responsibility for our guest's comfort and happiness for as long a time as he is under our roof.

We French recognize, of course, that a basic code of hospitality is respected by civilized men and women throughout the world, but we like to believe that we have a special genius for its interpretation. Throughout our history we have cultivated the social arts, and our receptions, while allowing for a maximum of fantasy and imagination, are built upon the solid foundations of a *cuisine* which is acknowledged to be the finest in the world, a roster of excellent wines, and an etiquette which is at once specific and flexible. We try to make life as agreeable as possible for those with whom we come in contact and, if there is no conflict of aims, for ourselves as well.

Moreover, we prefer our own expression "to receive" to that of current Anglo-Saxon usage "to entertain". Naturally, when we have greeted our guests and made them as comfortable as we can, when we have shared with them our most carefully prepared *cuisine* and choicest wines, we hope to be able to divert and amuse them as well, for brilliant conversation and tasteful gaiety are a notable part of our tradition. But the idea of "entertaining" is not broad enough; to "receive" is far better, for it means that we admit our guest and more, that we take him to ourselves, that his interests and needs become and are felt as keenly as our own.

The kind of hospitality we have in mind is never—indeed cannot ever be—forced. It is offered out of a sense of abundance and well-being and has but one aim: to give our guests the maximum of pleasure. It is the spirit that reigns in all of our receptions, from the intimate, closed, family celebrations of christenings and first communions, to the brilliant late evening dinners or the gala receptions of heads of foreign states in the halls of Versailles.

Moreover, if you have read the French newspapers you have seen how the menu and setting of an official dinner is described in almost as much detail as the political implications of the occasion.

This latter tradition of the sumptuous formal dinner is still alive in the great homes of France. No other social gathering can ever completely equal it. It is the time when men in evening dress stand like punctuation marks among women whose gowns bear the labels of our *grands couturiers* and whose jewels reflect the candles which light the festive table. The table itself is mounted like an exquisite piece of jewelry, with sparkling crystal, the sheen of damask, the soft gleam of silver, and a profusion of fresh flowers, attended by a staff of servants magically present when

Entertaining

needed and discreetly absent when not. On such an evening, one of the following menus might be served:

Consommé aux Cerises	Potage Germiny
Homard à la Nage	Brochet au Vin Blanc
Canard aux Pêches	Selle Maria Callas
Asperges à la Crème	Pommes Maxim's
Salade	Salade
Fromages	Fromages
Poires Belle Hélène	Crêpes Madame de...

More often, of course, the small intimate dinner is offered. One or two guests, and never more than six or eight, are invited, and the service is assured by the regular personnel of the household. This is a very pleasant way to receive, for the host and hostess are freed from many of the problems of organization which the important formal dinner imposes and they are thus at greater liberty to enjoy their guests. This is the moment to serve those excellent dishes which we call *Cuisine Bourgeoise*, or home cooking—a simple unpretentious *cuisine*, distinguished, however, by the excellence of its ingredients and its painstaking preparation. For example :

Potage Crème d'Artichauts	Moules à la Marinière
Steack au Poivre	Tournedos Henri IV
Pommes de Terre Vapeur	Pommes de Terre Frites
Salade	Haricots Verts à la Française
Crème Marbrée au Caramel	Quartiers d'Orange au Cointreau

It is still feasible in France to receive at a week-day luncheon, but it is preferable that the luncheon menu be a rather light one. For example:

Tarte aux Oignons	Croûte aux Champignons
Ris de Veau aux Petits Pois	Côtelettes de Veau Chasseur
Salade Verte	Salade au Lard
Fromages	Fromages
Fruits rafraîchis	Framboises à l'Orange

Many a French hostess has made her reputation with her ingenious after-theater suppers. The menu should be short and simple, as the hour is already advanced and no one wants to stay up until dawn. In winter it is nice to start with a hot soup: a *Soupe à l'Oignon* or a *Consommé au Foie Gras*. In summer a cold *Germiny* or *Consommé aux Piments* would be more appropriate. This should be followed by a cold dish prepared ahead of time: *Filet de Bœuf en Croûte*, *Dindonneau en Daube Froid*, or *Chaud-Froid de Volaille*. Finally, a light dessert: *Framboises à l'Orange* or *Poires Bourdaloue*.

On three occasions in France—christenings, first communions, and weddings—the table literally groans under the best the family can provide. Ordinarily thrifty, the French housewife throws caution to the winds and orders staggering quantities of *foie gras* and truffles. Eggs are not counted nor is the rich cream spared in the preparation of the ceremonial cake.

A French wedding luncheon, as you will see, has a longer and more elaborate menu than even a gala dinner:

> Foie Gras en Gelée
> Brochet au Vin Blanc
> Poulet à l'Estragon
> Petits Pois à la Française
> Cœurs de Laitue en Salade
> Poires Belle Hélène
> Gâteau de Mariage
> Fruits

If you have the good fortune to be extremely close to a French family, you may be invited to the son's or daughter's first communion. The communicant, if it is the son, will be angelic beyond all recognition in an Eton jacket and his first long trousers, with the traditional white satin communion sash tied in a huge bow on his left arm; if it is the daughter, she will wear an innocent long white organdy dress and veil which seem to foreshadow her wedding gown. On this day of days, the French child steps forward from his usual last place in the order of things and presides over the table of relatives, god-parents and a very few of the most intimate family friends.

For the first communion, the table linen, flowers, and candles are white; white or the palest pastels are used for the luncheon which brings together the families, god-parents and the priest after a christening. At the end of this latter type of celebration, there are coffee and liqueurs as well as the traditional *dragées*, or sugared almonds.

Some of you may have seen Jean Renoir's film, *Le Déjeuner sur l'Herbe*, and must wonder whether or not it exaggerated the French *pique-nique*. It would be more exact to say that this was a parody of the extremes to which French picnicking could go, aided and abetted by an over-fanciful imagination. However the French picnic has little in common with the hearty, open air, plain-eating variety common in America, or its barbecue variation.

But the two extremes are possible. It can be as simple as a loaf of French bread with a slice of ham and a bottle of *vin ordinaire*; or, it can be a complete and elaborate cold meal, accompanied by appropriate wines kept at their proper serving temperatures, and served elegantly in some suitably rustic spot on a folding table surrounded by folding chairs, or on a fine tablecloth spread out on the grass. The first act of an intrepid French mountain climber when he attained the summit of Mont-Blanc was to calmly spread out just such a picnic for himself, not forgetting the *Foie Gras en Aspic!* For the English or American hostess who would like to surprise and delight her picnic guests by the refinement of her menu, we propose the following:

> Saucisson, Radis Roses, Beurre
> Truites en Gelée de Rubis
> Rôti de Porc Frais
> Salade aux Raisins
> Fromage de Gruyère
> Fruits

But whatever the occasion or character of reception, gala dinner, or *déjeuner sur l'herbe*, the secret of its success is in the planning. It must

Whatever the season, bring a breath of springtime to your table. (Flowers by Fioralie, Lace from A la Ville du Puy, Crystal by Baccarat)

be planned well in advance and so carefully that it appears not to have been planned at all.

Invitations in France go out at least ten days before an important dinner. For informal occasions, it is entirely acceptable to telephone an invitation, but in this case it is customary to send out a little reminder card *(carte-mémoire)* to the invited guests.

For these important occasions the mistress of the household is transformed into the feminine counterpart of a field marshal planning a campaign. No detail is too trivial to command her attention. She will recall, in planning her menu, that the delights of the table begin with the sense of sight, and she will never be caught in the pitfall of serving a menu composed of cream of chicken soup, steamed fish fillets, boiled potatoes with drawn butter, and vanilla ice cream! No matter how delightful each individual dish, the most indifferent eater could hardly face such a bland, colorless meal. Nor will she go to the opposite extreme and add artificial coloring to foods; the poisonous greens and purples of bottled coloring matters are strictly taboo in French *cuisine*, and a French cook will rarely go beyond adding a drop of caramel to the golden brown of a sauce. But, whenever possible, she will be alive to the possibilities of natural nuances. The thin slice of ripe red tomato molded into the amber jelly of an *Œuf en Gelée*, for example, is as necessary to delight the eye as the palate.

She will alternate textures as well as colors, and will remember that the dessert is an integral part of the meal. If the first and main courses are light, she will serve a rich chocolate cream or a chestnut cake for dessert; if heavy, she will end the dinner with a frothy fruit *mousse* or refreshing sherbet.

The menu completed, she brings the host into the strategy; it is his mission to look over the wine-cellar and help her choose wines in perfect harmony with the menu.

Flowers, cigarettes and liqueurs must be readied. The linen must be examined, the china and glassware accounted for, the silver polished, and the personnel thoroughly briefed. And then comes the moment for the hostess to calmly unlearn her role of strategist, as an actress unlearns a part which has absorbed her on the stage. She will spend several hours alone with herself, resting, dressing, and getting in the mood to enjoy her own party—in a phrase, to be her own guest.

The first guests arrive, never precisely on the dot, but never more than fifteen minutes late. The host and hostess rise and welcome each new arrival, and the hostess introduces him or her to the guests already assembled.

The dining-room door opens: "Madame est servie".

If it is a large dinner, a butler will stand at the entrance with a seating chart to help each guest find his or her place with a minimum of confusion. For six or eight guests, place cards may be used. Places of honor are at the right and left of the host and hostess, and everyone waits to sit down until the hostess has been seated.

Soup, if it is the first course, is served before the guests are seated and the hostess gives the signal to begin when she lifts her spoon. Water, too, is already on the table in large glasses, and the wine has been decanted if necessary.

The servant removes simultaneously the soup plates and the large plates beneath them and replaces them with other plates immediately. The ladies at the table are served first, beginning with the guest of honor at the right of the host and ending with the hostess; then the male guest of honor is served, the other men at the table, and finally the host.

In France, salad is normally served in a small crescent-shaped crystal bowl or salad plate placed to the left of the dinner plate. It is passed only once, either with or after the meat course, and is eaten with the fork and the fork only. Cheese is a separate course and is never served with the salad.

The French gourmet has little charity for the habit of smoking between courses, for it not only dulls the palate but the smoke masks the aroma of well-prepared food for everyone present, smokers and non-smokers alike.

Smoking is allowed only after the last red wine, and then only if ash trays are placed on the table.

After dinner, liqueurs are served with coffee in the salon. A good trio to choose: Cognac or Armagnac brandy, a distilled Kirsch or plum brandy, and a sweet liqueur. The brandies are served in large snifters and the fruit liqueurs in small glasses which have been chilled beforehand.

All of this is tradition which must of course be observed. But tradition alone does not make a lively, successful dinner party. The following is a commentary by Maggie Vaudable which gives some insight into the personal ideas of a vivacious and imaginative Parisian hostess.

"When all is said and done, the most important thing to me about a dinner party is the company.

"There is no table so elegant, no banquet so splendid, no fare so sumptuous that they can replace the one remaining luxury of our age: conversation.

"I remember a dinner I gave a few years ago in honor of a brilliant American lawyer. We had invited a few prominent Parisians, and among them Louise de Vilmorin, who stood out like a rare and exquisite flower. As he took his leave, the guest of honor paid me the usual compliments and then, recalling some of the sallies exchanged during dinner, he said with a glow: 'And... the conversation...'

"However, one must be careful not to overdo it. It is preferable not to have too many brilliant conversationalists at one table.

"Once, when Jean Giono happened to be in Paris, we were fortunate enough to have him as our guest, together with our Palais Royal neighbors, Colette and Jean Cocteau, and, very exceptionally, Henry de Montherlant. It was an extraordinary combination, but Giono monopolized the conversation. He talked a blue streak with such rugged, impetuous eloquence that there was simply no stopping him, and I am afraid that none of our guests enjoyed the evening as much as they might have.

"One should be as careful blending one's guests as one is in mixing a cocktail.

"Two good conversationalists are better than one; between them they keep the ball rolling. Then, too, there should be a special attraction, someone who is currently in the news or some rare out-of-towner.

"As in Greek tragedy, there must be a chorus around the protagonists. Of course, it is easy to fill in with people who know one another, but this is likely to become a bit cliquish, with conversations seemingly obscure to an outsider.

"If the party is confined to six or eight guests, it is easy to warm the atmosphere. It is with larger numbers that the very careful mixing of groups becomes necessary. Quick and relaxed table conversation is the reward of thoughtful planning. The effort and strain are over and the hostess can finally relax a bit herself, although it is of course up to her to avoid pitfalls and introduce subjects which will give all her guests a chance to say something.

"To go behind the scenes for a moment, there are the preparations. I am one of those fortunate women who never have palpitations over the cooking. In the first place, it is not my department. Most hostesses let their husbands choose the wines, and since mine is more expert than I in both food and wine, I leave all the decisions up to him. I may offer a few suggestions, but in the final analysis it is he who makes out the menu.

"My chief responsibility is the flowers. The size of the party determines my decorative scheme. When we have six or eight guests, I like to decorate the table with three Bohemian glasses of spring flowers (especially in winter!) or a small silver bowl with, on either side, an antique mug filled with anemones, hyacinths or freesias. Although I am very fond of narcissuses and other extremely fragrant flowers, I refrain from putting them on the table. Their perfume would interfere with the appreciation of the food and wine. For more formal dinners, I like to have silver candelabra decorated with fresh cut flowers or a combination of small fruits and flowers (grapes, for example).

"In a large house, there is nothing so lovely as immense bouquets of long-stemmed flowers in vases on the floor. But when dimensions are smaller, it is wiser to forego flowers in great quantities. In my appartment, I like to have one large bouquet made up of three or four different kinds of flowers and several small bouquets in glasses or silver bowls to provide additional spots of color.

"Like everyone else, I like candles on the dinner table, on other tables, in sconces, and just about everywhere. And as I can never resist the temptation to light a fire in the fireplace, we cool off the rooms until dinner-time so that the party will not end up like a Turkish bath.

"My husband and I have done away with cocktails before dinner. We prefer to serve whisky and of course Champagne, which produces a gay light-hearted atmosphere. We also serve old Port and Sherry. When we are entertaining connoisseurs, my husband likes to serve them a rare, well-chilled Sauternes (a Château, of course!). It always surprises people who have nothing but contempt for this sort of wine because they have drunk it the wrong way at the wrong time. After dinner, towards the end of the evening, Champagne is pleasant and there are always partisans of whisky. But I think that fresh fruit juices (plain, or mixed with Champagne) are the most refreshing way to end an evening. A delicious mixture can be made with the syrup of canned raspberries, pineapple juice, freshly squeezed orange juice, and that dash of lemon juice which is essential.

"For several years now, the question of parking has been one of our major problems. Anyone unlucky enough not to have parking space and who, like ourselves, lives on a street lined with parked cars twenty-four hours a day, should relieve their guests of their parking worries. Our solution is to have a chauffeur at the door who takes each car, parks it, and goes and gets it at the end of the evening. One chauffeur is enough for as many as twelve guests (if you telephone your closest friends and have them stagger their arrivals)."

Every now and then a host or hostess might want to receive his friends or business acquaintances in a restaurant. The arrival of friends in the city may coincide disastrously with the cook's illness or the redecoration of the dining-room, for even the best organized of households is not immune to domestic crises. A restaurant is likewise the solution for the traveler living in a hotel, who desires to return hospitality, or for the resident of a city who wishes to introduce friends from out-of-town or abroad to its amenities. Restaurant reception is also ideal for those occasions when guests come from diverse backgrounds or cultures, or when difficulties of language, for example, might create disconcerting holes in the conversation

The warm play of lights and shadows in a centerpiece worthy of an old Dutch Master.

around the dinner table in a private home. The coming and going of other diners, the saving grace of music, and the opportunity to dance may come to the rescue of many a flagging conversation.

A restaurant can be much more than a mere solution for emergencies however. While certain occasions of a particularly familial nature are meant to be celebrated in the intimacy and privacy of the home, others gain immeasurably from moving out into the semi-public atmosphere of a restaurant. Celebrations of success, for example, belong there: the publication of a novel or the first night of a play, a reunion to wish *bon voyage* to a lucky traveler, all are outward, expansive, and social expressions of joy and well-being. The special atmosphere of a smart restaurant has the paradoxical effect of strengthening the lines of intimacy among members of a party while bearing their joyous mood out to meet and blend with the general gaiety.

Excellence of *cuisine* and cellar, distinction of service, refinement of atmosphere, and originality determine the choice of a restaurant, and the nature of the gathering will decide whether a luncheon or dinner is given.

For a particularly elegant occasion, the faultless finesse of tradition. (Coll. Bensimon)

As a rule, any event that is more business than pleasure will be held at mid-day, for it is almost a law that the serious discussion of business and politics be banished from the dinner table.

The host in the restaurant should be moved by the same considerations and bound by the same rules of hospitality as when receiving in his own home. If he is known in the restaurant, he will telephone several days in advance to inform the manager of the date and size of his party and, discreetly, the identification of its members. If they are to be six or more, he will ask the director to propose a menu, suggest wines, and perhaps arrange for special floral decorations and music.

If the party is more friendly than formal, the dinner should be in one of the restaurant's public rooms. If, on the contrary, it is of a more formal nature, the host should book a private dining-room. In both cases, the host should somehow add his own personal touch—his own special cigars, for instance or, for the private room, a centerpiece brought from his own dining-room.

When one hires a private dining-room, should one have music or not? Above all, avoid the type of ridiculous trio that pours out a continual flood of music. If it seems appropriate, hire an accordionist, or get the most famous tzigane soloist flown over from Vienna if you can afford it.

A party in one of the public rooms should not exceed twelve (never plan a party of fourteen; you risk a missing guest leaving you with thirteen). If there are more than twelve it should be in a private room with several tables—a good number for a table is eight, or nine if the guests are not exactly in couples.

If you do not know the director of the restaurant, try and find a friend who can introduce you. A good restaurant is like a club; regular patrons are like members, new patrons must be introduced and initiated. If you are new, it is in your interest to go in person to get the arrangements under way. Personal contact under these circumstances is very important.

Much has been said about the reception at Maxim's, both compliments and complaints. But when there are complaints, it is because people have not abided by the rule. What is the rule? The rule is to present one's credentials and this can be done in several ways: by being brought for the first time by someone who is known at Maxim's, by finding Maxim's banker and getting a good word from him, by simply coming with Brigitte Bardot...

Louis Vaudable himself tells the following story: "A business friend from abroad once came to Maxim's with a group of friends and neglected to call me. It was in August, a bad time for glamor or good service everywhere. He was very disappointed with his reception. I hastened to make amends and a few days later arranged a special dinner party for him and his friends. We were eighteen. When he left Maxim's, he turned to me and said: 'Now I know that to be well treated at Maxim's you have to be the boss's guest.' I replied: 'There's where you're mistaken; you simply have to be known.' "

When all questions concerning the menu and wines have been settled, arrange for the bill to be sent the next day and not presented at the table; the same for the tipping, about 12% for the waiter who serves you, 5% for the captain who supervises the service, and, depending on the wines, about the same for the wine steward. If the party is very elaborate, you should think of the Maître d'Hôtel as well. These rates are obviously higher than for an impromptu restaurant dinner where there is no special ahead-of-time planning. One final hint: pay the cloak-room attendant in advance so that she will refuse tips from your guests.

All the romanticism of the nineteenth century is recalled by this setting for a dinner by candle-light. (Flowers by Fioralie, Lace from A la Ville du Puy. Silver by Puy-forcat.)

230 Great French

From France's centuries-old gastronomic tradition, it seems that more recipes have evolved than there are stars in the firmament. Our culinary archives contain thousands of recipes. For example, Escoffier's Guide, listing and classifying the traditional recipes of his day (1900), includes nearly 5,000 entries, among which the following can be found: 100 recipes for consommés, 150 recipes for eggs, 60 recipes for omelettes, 185 recipes for sole, 200 recipes for chicken, 40 recipes for *foie gras*, and 175 recipes for ice cream and its variations. This Guide is the standard dictionary of the culinary language and the handbook most frequently referred to today by professional French chefs. A good chef should be familiar with all of these recipes as a good writer should be familiar with all of the words in his language. But even Escoffier's cookbook is not up to date. Since 1900, new French cookbooks have been published containing additional recipes, most of which come from what is known as regional French cooking.

This is enough to make any prospective cook give up in despair, or at least be painfully discouraged. But fortunately, daily use has much shortened and simplified the repertoire. After all, ingredients are not unlimited in variety and, practically speaking, can only be blended in some fifty manners. If you replace white wine with red wine or Cognac with whisky in the preparation of a special dish, your recipe may be different, but the principle or guiding spirit of the recipe has not changed. The merits of good classic cooking are undisputed, but tasteful variation and imagination are also desirable on occasion. And one does not necessarily exclude the other.

Gastronomically speaking, Maxim's is almost unique among restaurants; not only does its menu change every day, but at every meal. This is a tradition which, once scrupulously obeyed by all great Paris restaurants, is now disappearing. Today, most restaurants known for their gastronomic merits stick to a series of ten to twenty recipes which they present year in and year out. Maxim's, on the other hand, has a list of 600 different recipes from which to choose, from the simple *Côtes d'Agneau à l'Estragon* to the elaborate *Pot-au-Feu Dodin Bouffant*.

About one third of the recipes in Maxim's repertoire are quite simple, based on roasted, broiled, or sautéed meats. For there are a large number of steady customers who are not interested in an elaborate meal every day. Another third of the recipes are more complicated but still quite classic, the Escoffier type, more or less. The remaining third are original recipes, gleaned during travels in France and abroad, contributed by the various chefs who have worked in Maxim's kitchen, and dreamed up or modified by and with the help of certain customers, such as the members of the *Club des Cent* who meet every week at Maxim's. The recipes in the section of this book *The Haute Cuisine of Maxim's* are taken from all three categories: the fairly simple, such as the *Entrecôte Bercy*, the traditional, such as the *Poulet Strasbourgeoise*, and the entirely original, such as the *Sole Albert*. All of

Recipes

Introduction by Louis Vaudable

them are served regularly in the dining room at Maxim's.

As you will notice, the recipes which follow are divided into two main parts: *The Haute Cuisine of Maxim's* and *The Home Cooking of France*. The former has already been described. The recipes generally yield six servings. The latter is a selection of recipes with a flair, yet simple enough for everyday use, among them many regional recipes. In compiling this chapter, I called upon my old friend, the Countess of Toulouse-Lautrec, first known in France for stealing her grandmother's book of recipes for which her five brothers and sisters would gladly have given their portions of the inheritance. Forever on jaunts around the French countryside, she always comes back with one or two new recipes. "Mapie", (as we call her), was kind enough to give me her valuable assistance. These latter recipes generally yield four servings.

There are naturally many basic preparations which reappear frequently in any selection of recipes: meat stocks, sauces, pastry doughs, and the like. I have included those I consider the most essential to this book. If certain recipes of this sort are omitted, however, it is because they can be found in any basic cookbook, French or English.

One item which may surprise you is that there is little strong use of garlic and seldom the word *flambé* in this collection of recipes. French *cuisine* is often represented abroad by an erroneous overemphasis of these two elements. But the truth of the matter is that to offer a guest a dish highly seasoned with garlic is usually considered impolite. Garlic is an ingredient which some people despise. However, it must be admitted that in some regions of France, it is almost a staple. Therefore, if you are a garlic-loving family, there is no reason to deprive yourself of snails or frogs' legs or other dishes strongly flavored with garlic. But keep it within the family circle. Unsuspecting outsiders are strictly taboo. As for the famous French dishes known as *flambé*, some restaurants serve them for an excuse to show off in front of the customer. They pour so much Cognac... and what Cognac!... over the dish that the customer might just as well be faced with a bad cocktail! The same holds true for Madeira and other ingredients added at the last minute. A good recipe, if well executed, should defy all detection of its components. The over-all savor should be a harmonious blend.

In the following recipes, you will find a little of everything: peasant soups and stews, traditional roasts and soufflés, exotic curries, and iced desserts; meals for every occasion, every taste, and every purse. Some require hours of painstaking preparation: others can be whipped up in a matter of minutes. *Chez Maxim's* is designed to bring elegant French *cuisine* into your home, a high classic tradition adapted to twentieth-century standards. As the 1900 Escoffier is the basic guide of every French chef, I hope that *Chez Maxim's* will be your guide to more enjoyable living in 1963 and the years to come.

Some basic recipes

Below are some basic definitions and recipes often referred to (in italics) in the recipes which follow. Although stocks and sauces are indisputably better when made at home, their preparation is often long and painstaking. If you find yourself short for time, a good commercial preparation may be substituted.

Bouquet garni: a sprig of parsley, a sprig of thyme and a bay leaf tied together.

Fines herbes: Chopped parsley, tarragon, chervil and chives.

Croûtons: Small rounds or squares of bread, fried lightly in oil or butter.

● JUS BRUN (MEAT STOCK)

(about 1 qt.)
2 lb. veal and beef bones
1/4 lb. cut-up bacon rind
4 onions, 4 carrots
1 bouquet garni
Salt, pepper

Slice the onions and carrots and put them in a pan with the bones and bacon rind. Brown in the oven for a few minutes. Add the *bouquet garni* and 3 quarts of cold water. Season lightly. Partially cover and cook slowly for at least 4 hours.

Skim and strain; reserve the fat for a *Sauce Demi-Glace* and the meat and vegetables for a *Glace de Viande* if desired (see below).
PREPARATION: 4 hrs.

● SAUCE DEMI-GLACE (CONCENTRATED MEAT STOCK)

(about 2 qt.)
4 qt. Jus Brun
1/4 cup fat
1/2 cup flour
2 tbsp. tomato purée

Fat from a boiled or roasted meat, meat juice or gravy, is the ideal basic ingredient for this sauce. Lard may also be used.

Heat the fat and flour over a low flame, stirring constantly. When brown, add the *Jus Brun* and then stir in the tomato purée. Bring to a boil, stirring continually with a wooden spatula, and simmer for at least 2 hours 30 minutes. The longer it cooks, the purer it will be. Do not stir, but skim off the fat from time to time.

After 2 to 3 hours, strain and set aside. This sauce will keep for quite a while in a cool place. Try and keep some always on hand.
PREPARATION: 3 hrs.

● GLACE DE VIANDE (CONCENTRATED MEAT ESSENCE)

(about 1 cup)
Left-over meat and vegetables
from Jus Brun
Meat scraps (except lamb)

After straining off the *Jus Brun*, pour in enough water to cover the bones and vegetables (about 2 quarts). Add other scraps of left-over meat, excluding lamb. Cook slowly for 3 to 4 hours. Skim off the fat and strain the liquid into a pot large enough for it to boil freely. Boil until only about 1 pint remains, strain into a smaller saucepan, and continue to reduce until you have a small quantity of black syrupy liquid. Put in a jar and keep in a cool place. Adds flavor to roasts, gravies, soups and sauces.
PREPARATION: 4 to 5 hrs.

BOUILLON BLANC (BASIC CONSOMME)

(about 1 qt.)
3 lb. shin of beef
1 1/2 lb. rump of beef
1/2 lb. carrots, 1/2 lb. turnips
1/4 cup parsnips
1/2 lb. leeks, 2 medium onions
2 garlic cloves, 2 cloves
1 stalk celery, 1 bouquet garni
Salt, peppercorns

Quarter the carrots, turnips, parsnips, and onions; slice the leeks. Place the meat in 4 quarts of cold water and bring slowly to a boil. Skim off all the scum and fat as it comes to the surface of the liquid. Add the other ingredients and simmer for 2 hours, skimming repeatedly. Strain and continue to simmer, reducing the liquid, for 1/2 hour. Pour through a cheesecloth to catch the fat.

This consommé is the ideal basis for soups and sauces. The meat and vegetables can be served alone in a little liquid. The consommé is delicious with small croûtons or noodles or with vegetables as a vegetable soup.
PREPARATION: 3 hrs.

FOND DE CUISSON (VEAL STOCK)

(about 1 1/2 qt.)
4 lb. shin of veal
2 calf's feet, 2 lb. chuckroast
1 medium carrot, 1 medium onion
1 stalk celery
1/2 lb. butter or lard
1 bottle dry white wine
1/2 tbsp. rock salt
Pepper

Blanch the calf's feet. Remove and drain. Cut up the veal and beef and sear in the butter or lard. Place the meat in a large pot along with the vegetables, calf's feet, pepper, and rock salt. Add 2 quarts of cold water to the white wine, add to the pot, and bring to a boil. Skim, lower the heat, cover partially, and simmer for 3 hours. Strain through a cheesecloth and reduce to about 6 cups.

The boiled meat which has been removed after the first 3 hours can be used in various manners: cold salads, hot chopped meat dishes, stuffed tomato or eggplant dishes, or cold, with mustard and pickles.
PREPARATION: 3 hrs. 20 min.

FUMET DE POISSON (FISH STOCK)

(about 2 qt.)
2 lb. fish bones and trimmings
1/2 cup chopped onions
2 tbsp. butter, 4 sprigs parsley
1 bottle dry white wine
2 1/2 pt. water
12 peppercorns, Salt

Put the fish trimmings in a buttered pan with the minced onion, parsley and peppercorns. Stew for a while with the lid on, then add the white wine, water, and a pinch of salt. Simmer uncovered for 25 minutes and strain. Halibut, flounder and/or whiting may be used for this recipe.
PREPARATION: about 40 min.

SAUCE BÉCHAMEL (WHITE SAUCE)

(about 1 1/2 cups)
2 tbsp. butter, 2 tbsp. flour
1 1/2 cups scalded milk
Salt, pepper

Stir the butter and flour over a medium flame until it starts to color. Add the milk slowly, stirring constantly with a wooden spatula. The sauce should gradually thicken. Simmer for 20 minutes. Finally season with salt and pepper. For a *Sauce Mornay*, sprinkle with grated cheese.
PREPARATION: 30 min.

SAUCE AURORE (TOMATO CREAM SAUCE)

(about 2 cups)
2 cups Sauce Béchamel
3-6 *tbsp. tomato purée*
1 /4 *cup butter*

Mix the *Sauce Béchamel* with the tomato purée. Bring slowly to a boil and simmer for 5 minutes. Remove from the fire and stir in the butter in small pieces. Good with various fish and rice dishes.
PREPARATION: 40 min.

SAUCE CHAUD-FROID (COLD CREAM SAUCE)

(about 1 1/2 cups)
1 1/2 cups Sauce Béchamel
1 /2 *cup gelatin*
1 /2 *tbsp. cream*
1 *egg yolk*

Add the liquid gelatin to the warm *Sauce Béchamel* and reduce the liquid over a low flame, stirring constantly with a wooden spatula. Remove from the fire and stir in the cream and egg yolk. Strain and cool.
PREPARATION: 40 min.

SAUCE MAYONNAISE (MAYONNAISE SAUCE)

(about 2 cups)
3 *egg yolks*
1 1/2 cups salad oil
3 *tbsp. vinegar (or lemon juice)*
Mustard
Salt

All the ingredients should be at room temperature. Beat the egg yolks in a bowl until creamy. Beat in half the vinegar, 1/4 teaspoon of mustard and 1/2 teaspoon of salt until blended. Add the oil, drop by drop, beating constantly. If the sauce becomes too thick, thin out with more vinegar. Finally stir in 2 tablespoons of boiling water which will keep your sauce from turning.

For a *Sauce Remoulade* (Cold Mustard Sauce), stir in 1 tbsp. French mustard, 2 tbsp. chopped pickles, capers, parsley, chervil and tarragon, and a few drops of anchovy essence. Chill.
PREPARATION: 10 min.

SAUCE HOLLANDAISE (HOLLANDAISE SAUCE)

(about 1 cup)
3 *egg yolks*
1 *cup butter*
Lemon juice
Salt

Place the egg yolks and 2 teaspoons of water in the top of a double-boiler over hot but not boiling water. Beat with a whip until creamy and thick. Slowly add the butter, little by little, stirring continually. Season with a pinch of salt and 2 drops of lemon juice. Keep warm until serving time. Be careful at all times not to overheat, as the sauce will become lumpy. Excellent with broccoli, asparagus and artichokes.
PREPARATION: 8 min.

RIZ A L'INDIENNE (STEAMED RICE)

(serves 6)
1 1/2 cups long-grained rice

Wash the raw rice and drain it. Pour slowly into 2 quarts of boiling salted water. The water should never stop boiling. Stir from time to time. After about 20 minutes, drain and rinse in cold water. Wrap in a damp towel and place in a covered baking dish in a moderate oven (350°) for about 15 minutes to reheat and dry out the rice. Fluff with a fork, add butter, and serve. Perfect with fish and creamed dishes.
PREPARATION: 40 min.

CRÈME ANGLAISE (CUSTARD CREAM)

(about 2 cups)
1 3/4 cups boiled milk
3 *egg yolks*
1 /2 *cup granulated sugar*
Vanilla

With the aid of a wooden spatula, mix the sugar and egg yolks vigorously in a mixing bowl. Boil the milk with a drop of vanilla, and pour it bit by bit into the sugar and egg yolks, stirring constantly. Turn the whole mixture back into the saucepan and heat over a low flame, stirring gently. Be careful that it does not boil. As soon as it starts to coat the spatula, remove from the fire. Cool slightly before serving.

If additional flavor is desired, cool and add 1 teaspoon of the liqueur of your choice or flavor with chocolate or coffee to taste.
PREPARATION: 15 min.

CRÈME PATISSIÈRE (PASTRY CREAM)

(about 2 cups)
2 cups boiled milk
1 cup granulated sugar
1/4 cup sifted flour
5 egg yolks, 1 tbsp. butter
Vanilla

With the aid of a wooden spatula, mix the sugar and egg yolks vigorously in a bowl. Beat in the flour. Boil the milk with a drop of vanilla and pour it slowly into the mixture, stirring constantly. Turn this mixture back into the saucepan and bring to the boiling point, stirring constantly. After 2 minutes of rapid boiling, (beat vigorously), pour the cream into a mixing bowl and smear the top with softened butter to prevent a skin from forming.
PREPARATION: 25 min.

PATE BRISÉE (SHORT-CRUST PASTRY)

(A 12-inch pie)
2 cups sifted flour
3/8 lb. butter
2 tbsp. granulated sugar (optional)
1/2 cup cold water
1/4 tsp. salt

Pour the flour into a mixing bowl. Place the softened butter and salt (and sugar) in the center and knead together quickly. Add the water and knead together delicately and rapidly, making a dough which is homogeneous but not elastic (the result of too much kneading). Roll into a ball, wrap in waxed paper, and refrigerate for at least 2 hours. If possible, chill overnight, as the longer it stands, the better your crust will be.
PREPARATION: 10 min. (plus standing).

PATE A CHOUX (CHOUX PASTRY)

(about 2 cups)
1 cup sifted flour
1 cup water
4 eggs
6 tbsp. butter
1 tsp. granulated sugar (optional)
Salt

Heat 1 cup of cold water with the butter in a saucepan, stirring until the butter is melted. Add the sugar and a pinch of salt and bring to a boil. Remove from the fire and add the flour. Stir briskly with a wooden spatula until the batter is blended. Return to a high flame for 2 or 3 minutes, stirring continually to prevent sticking. When the batter no longer tends to stick but comes away easily from the sides of the pan, remove from the fire again and let cool for a few minutes. Add the eggs, one by one, stirring constantly, and making sure that each egg is well incorporated into the batter before adding the following one. Use immediately.
PREPARATION: 20 min.

PATE FEUILLETÉE (PUFF PASTRY)

(about 4 cups)
2 cups sifted flour
2 cups softened butter
1/2 cup cold water
1 tsp. salt

Pour the sifted flour into a mixing bowl. Be sure the salt is free from lumps and put it in the center, add part of the water, mix, and continue to add water until the right consistency is obtained (the same as that of the softened butter). As all flours do not have the same absorption powers, it is difficult to indicate exactly how much water or butter is needed. The dough should be neither too soft nor moist. Knead as little as possible; roll into a ball, wrap in waxed paper, and chill, but not in the freezer.

After about 20 minutes, flatten out the dough in a square of about 8 inches per side. Place the softened butter in the center and fold over the 4 corners so the butter is completely enveloped in the dough. Chill again.

After 10 minutes, begin to "turn" the dough. This consists of rolling it out in a strip 3 times as long as it is wide (about 8 inches by 24 inches). Do not press heavily with the rolling pin, and do not sprinkle your working surface with too much flour as the proportions risk being destroyed. Fold the ends of the strip over towards the middle to form a three-tiered square. Turn the square around (do not turn over) and roll out in the opposite direction. Chill 10 minutes. "Turn" 2 more times, each time in the direction opposite the preceding one. Chill 10 minutes more. Finally 2 more "turns" (making 6 in all) and your pastry dough is ready. Chill 20 minutes before use.

This pastry should be put first in a very hot oven (450°) for about 10 minutes. Then lower the heat to about 350° and continue baking until golden brown and flaky.
PREPARATION: 1 hr. 15 min.

The Haute Cuisine of Maxim's

● **CONSOMMÉ DE FOIE GRAS (FOIE GRAS CONSOMMÉ)**

4 cups good chicken broth
3 /4 lb. foie gras
4 /5 cup Port wine
2 /5 cup Armagnac
Allspice

Remove all the fat from the *foie gras* and cut it into small cubes. Bring the broth to a boil and throw in the pieces of *foie gras*. Remove from the fire and add the Port wine, Armagnac, and seasoning. Leave to infuse for a few minutes.

* An original variation on a classic theme which dates from the Renaissance.

PREPARATION: 15 min. COOKING: 5 min.

● **CONSOMMÉ AUX CERISES (CHERRY CONSOMMÉ)**

4 cups Bouillon Blanc
50 ripe black cherries
1 1/2 cup cherry brandy
Freshly ground pepper

Neatly stone 30 large cherries. Take the 20 remaining cherries and pound them and their pits into a purée. Spoon this purée into the boiling bouillon, remove from the fire, cover, and leave standing for about 10 minutes. Strain, add the stoned cherries, and let stand 2 or 3 minutes more. Just before serving, add the cherry brandy and a little freshly ground pepper.

* This is a nice consommé to serve cold in the summertime.

PREPARATION: 20 min. COOKING: 15 min.

● **CONSOMMÉ AUX PIMENTS (JELLIED PIMENTO CONSOMMÉ)**

2 1 /2 qt. unsalted Fond de Cuisson
1 lb. veal shank
1 calf's foot
2 chicken drumsticks with feet
1 large red pimento
1 onion
Salt, pepper

The chicken feet should be thoroughly cleaned, boiled for a few minutes, and the claws removed. Brown the whole unpeeled onion for a few minutes in the oven. Place these ingredients, the cut-up veal shank, calf's foot and the *Fond de Cuisson* in a deep heavy saucepan and boil gently for 3 hours. By then the stock should be reduced to about 1 quart of liquid. Strain through a cheesecloth and let cool. The fat will form a solid crust on the surface which can be easily removed.

Dice the pimento coarsely, add it to your consommé and return to the fire. Boil for 15 minutes. Remove from the fire, let cool until luke-warm, and strain into a ceramic bowl. Season to taste. The consommé should be very clear. Before it has a chance to jell, dish it into individual cups, and put in the refrigerator.

*With the use of no artificial gelatin, you should obtain a smooth natural jelly.

PREPARATION: 10 min. (plus chilling). COOKING: 3 hrs. 15 min.

CONSOMMÉ AUX CERISES

POTAGE BILLY BY (CREAM OF MUSSEL SOUP)

1 1/2 cups Fumet de Poisson
2 qt. mussels
1 large onion
1 stalk celery
2 cups heavy whipping cream
1 cup dry white wine
2 sprigs parsley
1/2 tsp. ground peppercorns
Salt

Scrape and wash the mussels thoroughly. Mince the onion and place it in a deep saucepan along with the celery, wine, and pepper. Add the mussels, cover the saucepan, and boil over a high flame for 6 minutes. Shake the mussels in the pan 2 or 3 times during the cooking process so that those on top go to the bottom and vice versa. When the mussels are open, remove and drain them. Pour the liquid in the saucepan through a fine strainer, return to the saucepan, and reduce to about 1 quart of liquid. Add the *Fumet de Poisson* and cream and reheat over a low flame until the liquid comes almost to the boiling point, stirring continually with a wooden spatula. Season to taste.

Serve very hot without the mussels. This soup can also be served cold. The chilled mussels, removed from their shells, make an excellent hors-d'œuvre when accompanied by a *Sauce Remoulade*.

* It was Louis Barthe, the former chef at Maxim's, who told me the story behind the *Potage Billy By*. In 1925, he was working in the kitchen at Ciro's, a restaurant in Deauville known for a special mussels dish with a particularly succulent juice. One day a very good customer, Mr. William Brand, decided to invite some American friends to Ciro's. Mussels are generally eaten with the fingers in France, using one double shell as tongs to scoop the meat out of the others. As Mr. Brand wanted to spare his friends this delicate operation, he requested that the juice be served without the mussels. It was such a success that during the days that followed each of his guests returned separately to Ciro's and ordered the "Potage Billy Brand". For the sake of discretion, it was placed on the menu as *Potage Billy B.*, and thus was born the *Potage Billy By* which has since become a classic of the French culinary tradition.

PREPARATION: 20 min. COOKING: 25 min.

POTAGE GERMINY (CREAM OF SORREL SOUP)

6 cups Bouillon Blanc
20 leaves fresh sorrel
6 egg yolks
1/2 cup butter
1 cup heavy whipping cream
1 tsp. chopped chervil
Salt, pepper

Cut the sorrel leaves into narrow strips and soften them with a walnut-sized piece of butter in a deep saucepan. Pour in the bouillon, bring to a boil, and cook for 10 minutes.

Meanwhile, beat together the cream and egg yolks. Remove the saucepan from the fire and slowly add the egg and cream mixture to the soup. Season with salt and pepper. Put back over a low flame, stirring continually, until you obtain a smooth, creamy consistency. Be careful that the soup does not boil.

Remove the saucepan from the fire, add the rest of the butter cut into small pieces and the chervil. Stir well and serve at once.

PREPARATION: 15 min. COOKING: 10 min.

CRÈME AUX HUITRES (CREAM OF OYSTER SOUP)

36 small oysters
1 cup rice flour
1/2 cup butter
1 qt. milk
6 egg yolks
1 1/2 cups heavy whipping cream
Salt, pepper, red pepper

Open the raw oysters, remove them from their shells, strain the juice, and poach them in it for about 2 minutes. Strain and set juice and oysters aside for future use.

Prepare a light sauce by heating half the butter over a low flame until it begins to brown and smell of nuts; add the rice flour, and finally the milk, stirring constantly with a wooden spatula to avoid lumps. Strain and add the juice from the oysters. Add the 6 egg yolks one by one, the cream, the remaining 1/4 cup of butter, and stir until you obtain the consistency of a custard sauce. Be careful that the mixture does not boil.

Season lightly with salt and pepper, add a pinch of red pepper, and garnish with the poached oysters.

PREPARATION: 10 min. COOKING: 20 min.

6-9-1902

ŒUFS SUR POMMES PRÉCIEUSES (EGGS ON STUFFED POTATOES)

6 fresh eggs
6 large Idaho potatoes
1 1/2 cups heavy whipping cream
1/2 cup minced cooked ham
1 cup Sauce Mornay
1/2 cup melted butter
3/4 cup grated Parmesan cheese
3 truffles
6 mushroom caps
Salt, pepper

Wash and dry 6 large potatoes of even size and shape. Slice off the tops about 1/3 of the way down. Replace the tops and bake the potatoes in the oven, being careful that they do not burst. Remove and hollow them out, leaving a fairly sturdy shell. Mash the pulp through a strainer or in a blender, place in a bowl, and add the cream and minced ham. Season with salt and pepper and stuff the potatoes with this mixture. Scrape the tops and place then upside down on the potatoes. Poach the eggs and place a hot poached egg in each cap.

Arrange the stuffed potatoes with the poached eggs in an ovenware serving dish. Pour over a generous quantity of *Sauce Mornay*, sprinkle with cheese and moisten with the melted butter. Brown gently in the oven.

This dish is excellent accompanied by mushrooms and finely sliced truffles cooked in butter.

PREPARATION: 20 min. COOKING: 50 min.

ŒUFS FROU-FROU (COLD EGGS IN ASPIC)

6 fresh eggs
3 hard-boiled egg yolks
2 black truffles
3/4 cup fresh peas
3/4 cup asparagus tips
3/4 cup string beans
1 pt. meat or artificial gelatin
1/2 cup Sauce Mayonnaise
1 cup Sauce Chaud-Froid
Salt, pepper

Poach the eggs. Cool, put them on a plate, and smother with a *Sauce Chaud-Froid* to which a purée of the 3 hard-boiled egg yolks (ground in a blender or mashed through a strainer) has been added. Decorate the top of each egg with a thin notched disk of black truffle. Encircle the base of each egg with the remaining truffle finely chopped. Glaze with half-melted gelatin and chill.

Prepare a salad of cooked vegetables: fresh garden peas, green asparagus tips, cut-up fresh string beans, and *Sauce Mayonnaise* mixed with a little melted gelatin.

Put the salad in a mound in the center of a round serving dish. Encircle with chopped gelatin. Place the eggs around the salad and decorate the outer rim with more chopped gelatin.

PREPARATION: 30 min. (plus chilling). COOKING: 30 min.

ŒUFS A LA TRIPE (CREAMED HARD-BOILED EGGS)

12 fresh eggs
2 large onions
3/4 cup butter
1 pt. thin Sauce Béchamel
Salt, pepper

Dice the onions and stew them gently in the butter until tender. Add the *Sauce Béchamel* and simmer for 10 minutes. Hard-boil the eggs, slice them in thick rings, and add to the sauce. Mix together carefully. Try to heat the eggs thoroughly without breaking the slices. Season to taste and serve at once.

PREPARATION: 20 min. COOKING: 15 min.

OMELETTE HONGROISE (TOMATO OMELETTE)

12 fresh eggs
3 medium tomatoes
2 large onions
1 cup butter
Salt, paprika

Dice the onions and stew them gently without browning in half the butter along with the peeled, drained, and coarsely chopped tomatoes and a pinch of paprika. Season with salt. Remove from the fire and stir in the rest of the butter in small pieces. Season and beat the eggs and pour into a large buttered frying pan. Stir constantly with a fork, especially raising the edges, until the eggs begin to set but are still liquid. Just before folding over, stuff with the tomato and onion mixture.

Never attempt to use more than 12 eggs for this omelette. It is better, in fact, to make two omelettes of 6 eggs apiece.

* For the success of any egg dish, the eggs must be as fresh as possible.

PREPARATION: 10 min. COOKING: 20 min.

ŒUFS FROU-FROU

ANGUILLE AU VERT (EEL IN GREEN SAUCE)

A 2-lb. eel
3/4 cup butter
4 egg yolks
1 cup heavy whipping cream
2 onions
1 stalk celery
1 bottle dry white wine
1/2 cup sorrel
1/2 cup watercress
1/4 cup white nettles
3 mint leaves
1 tsp. chervil
1 tsp. parsley, 1 tsp. sage
1 tsp. savory
Salt, freshly ground pepper

Cut the skinned, cleaned, and well-washed eel into 2-inch slices. Brown them in butter in a shallow pan. Dice the onions and celery, add them to the eel, and allow to soften. Pour in enough white wine to cover. Season with salt and freshly ground pepper. Add the sorrel, watercress, nettles, fresh mint, chervil, sage, savory, and parsley, all finely chopped together, and boil for 15 minutes. Meanwhile beat the egg yolks and cream together.

Remove the pan from the fire and strain the contents carefully. Put the slices of eel on a serving dish and keep hot. Reheat the liquid and bind off the fire with the egg and cream mixture. Allow to simmer for a few minutes. Check the seasoning and pour over the eel. Serve at once.

* Just as France borrows words from other languages, so she borrows recipes from other cooking traditions. This dish is Belgian by origin, where it is served cold instead of hot.

PREPARATION: 30 min. COOKING: 25 min.

SAUMON BRAISE (BRAISED SALMON)

A 3-lb. salmon
6 large mushroom caps
1 truffle
1 carrot
1 onion
1 1/2 cups butter
1/2 bottle dry white wine
or Sherry
6 sprigs parsley
1 sprig thyme
2 bay leaves
Salt, pepper

Cut the carrot and onion in to thin slices. Remove the rack from the bottom of an appropriately sized oblong fish kettle and spread the sliced vegetables and herbs over the bottom of the pan. Replace the rack and place the salmon on it. Season with salt and pepper. Place the mushrooms around the fish. Pour over 1/2 cup melted butter and place in a moderate oven (350°). After 15 minutes, pour in enough white wine or Sherry to half cover the salmon. Cover and cook, basting frequently. Cooking time should be calculated at the rate of 10 minutes per pound, about one half hour in all. The salmon should be slightly browned on top.

If the liquid reduces too rapidly, add some more white wine or Sherry after 20 minutes. The salmon should be one-third submerged in liquid.

Slice the truffle in 6 thin slices. Ten minutes before removing the salmon from the oven, place the slices of truffle in the pan with the fish.

When done, lift out the rack and slip the salmon onto a hot serving dish. Strain the cooking liquid through a cheesecloth and reduce to 1 1/2 cups. Remove from the fire and stir in 1 cup of butter. Pour some of this sauce over the salmon and decorate it with truffles and mushrooms.

PREPARATION: 20 min. COOKING: 50 min.

COULIBIACS DE SAUMON (RUSSIAN SALMON TURNOVERS)

12 small boneless salmon fillets
3/8 cup chopped mushrooms
1 cup cooked rice
3 hard-boiled eggs
2 small onions
3/8 cup dried vesiga
2 cups Pâte Feuilletée
1 1/4 lb. butter
1 egg
1 tbsp. chopped parsley
Salt, pepper

Soak the vesiga* for at least 6 hours; overnight if possible. Cook for 4 hours in either very lightly salted water or bouillon. Drain and chop up fine. Heat 1 tablespoon of butter in a pan and sear the salmon. Let cool in the pan. Remove, and heat the chopped onions and mushrooms in the same pan, sprinkle with a little parsley and let cool.

Cut out 6 small disks of Pâte Feuilletée, about 6 inches in diameter and 1/4-inch thick. To one side of the center of each one, stack a layer of Vesiga, a layer of rice, a fillet of salmon, chopped hard-boiled egg, parsley, mushrooms and onions, Vesiga, salmon, rice. Fold over like a turnover and brush with beaten egg. Make a small hole to let out the steam and a few knife pricks on the surface, and bake in a hot oven (425°) for 35 minutes. Melt the butter and put 2 teaspoonfuls in the opening of each turnover before serving.

* Vesiga is the dried spine marrow of the sturgeon. As it is used almost solely in Coulibiacs, binding the other ingredients and contributing its own special flavor, your best chances of finding it are in a Russian grocery store or delicatessen. If you cannot find it, it can be omitted.

PREPARATION: 40 min. (plus Pâte Feuilletée). BAKING: 35 min.

SAUMON BRAISÉ

TRUITES FARCIES EN PAPILLOTES (BAKED STUFFED TROUT)

Six 1/2-lb. brook trout
2 cups fresh crustless breadcrumbs
1 cup butter
3/4 cup heavy whipping cream
1 egg
1/2 cup dry white wine
1 tsp. lemon juice
1 tbsp. chopped parsley, tarragon, chervil and chives
Salt, pepper

Have your fish dealer remove the backbone of the trout leaving the heads and tails on. Soak the breadcrumbs in the cream, squeeze out, and set the cream aside for later use. Season the breadcrumbs with salt and pepper and mix with the egg, 1/4 cup of butter and the herbs. Stuff the trout with this mixture and place them side by side in a well-buttered, salted and peppered ovenware dish. Pour the wine over the fish, warm on top of the stove, and place in a slow oven (300°) for 5 minutes. Drain the trout, setting the juice aside, wrap each one in slightly buttered aluminum foil, and return to the oven. After about 8 more minutes, remove the foil and place the trout on a heated serving dish.

Heat the cream and lemon juice with the cooking juices. Strain through a cheesecloth and serve on the side.

* Wrapping the trout in aluminum foil keeps the full flavor of the fish from escaping.

PREPARATION: 30 min. COOKING: 20 min.

TRUITES A LA GELÉE DE RUBIS (COLD TROUT IN RUBY ASPIC)

Six 1/2-lb. brook trout
A 3/4 lb. eel
2 eggs
1 bottle good red wine
1 carrot
1 medium onion
1 garlic clove
1 bouquet garni
Salt, pepper

Prepare the aspic in the following manner: dice the carrot, onion and garlic, place them in a saucepan, and heat very slowly so as to extract the juices. Add the *bouquet garni* and season with salt and pepper. Skin and slice the eel, add it to the vegetables, and pour in the warmed wine. Bring to a boil and simmer for 40 minutes. Remove from the fire and pour through a fine strainer into a bowl. Leave to cool, skim off all top fat, and check the seasoning. If the liquid is not absolutely transparent, clarify it by adding 2 beaten egg whites, and reheating to the boiling point, beating constantly. Once the boiling point achieved, lower the flame and cook slowly for 10 minutes; then strain through a cloth.

Place the trout in a deep pan, cover with the cooled red aspic, and poach gently for about 10 minutes. Let cool in the pan. Before the aspic solidifies, remove the trout and arrange them neatly on a serving dish, covering them evenly with aspic.

* This dish is excellent with a salad of fresh cucumbers macerated for 8 to 10 hours with a little salt. Season with oil, vinegar, chopped parsley, tarragon and pepper.

PREPARATION: 40 min. COOKING: 1 hr.

SOUFFLÉ DE LAITANCES D'ALOSES (SHAD ROE SOUFFLÉ)

3/4 lb. shad roe
1 cup thick Sauce Béchamel
4 eggs
1/4 cup butter
1 tsp. lemon juice
Salt

Spread the butter thickly over the bottom of a small saucepan and put in the roe. Season with salt, add the lemon juice and 1 tablespoon of cold water, cover with a buttered piece of paper, and put on the cover. Stew gently for about 5 minutes and then mash through a strainer. Put the resulting purée in a saucepan with the *Sauce Béchamel;* heat, stirring constantly, but do not boil. Remove from the fire. Separate the eggs, beat the yolks, and add them to the sauce. Beat the egg whites very stiff and fold them in carefully with a wooden spatula. Butter a deep straight-sided soufflé dish, pour in your soufflé mixture, filling the dish two-thirds full, and bake in a preheated moderate oven (350°) for about 20 minutes. Serve immediately; as everyone knows, a soufflé falls if made to wait.

* French proverb: Better the man should wait for the meal than the meal should wait for the man.

PREPARATION: 20 min. COOKING: 20 min.

TRUITE A LA GELÉE DE RUBIS

SOLES ILE-DE-FRANCE (SOLE IN CREAM-WINE SAUCE)

Six 1/2-lb. fresh sole
2 medium carrots
1 medium onion
1 medium turnip
1 1/2 cups butter
1 cup heavy whipping cream
1/2 cup dry white wine
1/2 cup Fumet de poisson
Salt, pepper

Cut the carrots, onion, and turnip in thin strips. Remove the heads, fins, and dark skins of the sole and clean them. Scrape the white skins; wash and dry.

Melt half the butter in a pan with a closely fitting lid; add the vegetables and a pinch of salt. Cover and cook very slowly. As soon as the vegetables have softened, add the dry white wine and concentrated *Fumet de Poisson* and reduce the liquid by half.

Spread the contents of the pan evenly over the bottom of an oblong, shallow ovenware dish, and place the sole on top. Season lightly with salt and pepper, melt the remaining butter, and pour it over the sole. Cover the dish with buttered wax paper and poach in a moderate oven (350º) for about 20 minutes.

Remove from the oven, place the sole on a serving dish, and keep hot. Strain the sauce, add the cream, and reduce until just enough remains to cover the fish. Pour over the sole and serve at once.

* One cannot say that the *cuisine* of the *Ile-de-France* is peculiar to the region, as its development started under Louis XIV and was subsequently spread all over France. Moreover, the attractions of Paris brought many chefs from other regions who added their culinary inspirations to those already existing.

When a distinction is made, however, the term most often used in reference to the *cuisine* of this central area of France is "sophisticated". The above *Soles Ile-de-France* is certainly worthy of its name.

PREPARATION: 30 min. COOKING: 25 min.

SOLES ALBERT (SOLE BAKED IN VERMOUTH)

Three 1-lb. fresh sole
1 lb. butter
3/4 cup fresh breadcrumbs
1 1/2 cups dry Vermouth
1/2 lemon
3 shallots
1 tbsp. chopped parsley and tarragon
Salt, pepper

Remove the heads, tails, fins and the skin from both sides of the sole and clean them. With a very sharp pointed knife make an incision along the dorsal bone. Melt 3/4 cup of butter in a large ovenware dish. Chop the shallots, mix with the herbs, and spread the mixture in the bottom of the dish. The dish should be large enough to hold the three sole placed side by side.

Melt 1/2 cup of butter in another pan, dip the side of the sole formerly covered with white skin in this butter, and then in the fresh breadcrumbs. Place the soles, breaded side up, in the hot ovenware dish. Season with salt and pepper. Pour in enough dry Vermouth to half submerge the fish without wetting the breadcrumbs. Pour another 3/4 cup of melted butter over the soles. Place in a hot oven (425º) and brown for about 30 minutes.

Remove from the oven and place neatly on a hot serving dish. Reduce the juice in the pan to almost 2 tablespoons. Remove from the fire and stir in the remaining butter, whisking vigorously, so as to obtain a light, frothy sauce. Add a squeeze of lemon; check the seasoning. Pour some of the sauce around the soles and serve the rest separately.

* Sole is the most well-known fish in France and England. As its flesh is tender and delicate in flavor, it is excellent at the beginning of a meal. It is equally good both hot and cold. Escoffier listed 185 recipes for preparing sole—150 different ways of poaching, 20 ways of grilling or broiling, and 15 ways of baking in the oven. According to Escoffier, sole can be poached in fish stock, white wine, or red wine. It is the other ingredients which go into the recipes that differentiate one from the other. *Soles Albert* is the 186th recipe, unlisted by Escoffier. Here, the fish is poached in Vermouth—a very dry Chambéry. It was Albert, reigning headwaiter and monarch at Maxim's for over twenty-five years, who perfected this recipe. I believe he got it originally from Paillard—a great Paris restaurant which disappeared right after World War I.

If you cannot get sole, substitute fillets of flounder.

PREPARATION: 25 min. COOKING: 30 min.

54

HOMARD A LA NAGE (BOILED LOBSTER WITH BUTTER SAUCE)

Six 1 1/4-lb. live lobsters
1/2 cup sliced carrots
1/2 cup sliced onions
6 garlic cloves
1 bottle dry white wine
1 cup butter
1/2 lemon
1 stalk celery
1 bouquet garni
2 tsp. coarsely ground peppercorns
3 tbsp. rock salt

Put the carrots, onions, celery, garlic, *bouquet garni*, salt and pepper, and dry white wine in 3 quarts of water in a large pot. Bring to a boil and cook for 25 minutes. Wash and rinse the live lobsters thoroughly; place them carefully in the boiling water and maintain at a boil for about 20 minutes.

Meanwhile, mix the softened butter with the juice of 1/2 lemon and season with salt and pepper. Beat briskly and set aside for future use. Remove the lobsters; take about 1 quart of the liquid from the lobster pot, including carrots and onions and 2 or 3 cloves of garlic, and keep hot.

Split the lobsters in half lengthwise. Remove the meat, discard the intestines and the small gritty pouch in the body of the lobster, and place in a heated serving dish, or in 6 hot soup-plates, along with the cracked claws. Cover with some of the cooked vegetables. Pour a little of the hot cooking liquid into a warmed bowl and whisk in the softened butter and lemon juice. Serve the sauce separately.

PREPARATION: 30 min. COOKING: 45 min.

HOMARD A L'ARMORICAINE (LOBSTER WITH TOMATO SAUCE)

Three 2-lb. live lobsters
1/2 cup olive oil
2 cups butter
2 cups dry white wine
1 cup Cognac
1 cup Fumet de Poisson
6 medium tomatoes
6 shallots
1/2 cup tomato purée
1 garlic clove
1 tbsp. chopped parsley
1 tsp. chopped chervil and tarragon
Salt, pepper, red pepper

"Sacrifice" the lobsters alive, severing the tails and cutting them in 5 or 6 slices. Slit the main part of the body in half lengthwise with a sharp, heavy kitchen knife and remove the small gritty pouch. Set the green coral and intestines aside in a bowl, season with salt and pepper, and reserve for the sauce. Detach the claws and crack their shells.

Meanwhile, peel, chop, and drain the tomatoes, chop the shallots, and crush the garlic. Heat the oil and 2 tablespoons of butter in a large shallow pan, and cook the cracked claws and sliced lobster tails over a high flame. When the shells are red, drain off the butter and oil. Sprinkle the lobster with chopped shallots and crushed garlic and a pinch of red pepper. Pour in the wine, the *Fumet de Poisson*, and the Cognac. Add the tomatoes, tomato purée, and 2 teaspoons of chopped parsley. Cover and cook for 20 minutes. When done, remove the shells, arrange the meat in a deep, round serving dish, and keep hot.

Reduce the liquid in the pan by two-thirds, and remove from the fire. Pound together the coral, intestines, and 3 tablespoons of butter and add this purée to the liquid. Bring to a boil; then mash through a fine strainer.

Reheat this sauce, remove from the fire, and add the rest of the butter bit by bit, stirring continually. Pour over the pieces of lobster. Sprinkle with finely chopped parsley, chervil, and tarragon, and serve very hot with *Riz à l'Indienne*.

PREPARATION: 30 min. COOKING: 30 min.

HOMARD AU WHISKY (LOBSTER WITH WHISKY SAUCE)

Three 2-lb. live lobsters
1 cup Scotch whisky
1 cup Cognac
1/2 cup Madeira wine
1/2 cup white Port wine
1/2 cup olive oil
1 cup butter
1 1/4 cups heavy whipping cream
4 egg yolks
6 shallots
1 garlic clove
Salt, pepper

"Sacrifice" and prepare the lobsters as indicated for *Homard à l'Armoricaine*. Chop the shallots and crush the garlic. Heat the oil and 1 tablespoon of butter in a large shallow pan, and cook the cracked claws and sliced lobster tails over a high flame. When the shells are red, drain off the butter and oil. Sprinkle the lobster with the shallots and garlic. Pour in the Cognac, Port, and Madeira and cover. Cook for 20 minutes, remove the shells, arrange the meat in a deep round serving dish, and keep hot.

Reduce the liquid in the pan by half and remove from the fire. Mix the cream and egg yolks, stir them slowly into the warm sauce, and reheat slowly. Do not boil, but cook until the consistency of a custard sauce. Remove from the fire and stir in the remaining butter in small pieces. Pour the whisky over the lobster, followed by the sauce. Serve with *Riz à l'Indienne*.

PREPARATION: 30 min. COOKING: 30 min.

HOMARD A LA NAGE

LANGOUSTINES SAUCE PUDEUR (CRAWFISH IN ASPIC)

2 lb. crawfish or shrimp
1 lb. bones and trimmings of
flounder, pike, and whiting
1/2 bottle Champagne (or dry
white wine)
1 large onion
2 truffles
1 cup mushrooms
2 sprigs parsley
2 sprigs tarragon
1 cup Sauce Mayonnaise
1/2 cup unsweetened whipped cream
Salt

Prepare the aspic well in advance: place the fish bones and trimmings in a pan with the sliced onion and mushrooms, parsley, the Champagne (or white wine), 1 quart of water, and a pinch of salt. Bring to a boil, skim, and simmer for 45 minutes. The resulting liquid should be transparent. Strain the liquid through a cheesecloth. Add 1 sprig of tarragon and leave to cool. Check to see if the aspic is firm enough; if necessary add a little commercial gelatin.

Cook the crawfish by throwing them in a cup of heavily salted boiling water and maintaining at a boil for 3 minutes, stirring once or twice. Drain, cool, shell and clean them, so that only the tails remain.

Line a mold with aspic and decorate with tarragon leaves and thin slices of truffle. Remember that the bottom of the mold will be the top of your aspic. Arrange a layer of crawfish on the layer of truffles. Cover with aspic. Continue alternating crawfish and aspic until no fish remains. Finish with a layer of aspic.

Chill to solidify before unmolding for serving. Excellent accompanied by a *Sauce Mayonnaise* to which the whipped cream has been added just before serving.

* The real *langoustine*, as known in France, is a small shellfish about six to eight inches long which is found only in the waters near Cherbourg. It is usually dressed up with a sauce. This particular dish was created by the great Parisian fashion-designer, Hubert de Givenchy.

PREPARATION: 1 hr. COOKING: 1 hr.

SCAMPI AU CURRY (CURRIED SHRIMP)

1 1/4 lb. Scampi (shelled bay
shrimp or crawfish)
1 large onion
1/2 cup butter
2 cups heavy whipping cream
1 egg yolk
1/2 tsp. curry powder
Salt, red pepper

Mince the onion and put it in a saucepan with 1/4 cup of butter and 1/2 teaspoon of curry powder. Cook the onion gently until it softens. Add the shelled and well-washed *scampi* and 1 1/2 cups of cream. Reduce the sauce slowly, stirring continually, until it starts to thicken. Remove from the fire and bind with the egg yolk beaten with the remaining cream, the rest of the butter, and a pinch of red pepper. Taste before adding salt, as the fish may provide enough natural salt.

Reheat and place in a deep, round serving dish. Serve with *Riz à l'Indienne*.

* Originally *scampi* was an Italian dish, named after a small shellfish of the same name which is found around Venice. Shrimp or crawfish tails are the best substitute.

PREPARATION: 10 min. COOKING: 15 min.

HOMARD A L'INDIENNE (CURRIED LOBSTER)

Three 1 3/4-lb. live lobsters
1 cup olive oil
1 cup butter
2 cups dry white wine
1/2 cup Cognac
1 large eating apple
1 cup Fumet de Poisson
2 tsp. curry powder
Salt, pepper

"Sacrifice" and prepare the lobsters as indicated for *Homard à l'Armoricaine* (p. 56). Peel, core, and dice the apple. Sauté the lobster in the oil and half the butter over a high flame. When the shells are red and the meat seared, pour off the oil and butter and add the wine and Cognac to the pan. Reduce the liquid by two-thirds. Season with salt and pepper, add the curry powder, the *Fumet de Poisson* and the diced apple.

Cover and cook for 15 minutes, after which take out the lobster, remove the shells, and put the meat in a warmed deep serving dish with a cover.

Pound the intestines, coral, and the remaining softened butter together. Add this purée to the sauce. Bring slowly to a boil; then mash through a fine strainer. Check the seasoning and pour over the lobster. Serve immediately, with *Riz à l'Indienne*.

PREPARATION: 30 min. COOKING: 20 min.

COQUILLES SAINT-JACQUES ALEX HUMBERT (SCALLOPS IN HOLLANDAISE SAUCE)

30 live scallops
3 fresh tomatoes
1/4 cup mushrooms
1 shallot
1 1/4 cup butter
1/4 cup Cognac
1/4 cup dry white wine
3 tbsp. Sauce Hollandaise
Salt, pepper, saffron

Open, wash, and clean the scallops, removing them from their shells. Reserve the red roe if there is any. Drain, dry, and season the scallops with salt and pepper.

Peel the tomatoes, remove the seeds, and chop them coarsely. Mince the shallot and cut the mushrooms in narrow strips. Warm the vegetables in 1/2 cup of butter in a pan. Heat the other 3/4 cup of butter in another large pan over a high flame and sauté the scallops. Add the warm vegetables, the wine and Cognac and, when almost boiling, add the scallop roe and a pinch of saffron. Boil for a few minutes.

Remove the pan from the fire and reduce the sauce, stirring constantly. Bind with 3 tablespoons of *Sauce Hollandaise*. Serve at once.

* It was after hearing one of his customers complain that *Coquilles Saint-Jacques* were always prepared "in the same old way" that M. Alex Humbert, the chef of Maxim's, created this dish in 1938. At that time, he was the owner of the Paris restaurant Les Cigognes.

PREPARATION: 20 min. COOKING: 15 min.

COQUILLES SAINT-JACQUES LES BAUX (SHELLFISH IN VERMOUTH SAUCE)

24 live scallops
1 qt. mussels
1 cup cooked shelled shrimp
1/2 cup heavy whipping cream
3/4 cup butter
1 oz. Vermouth
Salt

Open, wash and clean the scallops, removing them from their shells. Heat them in the Vermouth in a saucepan for 3 or 4 minutes. In this way the scallops will become more juicy. Simmer until the liquid is reduced to three quarters of its original volume and stir in the cream. When the sauce is thick and smooth, add the butter in small pieces.

Put the mussels in a saucepan with an ounce of salted water (or white wine). Heat until they open, remove the shells, and add the mussels and shrimp to your scallops. Mix well. Serve in individual shells or small ramekins.

* The first discovery of scallops in Europe was off the coast of the province of Galicia in the northwest corner of Spain. Pilgrims to Santiago de Compostela returned home with a scallop shell to prove that they had arrived at their destination. From this comes the French name for scallops: *Coquilles Saint-Jacques*.

PREPARATION: 20 min. COOKING: 15 min.

MOULES A LA DEAUVILLAISE (MUSSELS IN CREAM-WINE SAUCE)

5 qt. mussels
1 cup dry white wine
3/4 cup butter
1 pt. heavy whipping cream
1 large onion
3 shallots
1 garlic clove
1 tbsp. chopped parsley
Powdered thyme
1/2 bay leaf
Freshly ground pepper

Mince the onion and shallots separately and crush the garlic. Scrub the mussels, ridding them of all mud or other foreign matter. Rinse several times in cold water, drain, and place in a large deep saucepan with half the butter, the onion, half the parsley, pepper, garlic, 1/2 bay leaf, a pinch of thyme, and the white wine. Cover and heat over a high flame. When they come to a good boil, stir the mussels so that those on top slip to the bottom, and vice versa. Cover again, bring again to a boil, and remove from the fire.

Melt 1 tablespoon of butter in another saucepan, and cook the shallots until golden. Add the cream and reduce by half. Meanwhile, remove 1 shell from each mussel, stack these latter in a deep hot serving dish, cover with a plate, and keep hot. Pour the juice into a saucepan, add the creamed shallots and reduce again by half. Remove from the fire and mix in the remaining butter in small pieces and the remaining parsley. Pour over the mussels and serve.

* An excellent and unusual way of dressing up mussels.

PREPARATION : 20 min. COOKING: 20 min.

COQUILLES SAINT-JACQUES ALEX HUMBERT

ESCARGOTS A LA CHABLISIENNE (SNAILS BAKED IN CHABLIS)

72 *cooked snails*
2 1/2 *cups Chablis wine*
1/2 *cup chopped shallots*
1 *lb. butter*
1 *tbsp.* Fond de Cuisson
1 *garlic clove*
1 *tbsp. chopped parsley*
Salt, pepper

Remove the cooked snails from their shells. Place 1/4 cup of shallots and the wine in a pan and reduce by half. Remove and strain through a cheesecloth. Stir in the *Fond de Cuisson* and set aside while you are making your seasoned butter.

Take the softened butter, add the remaining shallots, the crushed garlic clove, and the parsley, and knead them together in a bowl; season lightly with salt and pepper. Put a little of your warm wine sauce in the bottom of each snail shell, insert the snail, and fill the opening with seasoned butter. Place the shells on a special snail tray and heat gently in the oven for about 10 minutes, being careful that the butter does not boil.

*Although many foreigners consider snails and frogs' legs the epitome of French *cuisine*, these dishes are not served by any current three-star restaurant in the *Guide Michelin*. Both are more suitably prepared at home where you can fully enjoy the high seasoning without worrying about your neighbors and where the sauce can be mopped up with a piece of bread.

PREPARATION: 1 hr. (with cooked snails). COOKING: 10 min.

GRENOUILLES AUX FINES HERBES (FROGS' LEGS WITH HERBS)

60 *frogs' legs*
1 1/2 *cups butter*
3 *tsp. flour*
4 *tbsp. olive oil*
1/4 *lemon*
1 *tsp. finely chopped parsley*
and tarragon
Salt, pepper

Wash the frogs' legs thoroughly and soak them in milk for about 2 hours. Remove and dry them and season with salt and pepper. Dust with flour, and throw them into a large frying pan containing the very hot oil and 3/4 cup of butter. Sauté the frogs' legs until nicely browned. Remove, drain, and place in a heated deep serving dish.

Pour off the hot butter and oil from the frying pan and brown the remaining 3/4 cup of butter until it begins to smell of nuts. Pour this over the frogs' legs followed by a squeeze of lemon juice. Sprinkle a little mixed fresh, finely chopped parsley and tarragon over the frogs' legs and serve immediately.

* Most recipes for frogs' legs call for a great deal of garlic and shallots. This is too bad, as such high seasoning completely camouflages the delicate flavor of the meat itself.

PREPARATION: 2 hrs. (soaking included). COOKING: 10 min.

GRENOUILLES A L'AURORE (FROGS' LEGS WITH TOMATO SAUCE)

60 *frogs' legs*
6 *tomatoes*
1 *onion*
2 *garlic cloves*
1/2 *cup butter*
1 *small bunch fresh fried parsley*
1 *tsp. olive oil*
1/2 *lemon*
1 *tsp. chopped parsley*
Oil for deep frying
Salt, pepper, paprika

Pâte à Frire :
1 *cup sifted flour*
1 *cup milk*
1/2 *cup beer or luke-warm water*
2 *tbsp. melted butter*
2 *egg whites*
Salt

Clean and trim the frogs' legs. Place in a large bowl and marinate for 1 hour in a solution of lemon juice, olive oil, 1 crushed garlic clove, and chopped parsley.

Prepare the *Pâte à Frire* by mixing carefully all the batter ingredients except the egg whites. When they are well mixed (but not beaten), beat the 2 egg whites very stiff and fold in.

Remove the frogs' legs from the marinating solution and coat them thoroughly in frying batter. Plunge, one by one, into a large pan of very hot deep frying oil. As soon as they are golden, remove and drain on absorbent paper. Sprinkle lightly with salt and arrange neatly in pyramid form in a deep round serving dish. Decorate with fried parsley.

Make a sauce by peeling the tomatoes, removing the seeds, and chopping in small pieces. Mince the onion, brown it slightly in butter with 1 crushed garlic clove, add the tomatoes, a pinch of paprika, salt, pepper, and cook over a low flame for a few minutes, or until hot. Serve on the side in a gravy boat.

* The frying batter should be prepared in advance so as to induce a slight fermentation.

PREPARATION: 30 min. (plus marinating). COOKING: 15 min.

67

GRENOUILLES AUX FINES HERBES

FILET DE BŒUF EN CROUTE (ROAST BEEF IN A PASTRY CRUST)

A 4-lb. trimmed beef tenderloin
2 cups Pâte Feuilletée
1 cup butter
1 egg
Salt, pepper

Sauce Périgueux
2 cooked truffles
1 1/2 cups Sauce Demi-Glace
1 tsp. Glace de Viande
1/4 cup Madeira wine
2 tbsp. butter
Salt, pepper

Prepare the *Pâte Feuilletée* ahead of time.

Season the tenderloin and sear rapidly on all sides in butter in a very hot oven (425°). Count on 3 minutes per pound, or 12 minutes. Remove from the oven and let cool. Roll out the raw pastry in a rectangular strip, depending for its dimensions on the size and shape of the roast. The dough should be about 1/8 inch in thickness. Wrap the raw pastry around the beef. Brush with beaten egg, put in the oven, and bake for about 20 minutes or until brown.

Prepare a *Sauce Périgueux*. Heat the Madeira in a saucepan, add the *Sauce Demi-Glace*, and simmer until only half the original volume remains. Add the *Glace de Viande* and boil for a few more minutes. Lower the heat, add the truffles cut in tiny cubes or strips, and cook gently until these latter are hot. Remove from the fire and stir in the butter in small pieces. Serve on the side in a gravy boat.

* "Searing" leads to coagulation or the formation of a protective skin enclosing all the juices, flavor, and nutritional value in a piece of meat. This can be done either in a hot pan on top of the stove or in a very hot oven, depending on the size of the piece of meat in question.

PREPARATION : 1 hr. 30 min. COOKING: 40 min.

POT-AU-FEU DODIN BOUFFANT (MAXIM'S BOILED FRENCH DINNER)

(serves 10)
14 lb. beef shin
A 6-lb. rump pot roast, larded with
larding pork, rubbed with rock salt
A 4-lb. dressed chicken
A 3-lb. pork and veal sausage
seasoned with thyme, bay leaves,
mint, and savory
2 marrow bones
2 veal knuckles
A 3-lb. goose foie gras
1 bottle good red Burgundy wine
3 lb. carrots
2 1/2 lb. turnips
1/2 cup leek whites
1/2 lb. parsnips
2 large onions
3 stalks celery
2 garlic cloves
2 cloves
1/4 cup salt

Macerate the *foie gras* in the red wine for at least 3 hours. Take a 12-quart earthenware casserole or pot with a cover and fill with the beef shin, marrow bones, salt, and 9 quarts of cold water. Bring to a boil, skim, and simmer for 3 hours. Remove from the fire, let cool slightly, and add the rump roast. Peel and slice half the vegetables and add them tied in a cheesecloth; scrub the remaining vegetables and add them loose to the pot. Spike the onions with the cloves. Add the leek whites in a separate cheesecloth. Bring to a boil, skim, and simmer slowly for 1 hour 30 minutes, or 1/4 hour per pound. The roast should remain slightly pink. After the first hour, add the sausage.

While the beef is cooking, place the veal knuckles in another heavy container, cover with some of the liquid from your original *Pot-au-Feu*, and simmer for 1 hour 30 minutes. Stuff the chicken with the *foie gras* and, when the veal has simmered for 40 minutes, add the chicken. After 40 more minutes, remove the chicken and keep hot. If the veal is not yet tender, continue cooking, but for no more than 20 minutes. In the meantime, heat and reduce the wine in which the *foie gras* macerated.

Put a few tablespoons of cooking liquid from the 2 pots in the bottom of a large oval serving dish. Cut the chicken in small portions and the sausage, beef, and veal in medium slices and arrange them on the serving platter. Garnish with slices of *foie gras* and pour over the reduced wine. Serve the cut-up vegetables in a separate serving dish.

* This variation of an ultra-classic in French cuisine is most successfully prepared for at least 10 persons. Traditionally, the cooking juice is served first for the soup course, followed by the meat and vegetables, mustard, pickles, and rock salt.

Although the quantity of ingredients seems enormous, many of them are to provide the meat, vegetables and broth with a good strong flavor.

Meat (vegetables and fish as well) which is put in cold water and then brought to a boil loses its nutritional and savory juices to the cooking liquid. This is the principle for making a good broth. Meat which is put in boiling water forms a skin of coagulated juices which keeps the meat pink inside and retains all its flavor. If, however, this latter meat is boiled for 3 or 4 hours, the protective skin is broken and some of the juices escape. Result: a savory broth and a roast which still retains much of its original flavor.

PREPARATION: 3 hrs. (macerating included). COOKING: 4 hrs. 30 min.

FILET DE BOEUF EN CROUTE

CARBONADE FLAMANDE (FLEMISH BEEF STEW)

A 4-lb. round steak, cut in
2 thick slices
6 large onions
4 large tomatoes
1 1/4 cup butter
1/4 cup brown sugar
1 level tbsp. flour
1 bottle strong beer
2 cups Bouillon Blanc
1 bouquet garni
Salt, pepper

Peel and chop the tomatoes; remove the seeds. Heat half the butter in a large deep stewpan. When it starts to bubble, add the meat seasoned with salt and pepper and brown on both sides, being careful not to burn the butter. Remove the meat and keep hot.

Slice the onions and brown them lightly in the same butter. Sprinkle in the flour, mix well with the juice in the pan, and cook gently for 5 minutes.

Remove from the fire and allow to cool slightly; add the brown sugar, beer, *Bouillon Blanc*, and chopped tomatoes. Reheat to a boil, stirring constantly. Add the steaks, the *bouquet garni*, and, if necessary, more beer and bouillon, so that the meat is covered by the liquid. Cover and cook gently in a slow oven (300°) for about 3 hours, basting frequently. If the liquid in the pan reduces too rapidly, add a few tablespoons of hot water.

The meat is cooked when a sharp-pronged fork pierces it almost as easily as butter. By then, the juice in the pan should be reduced to about 1 1/2 cups. Strain the sauce through a fine strainer, pour over the meat, and serve at once with boiled potatoes.

PREPARATION: 1 hr. COOKING: 3 hrs.

ENTRECOTES BERCY (SIRLOIN STEAKS WITH BUTTER SAUCE)

Three 1-lb. sirloin steaks
8 sprigs watercress

Beurre Bercy :
1 1/2 cups beef marrow
1 cup dry white wine
3 shallots, 1 cup butter
3 tbsp. lemon juice
1 tbsp. chopped parsley
Salt, pepper

Prepare the *Beurre Bercy :* poach the beef marrow in boiling water, cool, and cut into tiny cubes. Mince the shallots and cook them slowly in the wine, reducing the liquid by half. Cool. Reheat, incorporating the softened butter, diced marrow, parsley, lemon juice, salt, and pepper. Mix well and keep hot.

Broil the steaks to suit your taste and place on a hot serving dish garnished with watercress. Serve the *Beurre Bercy* either on the side in a gravy boat, or spread over the steaks just before serving.

PREPARATION: 10 min. COOKING: 25 min.

BŒUF A LA LYONNAISE (SAUTÉD POT ROAST)

6 slices cooked pot roast
6 medium onions
1 cup butter
1 tbsp. wine vinegar
1 tbsp. chopped parsley
Salt, pepper

Mince the onions and cook them slowly in 1/2 cup of butter until slightly golden. Heat the remaining butter in another pan, sear the meat on both sides, and season. Place the meat on the onions and pour over the vinegar. Raise the heat, cover, and boil for 2 minutes, thus reducing the sauce. Save the butter from the meat for later use.

Lay a bed of onions on the bottom of a hot serving dish and place the steaks and juice on top. Sprinkle with finely chopped parsley and finally pour over the warm butter in which the meat was cooked.

PREPARATION: 20 min. COOKING: 10 min.

RUMPSTEAK A LA MOUTARDE (RUMPSTEAK WITH MUSTARD SAUCE)

3 thick 3/4-lb. rumpsteaks
3/4 cup butter
1 tbsp. mustard
1/2 cup dry white wine
1/2 cup Bouillon Blanc
1 tsp. chopped tarragon
Salt, freshly ground pepper

Trim and remove all fat and sinews from the steaks. Season both sides with salt and plenty of pepper. Heat 1/2 cup of butter in a pan large enough to hold the 3 steaks side by side. Sear the steaks quickly and finish cooking according to your taste, being careful not to burn the butter. Transfer the meat to a serving platter and keep hot. Pour the wine into the pan, bring to a boil, and reduce almost entirely. Add the *Bouillon Blanc* and reduce by half.

Spread the steaks with mustard. Sprinkle with finely chopped tarragon. Remove the pan from the fire, stir in the remaining butter, and pour the sauce around the steaks.

PREPARATION: 15 min. COOKING: 10 min.

BŒUF A LA LYONNAISE

MÉDAILLONS DE VEAU ORLOFF (VEAL STEAKS WITH WINE SAUCE)

6 *veal tenderloin steaks*
1 1/4 *cups butter*
6 *shallots*
1/2 *cup flour*
1/2 *cup dry white wine*
1/2 *cup Port wine*
1/2 cup Fond de Cuisson
Salt, pepper

Season the steaks with salt and pepper, dust lightly with flour, and sear them on both sides in a shallow pan containing most of the hot butter. Lower the heat and cook slowly for 10 to 12 minutes. Remove and keep hot.

Chop the shallots and soften them in the juice in the pan; add the white wine and the Port wine. Reduce by half and add the *Fond de Cuisson*. When hot, but not boiling, remove from the fire and stir in the remaining butter in small pieces. Slit the steaks horizontally. Place a *Purée de Champignons** between the two slices, pour over a *Purée Soubise**, and pour the wine sauce around the meat in the serving dish.

* Unless dressed up, veal is a sad and colorless meat. In the hey-day of the cabaret Le Bœuf sur le Toit, a pale and puny customer used to come in almost every evening and order a slice of cold veal, a perfect phenomenon of mimicry and highly incongruous in this mecca of merry-making.

On the other hand, veal lends itself well to almost any kind of dressing which might brighten it up: ham, cheese, mushrooms, tomatoes, tarragon, mustard, curry, Cognac; the choice is open to flights of fancy which would not be feasible with meats of a more pronounced flavor.

PREPARATION: 10 min. COOKING: 15 min.

1/2 *lb. mushrooms*
1/4 *cup butter*
1 1/2 *cups heavy whipping cream*
Salt

* *Purée de Champignons (Mushroom Purée)* Wash and mince the mushrooms, and cook them in the butter with a pinch of salt over a high flame. When the liquid in the pan has almost evaporated, mash them through a strainer, add the cream, and reduce, stirring constantly, until the desired consistency is attained. Check the seasoning.

Keep hot in a double-boiler until ready to serve. PREPARATION: 10 min. COOKING: 15 min.

1 *lb. onions*
1 *cup butter*
1 cup Sauce Béchamel
1 *cup heavy whipping cream*
Sugar
Salt, pepper

* *Purée Soubise (Onion Purée)* Mince the onions and blanch them for 5 minutes in boiling salted water. Remove and drain. Season with salt and pepper, add a pinch of sugar, and stew slowly in most of the butter in a small pan with a closely fitting lid. When soft, add the thick *Sauce Béchamel*. Simmer a few minutes and mash through a strainer. Add the remaining butter and check the seasoning.

Keep hot in a double-boiler until ready to serve. PREPARATION: 15 min. COOKING: 25 min.

FRICANDEAU DE VEAU (BRAISED VEAL)

A *3-lb. veal tenderloin*
1/2 *lb. fresh larding pork*
2 *medium carrots*
2 *large onions*
1 *lb. cut-up shank bones of veal*
1 *cup butter*
1 *bouquet garni*
Salt, pepper

Following the grain of the meat, have your butcher cut you a large steak from the veal tenderloin, about 2 inches thick and weighing about 3 pounds. Have him beat it with a heavy chopper to break the meat fibers. Cut the larding pork in thin strips and lard the veal with a larding needle.

Heat half the butter in a large deep casserole dish and add the pieces of veal shank bones. Slice the carrots and chop the onions and add them and the *bouquet garni* to the pan. When these ingredients are slightly browned, lay the piece of veal on top. Season with salt and pepper, melt the remaining butter, and pour it over the veal. Cook in a moderate oven (350°). The meat should gradually brown; there should be plenty of natural juice but it should never cover the meat. If, however, the meat seems to be drying out, add a few tablespoons of hot water, and put on the cover. The resulting veal should be as tender as butter!

* The *fricandeau* is a traditional French recipe. In the eighteenth century, Beaumarchais wrote:

"Dans vos nouveaux restaurants
Tous vos plats sont suprêmes
Et pourtant les fricandeaux
Sont toujours les mêmes."

PREPARATION: 30 min. COOKING: 2 hrs.

FRICANDEAU DE VEAU

SELLE D'AGNEAU MARIA CALLAS (TRUFFLED SADDLE OF LAMB)

A 4-lb. saddle of lamb
(plus bone and trimmings)
1/2 lb. small, fresh mushrooms
6 large black truffles
2 1/2 cups Fond de Cuisson
1 cup butter
1/2 cup heavy whipping cream
1/2 cup Madeira wine
1 tsp. cornstarch
Salt, pepper

Ask your butcher to bone the saddle of lamb from the inside and trim the flap edges neatly. Bring home the bones and trimmings. Season the saddle with salt and pepper. Wash about 12 small mushroom caps thoroughly and cut them in thick slices. Cook in the butter and 1 tablespoon of cream over a high flame. Reduce the sauce to a syrupy consistency and set aside for later use.

Cut the truffles in strips. Turn the saddle of lamb on its back and place half the mushrooms on either side of the fillets and the truffles in the center. Roll and truss the saddle, season lightly with salt and pepper again, and place in a roasting pan with the broken bones and trimmings from the meat. Roast in a hot oven (425º), 12 minutes per pound or about three-quarters of an hour in all. Transfer to a serving dish and keep hot.

Skim off the fat in the roasting pan. Pour the *Fond de Cuisson* in with the bones and cook slowly until only about 1 1/2 cups of liquid remain; strain and bind with the cornstarch and the Madeira.

Remove the string from the saddle of lamb. Serve the juice separately in a gravy boat. Excellent with spring vegetables: green peas, string beans, celery, or small browned potatoes.

* In December, 1958, when Maria Callas sang at the Paris Opera House for the first time, a huge dinner was given in her honor at Maxim's. It was for this occasion that the *Selle Maria Callas* was created by Maxim's chef, M. Alex Humbert, and it has been served there ever since.

PREPARATION: 30 min. COOKING: 45 min.

COTES DE MOUTON CHAMPVALLON (MUTTON CHOP CASSEROLE)

6 thick mutton chops
5 large onions
1 lb. potatoes
1/2 cup butter
2 cups Bouillon Blanc
2 garlic cloves
1 bouquet garni
Salt, pepper

Mince the onions and brown them slightly in a little butter. Spread them evenly over the bottom of a preheated ovenware dish. Keep hot. Season the chops with salt and pepper and, with the remaining butter, sear them quickly on both sides in a frying pan. Lay them on the minced onions and pour over enough *Bouillon Blanc* to cover the chops. Add the 2 crushed garlic cloves and the *bouquet garni*. Bring to a boil, place in a moderate oven (350º), and bake for 30 minutes.

Peel and slice the potatoes and place them on top of the chops. The meat should be half submerged in the juice. Season lightly and return the dish to the oven for another 15 to 20 minutes or until the chops and the potatoes are cooked. Baste frequently during the cooking process so that neither meat nor potatoes dry out. Serve directly from the baking dish.

PREPARATION: 30 min. COOKING: 1 hr. 15 min.

COTES D'AGNEAU A L'ESTRAGON (LAMB CHOPS WITH TARRAGON)

12 lamb chops
1/2 cup butter
1 cup Fond de Cuisson
1 sprig tarragon
Salt, pepper

Heat half the butter in a shallow pan large enough for 12 chops placed side by side. Season the chops with salt and pepper. When the butter is good and hot, put in the chops and cook on both sides, leaving them quite rare. Remove and place on a hot covered serving dish, where they will continue to cook slowly.

Pour off the juice from the pan. Pour in the *Fond de Cuisson*, bring to a boil, and reduce slowly by half. Meanwhile, blanch the leaves of tarragon in boiling water, dry them, and place neatly on top of the chops.

Add the remaining butter bit by bit to the juice in the pan. Pour over the chops and serve at once.

* Serve broiled lamb chops to guests with small appetites and lamb chops sautéd with tarragon to guests with small but sophisticated appetites!

PREPARATION: 15 min. COOKING: 15 min.

SOUFFLÉ DE JAMBON PARISIEN (HAM SOUFFLÉ)

2 cups gro nd, lean, cooked ham
1/4 cup butter
4 eggs
1/2 cup Sauce Béchamel
Paprika

Pound the ham and softened butter together and put in a blender or press through a fine strainer into a bowl. Stir in the *Sauce Béchamel* and a pinch of paprika. Separate the eggs, add the yolks to the purée, and mix thoroughly. Beat the egg whites stiff and fold in very carefully with a wooden spatula.

Pour this batter into a buttered deep straight-sided soufflé dish, filling it three-quarters full. Bake in a pan of water in a hot oven (425°) for 30 to 35 minutes. Serve immediately.

* Ham soufflés used to be devilishly complicated. Mashing the cooked ham through a very fine strainer was pure torture; every time, you inevitably ruined both the strainer and your finger-tips. Today, with a blender or similar device, it is as easy as pie and the recipe is well worth trying. It is particularly good because the ham retains its full flavor. Virginia ham should be excellent for this dish and, as it is very light, it is perfect for parties, accompanied by a salad, crisp warm French bread, and sweet butter.

PREPARATION: 30 min. COOKING: 35 min.

CARRÉ DE PORC AUX 4 PURÉES (ROAST PORK WITH VEGETABLE PURÉES)

A 2 1/2-lb. loin of pork
1/4 cup butter
Salt, pepper

Season the loin of pork with salt and pepper and smear with softened butter. Place the meat in a roasting pan and roast in a hot oven (425°) for about 40 minutes. Meanwhile, prepare the four purées which should accompany the pork. It is actually a good idea to prepare, or at least start your purées ahead of time. Keep them hot in double-boilers.

PREPARATION: 5 min. COOKING: 40 min.

3/4 lb. potatoes
1 cup milk
3/4 cup butter
2 tbsp. heavy whipping cream
Salt, pepper, nutmeg

Purée de Pommes de Terre (Potato Purée) Peel and quarter the potatoes. Cook in salted water, being careful not to boil too rapidly. Drain. Return to a very low flame to dry them out, stirring to prevent sticking. Mash through a strainer into a saucepan. Gradually add the softened butter, reheating slowly. Beat vigorously with a wooden spatula. Heat the milk to a boil and add it gradually, stirring constantly, until the desired consistency is obtained. Finally incorporate the cream. Add a pinch of nutmeg, and salt and pepper to taste. PREPARATION: 15 min. COOKING: 20 min.

3/4 lb. celeriac
1 cup milk
3 tbsp. butter
1/3 cup heavy whipping cream
Salt, pepper

Purée de Céleri Rave (Celeriac Purée) Peel and cube the celeriac. Season with salt and pepper and cook in boiling salted water. When three-quarters cooked (about 15 minutes), remove, drain, and stew in a little butter in a small pan with a closely fitting lid. When tender, remove and press through a strainer. Reheat slowly. Heat the milk and cream to a boil and add to the purée until the right consistency is obtained. Season to taste. PREPARATION: 15 min. COOKING: 30 min.

1 lb. chestnuts
1 small stalk celery
1 cup milk
2 tbsp. butter
1/3 cup heavy whipping cream
Salt, pepper

Purée de Marrons (Chestnut Purée) Slit the chestnuts all around and heat them in the oven in a pan until the shells pop open. Remove the shells. Plunge the chestnuts into boiling water, cover, and boil for 5 minutes. Rinse in cold water and remove the inner skin. Boil the chestnuts in salted water along with a small stick of celery. When they start to get tender (after about half an hour), drain them, press through a strainer, reheat, and stir in the butter, hot milk, and hot cream until the desired consistency is obtained. Season to taste. PREPARATION: 25 min. COOKING: 25 min.

1 lb. lentils
1 carrot, 1 onion
1 cup milk
2 tbsp. butter
1/2 cup heavy whipping cream
3 garlic cloves, salt, pepper

Purée de Lentilles (Lentil Purée) Soak the lentils in fresh water for 2 hours. Drain thoroughly, place in salted water, bring to a boil, add the carrot, onion, and garlic, salt and pepper, cover, and cook gently for about 1 hour 30 minutes or until tender. Remove the carrot, onion and garlic. Drain the lentils and press through a strainer. Reheat slowly and add the butter, hot milk, and hot cream to make a purée. Season to taste. PREPARATION: 2 hrs. 30 min. (soaking included). COOKING: 1 hr. 30 min.

CARRÉ DE PORC AUX 4 PURÉES

LANGUE DE BŒUF SAUCE CUMBERLAND (OX TONGUE WITH CUMBERLAND SAUCE)

1 *small cured ox tongue*
2 *medium carrots*
2 *large onions*
3/4 *cup chicken or pork fat*
1/2 *bottle dry white wine*
2 *qt. Bouillon Blanc*
1 *garlic clove*
1 *bouquet garni*
Salt, pepper

Sauce Cumberland:
6 *tbsp. red currant jelly*
1 *cup Port wine*
1 *orange*
1 *lemon*
1 *tsp. mustard*
Powdered ginger
Red pepper

Slice the onions and carrots and brown them in the fat in a shallow pan. Remove and keep hot. Brown the trimmed tongue lightly on all sides. Put the onions and carrots back in the pan along with the garlic and cut up tongue root. Lay the tongue on top, pour over the dry white wine, bring to a boil, and simmer until the liquid is almost completely reduced. Pour in the bouillon, covering the tongue entirely, bring to a boil, cover, and cook in a moderate oven (350°), turning often, for about 3 hours.

In the meantime, make the cold *Sauce Cumberland*. Cut tiny thin strips of peel from th orange and the lemon, 1 tablespoon of each. Blanch them in boiling water for 3 minutes, drain, and leave to cool. Melt the jelly; transfer to a bowl, stir in the Port, citrus peels, and the juice of the whole orange and half the lemon. Add the mustard, a pinch of red pepper, and one of powdered ginger. Mix well. This sauce may be served either hot or cold, but is usually served cold.

When the tongue is done, the liquid should be reduced to about 1 1/2 cups. Place the meat on a serving platter; strain the juice through a cheesecloth and pour over the tongue. Serve the sauce separately in a gravy boat.

* Tongue may also be served with a raisin sauce. Simmer 1/2 cup blanched almonds in 2 cups water for 1/2 hr. Add 3/4 cup raisins and simmer 1/2 hr. more. Strain. Melt 6 tbsp. butter, stir in 3 tbsp. flour, the liquid from the raisins and almonds and 2 tsp. sugar melted in 2 tsp. water. Finally add the juice of 1/2 lemon and the raisins and almonds.

PREPARATION: 30 min. COOKING: 3 hrs.

QUEUE DE BŒUF EN HOCHEPOT (OXTAIL STEW)

1 *large oxtail (for 6)*
2 *pig's feet, cut in thirds*
1 *pig's ear*
1 *lb. Chipolata sausages (grilled)*
1 *medium firm cabbage*
12 *small onions*
2 *medium turnips*
2 *medium carrots*
1 *cup sorrel leaves, stewed in butter*
20 *small potatoes*
Salt, pepper

Wash the oxtail thoroughly and cut into 4-inch sections. Blanch the pig's feet and pig's ear for 10 minutes in boiling water. Place them all in an earthenware casserole dish and pour in enough warm water to cover. Season with salt and pepper. Bring to a boil, skim off the fat, cover, and cook gently for 3 hours.

Meanwhile, quarter the cabbage and blanch it. Cut the carrots and turnips into small pigeon eggs. When the meat has cooked for 3 hours, add these vegetables as well as the peeled onions. Cover and cook gently for 1 more hour.

Remove the casserole dish from the fire. Place the pieces of oxtail in a circle on a warmed deep serving dish. Place the vegetables in the center with a border of sorrel, grilled Chipolata sausage, strips of pig's ear, and the meat from the pig's feet. Serve with small, steamed potatoes and a gravy boat of the hot cooking juice.

PREPARATION: 25 min. COOKING: 4 hrs.

PIEDS DE MOUTON POULETTE (SHEEP'S FEET IN CREAM SAUCE)

36 *very white mutton feet*
1 *tbsp. flour*
1 *tbsp. vinegar*
1 *pt. heavy whipping cream*
1 1/2 *cups cooked mushrooms*
4 *egg yolks*
1 *tbsp. lemon juice*
1 *sprig thyme*
1 *bay leaf*
1 *tbsp. chopped parsley*
Salt, pepper

Trim and singe the feet. Be careful to remove any hairs around the hoof. Rinse in cold running water and remove the larger bones.

Mix the flour and vinegar in a large saucepan over a low flame. Add 2 quarts of water, a pinch of salt, the thyme and bay leaf, and bring to a boil, stirring constantly. Put in the feet, bring again to a boil, and simmer for about 3 hours. The feet should become very soft so that the small bones can be removed easily. Remove and drain thoroughly.

Put the meat in a shallow pan with the cream and mushrooms, season with salt and pepper, and simmer for a few minutes. Just before serving, take off the fire, pour a little of the sauce into a dish with the egg yolks, beat together, and return to the pan, which should be slightly cooled. Reheat gently for a few minutes; do not boil. Add the lemon juice and chopped parsley and serve immediately.

PREPARATION: 15 min. COOKING: 3 hrs. 30 min.

LANGUE DE BŒUF

FOIE DE VEAU AUX RAISINS (CALF'S LIVER WITH RAISINS)

6 slices calf's liver
1/2 cup white raisins or
1 cup white grapes
1 cup butter
1 tsp. brown sugar
1 cup Demi-Glace
1/2 tbsp. vinegar
1 tbsp. flour
Salt, pepper

If using raisins, soak them in warm water for at least 1 hour. Drain and remove the seeds. If using fresh grapes, peel and remove the seeds.

Season the slices of liver with salt and pepper. Dust with flour and cook rapidly on both sides in 1/2 cup of butter. They should be slightly rare. Remove and keep hot. Pour the vinegar into the pan. Add the *Demi-Glace* and brown sugar. Reduce by half and throw in the drained raisins or grapes. If using raisins, simmer for 3 minutes. If using grapes, bring to a boil once. Meanwhile, heat the remaining 1/2 cup of butter in a saucepan until it is bubbly. Pour the grape sauce over the hot liver followed by the hot butter. Serve immediately.

* Both liver and kidneys are better if dipped in milk before cooking. It seems to make them more tender.

PREPARATION: 15 min. COOKING: 10 min.

RIS DE VEAU A LA PALOISE (SWEETBREADS WITH HAM)

1 large sweetbread (for 6)
6 slices smoked ham
1 cup butter
3/4 cup fresh breadcrumbs
2 eggs
1 tbsp. olive oil
1/4 lemon
1/2 cup flour
Salt, pepper

Soak the sweetbread in cold water for 1 hour; then blanch it by placing in cold water, bringing to a boil, and boiling for 5 minutes. Remove and rinse in cold water. Drain, remove the membrane, any gristle and fat, and cut the sweetbread in 12 even slices. Season with salt and pepper.

Beat the eggs and oil together. Dip each slice of sweetbread first in flour, then in the beaten egg, and then in breadcrumbs. Brown the slices on both sides in 1/2 cup hot butter. When cooked, remove and keep hot on a serving dish.

Warm the slices of ham in the hot butter in the pan. Remove at once and place on top of each slice of sweetbread. Add the rest of the butter to the pan. Squeeze the juice of 1/4 lemon over the meat and pour over the hot pan juice. Serve immediately

* Sweetbreads, considered a delicacy by the French, are seldom seen on American tables. With a little imagination, this economical dish can be turned into an elegant *plat de résistance*.

PREPARATION: 15 min. (plus soaking). COOKING: 15 min.

ROGNONS SAUTÉS AU CHABLIS (LAMB KIDNEYS WITH CHABLIS SAUCE)

18 lamb kidneys
1 cup butter
1/2 lemon
2 cups Chablis wine
1/2 cup Bouillon Blanc
1 tsp. chopped parsley
Salt, pepper

Remove the membrane from the kidneys and cut them in two. Season with salt and pepper and sauté them rapidly on both sides in 3/4 cup of butter. Remove and keep hot in a deep round serving dish.

Pour the Chablis into the pan and reduce slowly until only a quarter of the original amount of liquid remains. Add the bouillon, bring to a boil, remove from the fire, and incorporate the rest of the butter, bit by bit; add a few drops of lemon juice as well.

Pour off the kidney juice that will have collected in the serving dish. Cover the kidneys with the prepared sauce, sprinkle with chopped parsley, and serve immediately.

* These recipes should be handled with extreme discretion. Many people are allergic to giblets and either the insides of animals in general or one type in particular. I know from experience that these complexes can be overcome, but you have to be clever about it. One day our chef, M. Humbert, swore that he would make me eat cucumbers (something I never could stand). He dreamed up a special chicken cooked with cucumbers *(Poulet aux Concombres)* and, after enjoying it thoroughly, I congratulated him on his succulent turnips! As far as these dishes are concerned, however, it is better to warn your guests in advance.

PREPARATION: 10 min. COOKING: 15 min.

ROGNONS SAUTÉS AU CHABLIS

POULARDE ALBUFÉRA (CHICKEN WITH FANCY RICE STUFFING)

A 3 1/2-lb. dressed roasting chicken
(with giblets)
1 cup rice
7 large truffles
1/2 lb. goose foie gras
2 strips fresh larding pork
3 cups Bouillon Blanc
1/2 lemon

Rinse the rice in cold running water. Pour it into a saucepan of boiling salted water and boil for 10 minutes or until done (test by tasting). Be careful not to overcook. Drain, rinse in warm water, separating the grains with a fork, and steam in a covered strainer over a pot of boiling water, thus drying it out. Dice 4 truffles and the *foie gras*, mix with the cooled rice, and stuff and truss the dressed chicken. Rub the breast with lemon, cover with larding pork, and bind with string. Place chicken and giblets in a deep stewpan just large enough to hold them. Pour in enough *Bouillon Blanc* to cover, bring to a boil, cover, and simmer gently. The fowl should poach, not boil.

Prepare a pimento butter: mince the pimentos, mix until smooth with 1/4 cup of softened butter, and mash through a strainer. Set aside.

90

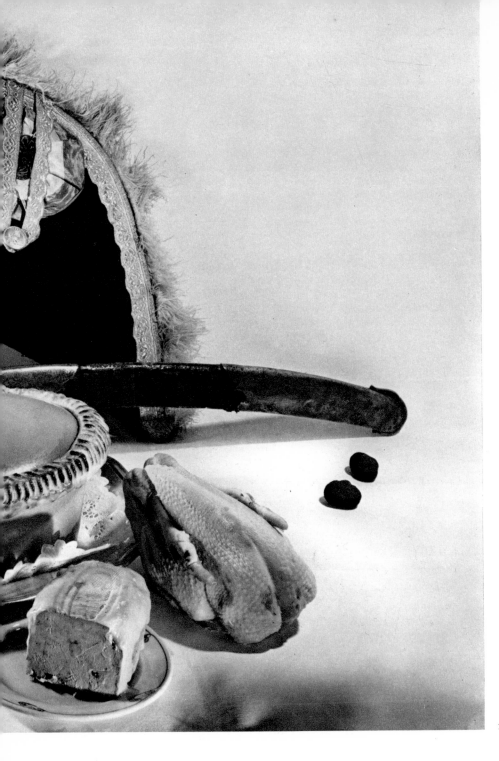

POULARDE ALBUFÉRA

When the chicken is done (about 30 minutes), remove from the liquid and keep hot. Set the giblets aside. Heat 1/2 cup of butter with 1/2 cup of flour over a low flame. When they begin to bubble, add the bouillon from the chicken, stirring constantly. Bring to a boil and simmer for at least 30 minutes. Skim the fat. Bring again to a boil and add the egg yolks and cream off the fire, stirring vigorously. Lower the heat and stir in the pimento butter. Keep hot.

Dice the giblets and the remaining truffles and heat them with the mushrooms and about 3 tablespoons of the sauce in a separate saucepan. Place the chicken on a serving platter and surround it with small heated pastry shells filled with creamed giblets. Pour some of the sauce over the chicken, and serve the rest on the side.

PREPARATION: 1 hr.   COOKING: 1 hr.

2 *small pimentoes*
1/2 *cup button mushrooms*
12 *small pastry shells*
1 1/2 *cups butter*
1/2 *cup flour*
1/2 *cup heavy whipping cream*
2 *egg yolks*
Salt, pepper

POULET AUX CONCOMBRES (CHICKEN WITH CUCUMBERS)

A 4-lb. dressed tender chicken
(with giblets)
1 lb. cucumbers
1 1/4 cups butter
1 cup heavy whipping cream
2 large firm tomatoes
1 medium carrot
1 medium onion
Powdered thyme, bay leaf
Salt, paprika

Cut the carrot and onion in thin slices, chop the giblets, and place them all in the bottom of a well-buttered ovenware dish. Heat gently for 5 minutes, then place the chicken brushed with 1/2 cup of melted butter on the vegetables. Put in a medium oven (350°) for 45 minutes, and, as it cooks, turn the chicken 4 times, basting well each time, and sprinkling with a pinch of salt. Fifteen minutes after putting in the chicken, add a pinch of herbs and 1 tomato, peeled, seeded, and coarsely chopped.

Meanwhile, peel the cucumbers, cut them in quarters, and remove the seeds. Round off the edges to make large nut-like forms. Blanch in boiling salted water for 3 minutes. Remove, drain, season with salt and pepper, and stew gently in the remaining butter and 1/2 cup of cream in a small pan with a tight-fitting lid. Season with salt and paprika.

When the chicken is done, put it on a warm serving dish. Pour the remaining cream into the dish in which the chicken cooked, bring to a boil, and simmer for 2 minutes. Pour through a fine strainer, check the seasoning, and pour over the chicken. Place the cucumber on and around the chicken, and decorate the breast with the other tomato sliced and slightly warmed in butter.

* This is the dish with which Alex Humbert cured me of an inveterate dislike of cucumbers!

PREPARATION: 30 min. COOKING: 40 min.

POULARDE HENRI IV (CHICKEN WITH WHITE WINE SAUCE)

A 4-lb. dressed tender chicken
(with giblets)
24 small raw leeks
2 lb. carrots
1 1/2 lb. turnips
1 lb. celery hearts
1 onion
1 cup butter
1 cup Bouillon Blanc
1 tsp. Glace de Viande
1 1/2 cups white wine
1 tsp. chopped shallots
1 tsp. chopped chives
1 garlic clove
1 bouquet garni
Salt, pepper

Truss the chicken and place the *bouquet garni* and garlic clove inside the carcass. Wash and peel the carrots and turnips (keep some of the peels), and cut them into small egg-like shapes. Blanch all the vegetables in boiling water, drain, season with salt and pepper, and stew slowly in 1/2 cup of butter until tender in a pan with a tight-fitting lid.

Place the vegetable trimmings and chicken giblets in the bottom of a saucepan. Place the chicken on top, add the remaining butter, and cook gently over a low flame until tender (about 1 hour). Meanwhile, cook the shallots in the white wine until practically no liquid remains. Add the *Glace de Viande* and chives and mix well. Pour into a gravy boat. Remove the chicken and keep hot. Strain the juice in the pan through a cheesecloth and add the bouillon. Bring to a boil and reduce by one-third. Remove and keep hot.

Place the chicken on a hot serving dish and arrange the vegetables around it, alternating colors. Serve with the reduced juice and the prepared sauce.

PREPARATION: 1 hr. COOKING: 1 hr.

POULARDE PETITE MARIÉE (SPRING CHICKEN WITH VEGETABLES)

A 3 1/2-lb. dressed tender chicken
(with giblets)
2 cups Fond de Cuisson
2 strips fresh larding pork
12 small new onions
12 small new potatoes
12 small new carrots
1 cup fresh peas
1 pt. heavy whipping cream
4 egg yolks
3 sprigs thyme
1 bay leaf
1 tbsp. chopped parsley
Salt, pepper

Boil the giblets in 2 cups of water and 2 cups of *Fond de Cuisson*. Plunge the chicken, the strips of larding pork across its breast, into a pot of boiling salted water for 5 minutes. Drain and place in a saucepan just large enough to hold it, along with the vegetables, thyme and bay leaf. Pour over the *Fond de Cuisson* and giblets. The liquid should just cover the chicken. Simmer for about 30 minutes.

When the chicken is done, remove it from the liquid and place it and the vegetables on a serving platter. Keep hot. Meanwhile reduce the liquid to about 2 cups. Remove the thyme and bay leaf. Take off the fire, stir in the egg yolks and cream, and reheat slowly over a low flame. Be careful that it does not boil. Pour over the chicken, sprinkle with chopped parsley, and serve.

PREPARATION: 30 min. COOKING: 40 min.

POULARDE HENRI IV

POULET SAUTE AU CURRY (CURRIED CHICKEN)

A 3 1/2-lb. frying chicken
2 medium onions
3 tbsp. oil
1 tsp. curry powder
1 cup coconut or almond milk
1 1/2 cups Sauce Béchamel
Salt, pepper

Cut up the chicken and sauté it in the oil until a golden color. Season with salt and pepper, add the chopped onions and curry powder, and cook gently for a few more minutes. Pour over the coconut or almond milk; add the *Sauce Béchamel*. Finish cooking the chicken by slightly reducing this sauce. Serve with *Riz à l'Indienne*.

PREPARATION: 20 min. (plus *Sauce*).   COOKING: 40 min.

POULET EN MEURETTE (CHICKEN WITH THICK WINE SAUCE)

A 4-lb. dressed roasting chicken
(with giblets)
1 bottle red Burgundy wine
6 oz. lean bacon
20 baby onions
1/2 cup small fresh mushrooms
1 tbsp. flour
1 tbsp. butter
(1/4 cup chicken or pig's blood)
2 garlic cloves
1 bouquet garni
Chicken bouillon
Croûtons
Salt, pepper

Cut the chicken into 6 pieces. Season them and the giblets (except the liver) with salt and pepper. Cut the bacon into thin strips and blanch it rapidly in boiling salted water. Drain and dry.

Melt 1/2 tablespoon of butter in a deep ovenware pot on top of the stove, and brown the bacon and onions. Remove, drain, and keep warm.

Brown the mushrooms in the same butter. Remove and keep warm with the bacon and onions. Place the pieces of chicken in the pot and brown them on all sides, then sprinkle with flour. Turn constantly. Crush the garlic, add it to the pot, and pour in the wine. Stir until the liquid starts to boil, then add the bacon, onions, mushrooms, and *bouquet garni*.

If the liquid does not cover the ingredients in the pot, add enough hot bouillon to cover. Put on the lid and cook gently for 45 minutes, after which time remove the solid ingredients from the pot and keep them hot. Throw away the *bouquet garni* and strain the sauce. If it seems thin, reduce it somewhat, but slowly.

Return the sauce and the pieces of chicken to the pot, but not to the fire. Dice the chicken livers, sear them rapidly in the remaining butter in a frying pan, and mash them through a fine strainer or in a blender, making a purée. Place in a bowl, add the chicken or pig's blood (optional) and 3 or 4 tablespoons of the juice from the chicken. Beat well together.

With the pot still off the fire, add this sauce, mixing the 2 liquids together through a rotating motion of the pot. Reheat gently, stirring constantly, and being careful the liquid does not boil. The sauce will gradually thicken.

Place the chicken on a warmed serving dish. Arrange the bacon, onions, and mushrooms around it, pour over the sauce, and encircle with croûtons.

PREPARATION: 35 min.   COOKING: 50 min.

POULET STRASBOURGEOISE (CHICKEN WITH FOIE GRAS AND TRUFFLES)

A 4-lb. dressed roasting chicken
(with giblets)
A 2-lb. goose foie gras
6 truffles
3/4 cup butter
1/4 cup Cognac
1/4 cup Madeira wine
2 strips fresh larding pork
1 carrot
1 onion
3 thin slices veal gristle
1 cup Fond de Cuisson
1 bouquet garni
Spices: prepared powdered mixture
of clove, nutmeg, cinnamon
Rock salt, table salt, freshly
ground pepper

Peel the truffles and season them with table salt, pepper, and spices. Season the *foie gras* in the same manner and place both truffles and *foie gras* in a bowl. Pour over the Cognac and Madeira and let stand for 24 to 48 hours.

Season the inside of the chicken with 1 teaspoon of fine rock salt. Place the macerated *foie gras* and truffles in the chicken, truss, and let stand in a cool place for 24 hours so that the fowl becomes impregnated by the flavor of the truffles. Keep the solution of Madeira and Cognac for future use.

When ready to roast, tie the 2 strips of larding pork across the chicken's breast and place it in a deep roasting pan on a bed of veal gristle, giblets, the chopped onion and carrot, and the *bouquet garni*. Melt the butter, pour it over the fowl, add a pinch of salt, cover, and put in a hot oven (425°) for about 1 hour 15 minutes. Baste frequently with the warmed *Fond de Cuisson*. When done, remove the chicken and keep hot. Skim the fat off the juice in the pan, add the Cognac and Madeira solution, and bring to a boil. Strain this sauce through a piece of cheesecloth.

Just before serving, remove the larding pork from the chicken and untruss it. Serve the sauce separately in a gravy boat.

PREPARATION: 1 hr. (plus 3 days).   COOKING: 1 hr. 30 min.

96

CANETON A L'ORANGE (ROAST DUCKLING WITH ORANGE SAUCE)

A 5 1/2-lb. dressed duckling
(with trimmings and giblets)
4 naval oranges
3 tbsp. sugar
1/4 cup wine vinegar
2 tbsp. butter
2 small onions
2 small carrots
3 cups Jus Brun
2 1/2 tbsp. cooking oil
5/8 cup Port or Madeira wine
3 tbsp. Curaçao
2 tbsp. arrowroot
1 tbsp. lemon juice
1 bouquet garni
Salt, pepper

Prepare some duck stock in the following manner: chop up the giblets and trimmings, onions and carrots, and brown them in the oil in a saucepan. Drain off the oil, add the *Jus Brun*, *bouquet garni*, and a little water, and simmer for at least 1 hour 30 minutes, skimming occasionally. Strain.

Cut the orange part of the orange peel in tiny slivers about 1 inch long. Blanch in boiling water for 15 minutes and dry. Season the inside of the duckling, add one-third of the orange peel, and truss. Prick the skin around the legs and lower breast. Brown in a hot oven (425°) for 15 minutes, then lower the heat to about 350°, turning the duck on one side for 30 minutes and the other side for 20 minutes. Skim the fat from the bottom of the pan occasionally. Return to an upright position and roast 15 more minutes. The juice from the duck should be a pale pink.

Meanwhile, prepare the sauce. Boil the sugar and vinegar over a medium flame until it becomes a dark brown syrup. Remove from the heat and pour in one-fourth of the prepared stock. Simmer a few minutes, stirring until the syrup is dissolved. Mix the arrowroot with 3 tablespoons of wine. Add the remaining stock and the arrowroot mixture to the hot sauce. Stir in the orange peel, simmer for 3 or 4 minutes, check the seasoning, and keep hot. Remove the white skin from the oranges, cut them in slices, and set aside.

Place the duck on a heated platter and keep hot. Skim all fat from the roasting juice, add the remaining wine, and boil, reducing to about 3 tablespoons. Strain into the sauce and simmer. Stir in the Curaçao. If the sauce seems too sweet, add a few drops of lemon juice. Remove from the fire and stir in the butter in small pieces. Garnish the platter with orange slices and pour over some of the sauce. Serve the rest in a gravy boat.

PREPARATION: 1 hr. 45 min. (stock).   COOKING: 1 hr. 45 min.

CANARD AUX PÊCHES (DUCKLING WITH PEACHES)

Two 3-lb. dressed ducklings
(with giblets)
6 large peaches
1 cup butter
3 tbsp. sugar
2 tbsp. vinegar
2 1/2 cups Bouillon Blanc
1 oz. peach brandy
Salt

Place the giblets in the bottom of a well-buttered pan and lay the ducklings on top of them. Add most of the butter and cook over a low flame, turning occasionally, for about 45 minutes. Remove the ducklings and giblets and keep them hot. Remove as much fat as possible from the remaining liquid in the pan. Add 1 tablespoon of sugar and cook until a pale caramel color, add the vinegar, reduce a little, and add the bouillon. Add the giblets and cook gently for 20 minutes. Remove from the fire and pour the sauce through a fine strainer. Stir in the little remaining butter.

If using fresh peaches, peel them, plunge them in boiling water for a few seconds, and drain them. Cut in half and remove the stones. Sprinkle with the remaining sugar and color them quickly over a high flame.

Place the ducklings on a hot platter with the peaches around them. Add the brandy to the hot sauce and pour over ducklings and peaches.

PREPARATION: 30 min.   COOKING: 1 hr.

SALMIS DE CANARD A LA ROUENNAISE (SLICED ROAST DUCKLING)

A 4-lb. dressed duckling
1 cup butter
1/2 cup good red wine
3 shallots
Spice mixture: nutmeg,
cinnamon, clove
Salt, pepper

Truss the duckling and place it in a roasting pan. Melt and pour over the butter, season with salt and pepper, and put in a very hot oven (450°) for 8 minutes, 4 minutes per side. Let cool for 5 minutes. With a sharp knife, detach the legs and second-joints.

Sprinkle a buttered oval ovenware dish with chopped shallots, salt, pepper, and spices. Cut the breast in thin slivers, and place them side by side in the dish. Season lightly with spices. Remove the meaty joints of the wings and pan-broil them with the drumsticks and second joints. Cut the remaining meat off the duckling, pour the red wine over the carcass, and press out all the juice. Pour this juice over the white meat.

Just before serving, dot with small pieces of butter and put in a hot oven (425°). The minute the meat begins to curl, remove from the oven, place the browned wings and legs at each end of the platter, and serve.

PREPARATION: 20 min.   COOKING: 30 min.

CANETON A L'ORANGE

DINDONNEAU AUX CELERIS (YOUNG TURKEY WITH BRAISED CELERY)

A 4-lb. dressed young turkey
(with giblets)
2 strips fresh larding pork
1 cup butter
1 stalk celery
1 medium onion
1 1/2 cups Bouillon Blanc
1/2 cup Madeira wine
1 bouquet garni
Rock salt, pepper

Truss the turkey and tie the pieces of larding pork over the breast. Sprinkle a little rock salt inside the carcass.

Chop up the onion and place it, the stick of celery, and the *bouquet garni* in the bottom of a well-buttered roasting pan with a cover. Arrange the giblets on the vegetables so that the turkey will not be in direct contact with the vegetables nor immersed in the butter in which it cooks.

Smear the softened butter over the turkey, season with salt and pepper, and lay it carefully on the giblets. Place in a medium oven (350°). As soon as the turkey has browned, cover and cook for about 50 minutes, basting frequently with a mixture of warmed bouillon and Madeira.

PREPARATION: 20 min. COOKING: 50 min.

12 celery hearts
1 carrot, 1 onion
2 lb. veal shank bones,
cut in small pieces
Bouillon or water
1 bouquet garni
Salt

Céleris braisés (Braised Celery). Clean and trim the roots of the celery and cut off the stalks about 3 inches from the base. Boil for 10 minutes, drain, and rinse well in cold running water. Line an ovenware dish with the veal bones, the sliced carrot and onion, and the *bouquet garni*, place the celery on the bones and vegetables, and pour in enough warmed bouillon or water to half cover the celery. Cover the dish and cook in a moderate oven (350°) for 1 hour or until the celery is tender. PREPARATION: 25 min. COOKING: 1 hr.

DINDONNEAU EN DAUBE FROID (COLD BONED STUFFED TURKEY)

A 4-lb. dressed young turkey
1 lb. lean sausage meat
1/2 lb. lean raw ham
1/2 lb. cured veal tongue
4 black truffles
3 strips fresh larding pork
1/2 cup Cognac
1 1/2 qt. Fond de Cuisson
Salt, freshly ground pepper, allspice

Have your butcher bone the turkey, cutting it down the back, and detaching the bone down to the breastbone. The legs, wings, and second joints remain intact. Season the interior with salt and pepper.

Cut the ham in small pieces and peel and quarter the truffles. Prepare a stuffing by mixing the sausage meat, ham, truffles, a pinch of allspice, and the Cognac all together. Place half of this mixture in the turkey; lay the piece of cured tongue wrapped in 1 strip of larding pork on top, and cover with the remaining stuffing. Reform the turkey, season the outside with salt and pepper, truss it, and tie the remaining strips of larding pork over the breast.

Put in a deep ovenware dish, pour in enough *Fond de Cuisson* to cover the fowl, and cook for about 2 hours 30 minutes. Cool, chill for 24 hours, and serve, like a *pâté*, directly from the dish.

PREPARATION: 40 min. COOKING: 2 hrs. 30 min. (CHILLING: 1 day)

DINDONNEAU FARCI A LA SAUGE (TURKEY WITH SAGE STUFFING)

A 5-lb. dressed turkey (with giblets)
2 1/2 cups fresh breadcrumbs
1 1/4 cups butter
1/2 lb. thick lean bacon
2 strips fresh larding pork
3 slices breast of veal
1 small bunch sage
3 carrots, 2 turnips
2 stalks celery
1 onion
2 garlic cloves
Bouillon or veal stock
1 tsp. powdered thyme, bay leaf
1 bouquet garni
Salt, freshly ground pepper, sugar

Prepare the stuffing in the following manner: mince 2 carrots, the turnips and celery, and stew them in 1 tablespoon of butter. Cut the bacon in small cubes and brown it. Cut up the sage and crush the garlic. Brown the breadcrumbs in butter until slightly golden, add the stewed vegetables, sage, garlic, bacon and bacon fat, stir together, and season with salt, pepper, and a pinch of sugar.

Stuff the dressed turkey with this stuffing, truss it, and cover the breast with larding pork. Cut up the remaining carrot, the onion and the giblets, and put them in the bottom of a roasting pan along with the *bouquet garni* and the breast of veal. Place the turkey on top. Melt a cup of butter and pour it over the fowl, add a pinch of salt, cover, and place in a hot oven (425°) for 1 hour 30 minutes. Baste frequently. If it seems to be drying out in the bottom of the pan, add a few spoonfuls of veal stock or bouillon.

When the turkey is done and golden brown, transfer it to a serving platter and remove the string and larding pork. Strain the juice through a piece of cheesecloth, skim off some of the fat, and serve separately in a gravy boat.

PREPARATION: 30 min. COOKING: 1 hr. 30 min.

103

FAISAN NORMANDE (PHEASANT WITH APPLES)

2 *pheasant*
4 *large sweet apples*
4 *strips fresh larding pork*
1 *cup heavy whipping cream*
3/4 *cup butter*
1 *tsp. Calvados*
Salt, pepper

Take 2 plump pheasant (for 6 persons). Truss and cover the breasts with larding pork. Brown in butter in a shallow pan. Peel and core the apples, cut in slices, and sauté them gently in butter until half cooked. Make a bed of the sautéd apples on the bottom of a hot ovenware dish. Place the pheasant on top. Season with a little salt. Arrange the remaining slices of sautéd apples around the birds. Cover and cook in a medium oven (350º) for 18 to 20 minutes.

Just before serving, pour over the warmed cream and Calvados. Serve directly from the baking dish.

* Thanks to the rich dairylands and plentiful apple orchards that adorn the Norman countryside, Norman cooking is typified by the use of heavy cream, apples, and Calvados (the Norman applejack). In general, the *cuisine* of Normandy is very rich, but it is saved from being labeled "heavy" by the imagination and delicacy of its variations.

PREPARATION: 30 min. COOKING: 25 min.

FAISAN FARCI MARYLAND (STUFFED PHEASANT)

2 *pheasant (with liver)*
1 *strip fresh larding pork*
3 *ears sweet fresh corn or*
1 *cup canned corn*
1/2 *cup diced lean bacon*
1 1/2 *cups heavy whipping cream*
1 *level tbsp. tapioca*
3/4 *cup butter*
1 *cup shelled peas*
1/2 *cup milk*
1/2 *cup Bouillon Blanc*
Salt, pepper

Have your butcher prepare the pheasant for stuffing through the gullet. Cut the liver into cubes. If using fresh corn, drop the ears in two-thirds water to one-third milk which is boiling and cook gently for 4-10 minutes. When tender, remove the kernels without crushing them. Set aside for later use.

Cook the peas in salted water until tender. Drain and set aside.

Brown the bacon lightly in a little butter. Just before removing from the fire, add the diced liver from the pheasant. In another pan, gently boil 1 cup of cream, stirring constantly, reducing it by half. Remove from the fire, let cool, and add the tapioca. Reheat slowly to the boiling point and remove immediately from the fire.

Place the corn, peas, bacon, and liver in a bowl. Season with salt and pepper and pour in the cream and tapioca. Mix well, being careful not to crush any of the ingredients, and stuff the pheasant with this mixture.

Truss the bird, tie the larding pork over its breast, and cook for 45 minutes in the remaining butter in a stewpan. Remove the pheasant and keep hot. Add the bouillon and remaining cream to the juice in the pan. Reduce slightly and pour over the pheasant just before serving. Serve the remaining sauce in a gravy boat.

* Birds with dark meat, such as duck, quail, pheasant or partridge, are usually served slightly rare. Birds with white meat, such as squab, are usually served well done.

PREPARATION: 30 min. COOKING: 45 min.

FAISAN BRAISÉ AU PORTO (BRAISED PHEASANT WITH PORT WINE)

2 *pheasant*
3/4 *cup butter*
1 *cup heavy whipping cream*
1/2 *cup Port wine*
Salt, pepper

Season the pheasant with salt and pepper and cook in the butter in a deep uncovered stewpan on top of the stove. When three-quarters cooked (about 20 minutes), add the cream, cover, and cook gently about 10 more minutes or until the birds are almost done.

Pour in the Port wine, mix well, baste, and replace the cover for 5 more minutes. Place the pheasant on a hot serving dish and pour over the sauce.

* Pheasant were originally imported from Asia. Unlike the partridge whose reproduction requires no artificial stimulant, their race has only been kept alive in Europe by intensive breeding. The flesh of the pheasant is considered less choice than that of the partridge.

PREPARATION: 15 min. COOKING: 20 min.

FAISAN FARCI MARYLAND

CAILLES AUX RAISINS (QUAIL WITH GRAPES)

6 quail
6 small strips larding pork
(6 vine leaves)
1/2 cup butter
2 cups white grapes
1/4 cup Cognac
1/4 cup Bouillon Blanc
Salt, pepper

Clean and truss the birds. Salt and pepper them lightly. If you have vine leaves handy, wrap one around each bird and cover with a thin strip of larding pork. Tie securely. Peel the grapes and remove the seeds.

Heat the butter in a shallow pan, sear the quail quickly; then put in a hot oven (425°) and roast for about 8 minutes. Remove from the oven, untruss, and place in a preheated uncovered ovenware dish with the cooking juice and the grapes. Return to the hot oven for another 5 minutes.

Just before serving, stir the warmed Cognac and bouillon into the juice in the pan, baste the quail with this sauce, cover, and serve immediately.

PREPARATION: 15 min. COOKING: 15 min.

RABLES DE LIÈVRE SAUCE POIVRADE (SADDLES OF HARE WITH PEPPER SAUCE)

3 saddles of hare
1 1/2 cups Sauce Poivrade
4 strips fresh larding pork
1 carrot
1 onion
3/4 cup butter
1 cup red currant jelly
1/2 cup dry white wine
1 1/2 cups Cognac
Powdered thyme, bay leaves
Salt, pepper

Trim the saddles of hare and insert small strips of larding pork into the meat. Set the trimmings to one side for later use. Place the saddles in a large bowl and season with salt and pepper, powdered bay leaves and thyme. Slice the carrot and onion, add them to the bowl, and pour over 1/2 cup of Cognac. Put in a cool place (not the refrigerator) and marinate for a good 12 hours, turning the meat from time to time.

Once marinated, remove from the solution (keep the solution for the sauce), drain, and roast in butter in a hot oven (425°) for about 20 minutes; the meat should remain slightly pink.

In the meantime, prepare your *Sauce Poivrade*, a *Sauce Grand Veneur* minus the currant jelly and heavy cream (see *Noisettes de Chevreuil* on the following page).

Place the saddles of hare on a hot serving dish and bring to the table. Warm the remaining cup of Cognac, pour it over the meat, and set a match to it. Add the marinating solution and the pan scrapings reduced with white wine to the *Sauce Poivrade* and serve separately. Serve a small dish of red currant jelly on the side.

* The hare is one of the most succulent of game meats. Its flesh has a really gamy taste. The best hares come from the mountain regions where they have no contact with mankind and feed on a variety of fragrant grasses.

PREPARATION: 12 hrs. 15 min. (marinating included). COOKING: 25 min. (plus *Sauce*).

PIE AU LAPIN (RABBIT PIE)

1 plump rabbit
2 cups Pâte Feuilletée
12 small highly spiced sausages
1/2 lb. thick lean bacon
4 onions
1 cup dry white wine
7 tbsp. butter
3 eggs
1 egg yolk
1/2 cup flour
1 sprig rosemary
1 sprig thyme
Salt, pepper

Have your butcher clean the rabbit and cut it into serving pieces. Peel and mince the onions and dice the bacon. Melt the butter in a heavy stewpan and cook the onions and bacon until golden brown. Dredge the pieces of rabbit in flour and sauté them in the same pan until nicely browned on all sides. Add the heated wine, the rosemary and thyme, salt and pepper. Cover and simmer for 1 hour.

Meanwhile, hard-boil the 3 eggs and cut each one in about 6 pieces. Brown the sausages in a frying pan. Pour the rabbit stew in an ovenware dish and add the eggs and sausages.

Roll out the *Pâte Feuilletée* in a 1/4-inch layer and lay it over the top of the baking dish. Seal the dough to the rim of the dish by dampening with cold water and pressing together. Cut a small hole in the crust and insert a chimney of heavy paper rolled like a cigarette. Brush with egg-yolk beaten with a little cold water. Bake in a hot oven (425°) for about 20 minutes. Serve directly from the baking dish.

PREPARATION: 10 min. (plus *Pâte Feuilletée*). COOKING: 1 hr. 30 min.

NOISETTES DE CHEVREUIL GRAND VENEUR (VENISON WITH CURRANT SAUCE)

12 *venison fillet steaks*
3/4 *cup butter*
Croûtons
Salt, pepper

Sauce Grand Veneur:
1 *small carrot*
1 *medium onion*
1 1/2 *cups vinegar*
1 *cup dry white wine*
1 *tbsp. olive oil*
1 *bouquet garni*
1 *qt.* Sauce Demi-Glace
2 *tbsp. heavy whipping cream*
3 *tbsp. red currant jelly*
Venison trimmings
Salt, freshly ground pepper

The meat should be carefully trimmed, removing all nerve fibers in particular. Keep the trimmings. Prepare the sauce by dicing the carrot and onion and heating them slowly in the oil. Add the *bouquet garni* and venison trimmings. When the ingredients are slightly browned, drain off the oil and pour in the white wine and vinegar. Reduce almost completely, add the *Sauce Demi-Glace* and simmer.

After 1 hour, add 1 tablespoon of pepper and a little salt. Remove from the fire, strain, and stir in the currant jelly. When it is well dissolved, add the cream, mix well, and keep hot until serving-time.

Place the steaks in a shallow pan containing the very hot butter. Cook on both sides, leaving slightly underdone. Take off the fire and let stand for 5 minutes before serving. Place on croûtons of the same size and shape, and serve with the sauce on the side.

* Rib chops may be substituted for fillets of venison in this recipe.

PREPARATION: 20 min. COOKING: 1 hr.

CIVET DE CHEVREUIL (VENISON STEW)

4 *lb. stewing venison*
1/2 *lb. lean bacon*
1 *cup small mushrooms*
24 *baby onions*
3 *large onions*
2 *bottles new red wine*
3 1/2 *tbsp. butter*
2 *tbsp. olive oil*
9 *tbsp. Cognac*
2 *tbsp. flour*
2 *garlic cloves*
1 *bouquet garni*
Powdered thyme, bay leaves
Chopped parsley
Croûtons
Salt, pepper

The venison should be boned and cut in large cubes. Mince 1 large onion, cut the bacon in thin strips, and crush the garlic cloves. Place the meat in a large dish with the olive oil, 1 tablespoon of Cognac, and the minced onion. Season with powdered herbs, salt and pepper. Leave the venison in this solution for 6 hours, turning the meat 2 or 3 times.

Brown the strips of bacon in 2 tablespoons of butter in a large frying pan over a high flame. Remove and keep hot. Cut the other 2 large onions in quarters. Place them in the frying pan in which the bacon browned. Cook over a low flame until a golden color. Sprinkle with 2 tablespoons of flour, mix well, and cook for 5 more minutes. Add the drained pieces of venison, raise the heat, and sear them rapidly, turning on all sides and stirring constantly.

Pour the contents of the frying pan into a large, warmed stewpan and add the bacon. Cover with the warmed red wine, add the crushed garlic and *bouquet garni*, and bring to a boil; cover and cook for just under 1 hour over a low flame. Remove the meat, bacon, and onions from the stewpan, strain the liquid, and return all ingredients to the rinsed pan. Reheat slowly.

Stew the mushrooms gently in the remaining butter and add them to the stew. Bring to a boil, cover, and cook gently for 45 minutes.

Shortly before serving, add the remaining Cognac to the stew. Continue to heat gently, stirring continually, until it starts to boil. Remove at once from the fire. Check the seasoning.

Arrange the stew in a deep serving dish surrounded by triangular croûtons in a saw-tooth pattern. Sprinkle with finely chopped parsley and serve at once.

* It is always a good idea to marinate venison as, although some consider its meat superior to all other game, one never knows under what conditions it was killed. Age, fatigue, and fear at the time of its death all play an important role in determining the flavor and quality of the meat.

Because of its intensely gamy flavor, venison lends itself to unusual and fragrant condiments: pepper and ginger, currants, oranges, pears, prunes, grapes and chestnuts. Broiled or roasted, both venison and hare should be served quite rare. Both are admirably complemented by a full-bodied red wine such as a Côtes-du-Rhône: Hermitage or Châteauneuf-du-Pape.

This stew, accompanied by a bottle of good red wine, is a perfect winter evening's meal, especially in the country, around an open fire-place.

PREPARATION: 6 hrs. (marinating). COOKING: 2 hrs.

CIVET DE CHEVREUIL

PURÉE D'ARTICHAUTS (ARTICHOKE PURÉE)

6 *large artichoke hearts*
1 *cup butter*
1 *tbsp. vinegar*
1 *tbsp. flour*
Croûtons
Salt, pepper

Mix thoroughly 1 tablespoon of vinegar with 1 tablespoon of flour. Add 4 cups of water, bring to a boil, and add the cleaned artichoke hearts. Season with salt and pepper, bring again to a boil, and cook for 20 to 30 minutes, or until half-cooked.

Remove from the fire, drain the artichoke hearts, and stew them gently in 1/4 cup of butter in a tightly-closed saucepan. When tender, mash them through a fine strainer into a warm pan and incorporate the remaining butter bit by bit, stirring continually. Season to taste.

* This purée can be thickened by adding the mashed pulp of baked potatoes. Delicious served with small croûtons fried in butter.

PREPARATION: 25 min. COOKING: 40 min.

ASPERGES A LA CRÈME (ASPARAGUS WITH CREAM SAUCE)

4 *lb. asparagus*
Salt

Sauce Crème:
1 1/2 *cups* Sauce Béchamel
1/2 *cup heavy whipping cream*
1/2 *lemon*
Salt

Peel the asparagus stalks carefully, wash in cold water, drain, and cook in gently boiling salted water. When the asparagus are tender, but still somewhat firm, drain, and place in warm water until ready to serve.

Reduce the *Sauce Béchamel* by half. Heat the cream and add it to the sauce. Stir until you have the consistency of sour cream. Season with salt and the juice of 1/2 lemon.

Drain the asparagus and place them on a napkin on a warmed serving dish. Serve the sauce in a gravy boat on the side.

* The water for the asparagus must not boil too fast or the tips will fall off. This is especially true for young, tender, green asparagus.

PREPARATION: 30 min. COOKING: 20 min.

AUBERGINES A LA SERBE (STUFFED EGGPLANT)

6 *small eggplant*
1 *cup ground left-over lamb*
or mutton
3/4 *cup cooked rice*
1 *large onion*
1 *tbsp. olive oil*
1/2 *cup melted butter*
1/2 *cup fresh breadcrumbs*
2 *garlic cloves*
Salt, pepper, chopped parsley

Heat the eggplant in a hot oven (425°) for 10 minutes. Meanwhile, chop up the onion and heat it in a little oil until soft. Remove the eggplant from the oven and slice them in half lengthwise. Scoop out the pulp, being careful not to break the skins. Chop up the pulp and mix it with the ground mutton, rice, and onion. Crush the garlic, and add it to the mixture. Season with salt and pepper, add 1 tablespoon of finely chopped parsley, and stuff the eggplant shells with this mixture.

Arrange the eggplant neatly in a hot ovenware dish. Sprinkle with breadcrumbs, pour over the melted butter, and brown in a hot oven.

PREPARATION: 30 min. COOKING: 15 min.

PAIN D'ÉPINARDS (SPINACH LOAF)

2 *lb. fresh spinach*
1 1/2 *cups heavy whipping cream*
3/4 *cup butter*
4 *eggs*
Croûtons
Salt, grated nutmeg

Cook the spinach in boiling salted water for 5 minutes. Rinse in cold water, drain, and squeeze dry. Mash through a fine strainer or in a blender. Melt half the butter in a saucepan; add the spinach and a generous pinch of nutmeg and boil for about 5 minutes, stirring constantly, thus eliminating any water. Remove from the fire and let cool slightly. Meanwhile, beat the eggs with the cream and whisk them and the remaining butter into the spinach purée. When the mixture is perfectly blended, taste and season.

Grease a deep round 10-inch mold and fill it with the purée. Place in a hot, but not boiling, water bath in a moderate oven (350°) for about 20 minutes. Let stand for about 10 minutes before unmolding for serving. Serve with crisp croûtons.

PREPARATION: 20 min. COOKING: 20 min.

114

TARTE AUX CHAMPIGNONS (MUSHROOM PIE)

1 *lb. mushrooms*
3/4 *cup grated Gruyère cheese*
1 *cup butter*
1 1/2 *cups heavy whipping cream*
1/2 *cup Port wine*
2 *cups Pâte Brisée*

Prepare the *Pâte Brisée.* Line a buttered pie pan with the chilled pastry dough, pricking with a fork in several places to avoid bubbles. Line with wax paper and spread with a layer of dried beans or uncooked rice so the crust will keep its shape. Bake in a hot oven (425º) until a light golden color, remove the paper and vegetables, and return to the oven for a few minutes.

Wash the mushrooms, drain and dry them. Cut in quarters and season with salt and pepper. Sauté them over a high flame in 1/4 cup of butter. When the liquid in the pan has almost evaporated, add the cream and Port wine. Stir briskly, remove from the fire, and incorporate the rest of the butter, stirring continually until a creamy consistency is obtained. Pour the mixture into the pastry shell, sprinkle with grated cheese and a little melted butter, and brown in a hot oven (425º).

* This same recipe can be made up in small tarts.

PREPARATION: 15 min. (plus *Pâte Brisée*). COOKING: 20 min.

GIROLLES AU GRATIN (BAKED MUSHROOMS)

1 *lb. mushrooms*
1 *cup butter*
1/2 *cup melted butter*
1/2 *cup olive oil*
1 *cup heavy whipping cream*
3 *shallots*
1/2 *cup grated Gruyère cheese*
1 *garlic clove*
1 *tbsp. chopped parsley*
Salt, pepper

Clean the mushrooms carefully, wash, drain them, and boil in plenty of salted water for 10 minutes. Meanwhile, chop up the shallots and crush the garlic. When the mushrooms are done, drain and dry them.

Heat the oil in a large frying pan and add 1/2 cup of butter. When the oil and butter are very hot, throw in the mushrooms, shallots and garlic. Season with salt and pepper and sauté them over a high flame. As soon as the liquid in the pan starts to evaporate, add the cream. Lower the heat and reduce the sauce to the desired consistency.

Remove from the fire and add the parsley and the remaining butter, bit by bit, stirring constantly. Pour the mixture into an ovenware dish. Sprinkle with grated cheese, pour over the melted butter, and place in the oven to brown.

* In France, wild apricot-colored mushrooms called *Girolles* are used in this dish.

PREPARATION: 30 min. COOKING: 25 min.

CÈPES FARCIS (STUFFED MUSHROOMS)

12 *large firm mushrooms*
4 *shallots*
1 *cup chopped cooked ham*
1/2 *cup fresh breadcrumbs*
3/4 *cup butter*
1/2 *cup oil*
1 *tbsp. chopped parsley*
Salt, pepper

Peel the mushrooms and blanch them in boiling water for 5 minutes. Rinse in cold water and drain. Cut off the stems and chop them up with the ham. Mince the shallots.

Heat the oil in a shallow pan and brown the mushroom caps quickly on both sides. Place them in a shallow ovenware dish, stem side up, and season lightly with salt and pepper.

Pour the chopped ham and stems into the warm oil in which the mushroom caps were browned, add the shallots and most of the breadcrumbs, setting enough of the latter aside for topping at the end. Finally add the chopped parsley, mix together and brown slightly. Season with pepper and a little salt (the ham being salty in itself), fill the caps with this mixture, and sprinkle with the remaining breadcrumbs. Melt the butter, pour it over the mushrooms, and place in a hot oven (425º) for about 10 minutes or until brown.

* In France, large flap mushrooms *(Cèpes)* about 2 inches in diameter are used in the preparation of this dish.

PREPARATION: 20 min. COOKING: 20 min.

FLAN DE CAROTTES (CARROT PIE)

1 3/4 lb. new carrots
1/2 cup cream
2 cups Pâte Brisée
1 cup butter
1/2 cup sugar
Salt, pepper

Line a 12-inch buttered pie pan with the chilled pastry dough. Press down firmly, trim the edges, and prick in several places with a fork to avoid bubbles. Line with wax paper and spread with dried beans or uncooked rice so the crust will keep its shape. Bake in a hot oven (425º) until the crust is a light golden color, remove the paper and vegetables, and return to the oven for a few minutes.

Peel and wash the carrots, and cut them in thin slices. Cook 1/2 cup of carrots in boiling salted water until tender. Stew the remaining slices in a little water with a pinch of salt, a pinch of sugar, and half the butter. When tender, the juice should be completely reduced. Make a purée by pressing the stewed carrots through a strainer and adding the remaining butter, bit by bit. Add the cream, mix thoroughly, reheat, and pour the purée into the pastry shell. Decorate with the slices of boiled carrots, sprinkle with a little sugar, and bake in a hot oven (425º) for 20 minutes.

PREPARATION: 30 min. (plus *Pâte Brisée*). COOKING: 1 hr.

COURGETTES PROVENÇALES (ZUCCHINI WITH TOMATOES)

1 1/4 lb. zucchini
2 large tomatoes
1 cup butter
1 garlic clove
1 tbsp. chopped parsley
Salt, pepper

Peel the zucchini, cut them in thick slices, and quarter the slices. Round off the edges, making small egg-like forms. Blanch in boiling salted water for 2 minutes. Drain and rinse well under cold running water. Heat half the butter in a large frying pan and sauté the seasoned zucchini. At the same time, peel and cut up the tomatoes, remove the seeds, and cook them slowly in the other 1/2 cup of butter. When the zucchini is tender, add the tomatoes, parsley, and the crushed garlic. Add a pinch of freshly ground pepper, mix well, and serve piping hot.

PREPARATION: 15 min. COOKING: 20 min.

BROCOLIS AU LARD (BROCCOLI WITH BACON)

4 lb. broccoli
1/2 lb. thick, rather fat bacon
3/4 cup butter
1 tbsp. chopped parsley
Salt, pepper, nutmeg

Cut off the heads of the broccoli; trim, wash, and dry them, and cook them in plenty of boiling salted water. Drain and rinse thoroughly. Cut the bacon in small strips.

Take a frying pan large enough to hold all the broccoli easily. Melt the butter, put in the bacon, and sauté it until slightly browned. Add the broccoli, mix well, and season with salt, pepper, and a pinch of nutmeg. Cook until the broccoli starts to color. Just before serving, sprinkle with finely chopped parsley.

PREPARATION: 25 min. COOKING: 20 min.

PURÉE DE FÈVES (LIMA BEAN PURÉE)

3 cups shelled Lima beans
2 small mealy potatoes
1/2 lb. butter
2 small sprigs savory
Salt

Heat half the butter in a saucepan, add the beans and savory, a little salt, a few tablespoons of water and the potatoes cut in small pieces. Cover and stew gently for about 40 minutes or until the beans are very tender and the water completely evaporated. Remove the savory and mash the beans and potatoes through a strainer or in a blender. Reheat over a high flame, then remove from the stove and stir in the remaining butter in small pieces. Check the seasoning and serve.

* Savory is a highly aromatic garden herb. Excellent in omelettes and salads as well.

PREPARATION: 15 min. COOKING: 40 min.

POMMES MACAIRE (MASHED POTATO CAKE)

15-18 *large potatoes*
3/4 *lb. fresh butter*
1 *cup melted butter*
Salt, pepper

Bake the potatoes in a moderate oven (350º) for about 40 minutes. Remove and mash the pulp with a fork, mixing in the fresh butter and seasoning to taste. The mixture should be quite lumpy. Take a 12-inch frying pan, heat half the melted butter over a high flame, and spread the potato pulp in a two-inch layer over the bottom. Brown on both sides, adding melted butter when needed.

PREPARATION: 50 min. BROWNING: 10 min.

POMMES MAXIM'S (SCALLOPED POTATO CAKE)

1 *lb. potatoes*
1 1/4 *cups butter*
Salt, freshly ground pepper

Melt the butter. Peel the potatoes, wash and dry them, and cut them in small thin slices. Put in a bowl, season with salt and pepper, pour in the melted butter, and mix thoroughly together.

Spread a shallow layer (about 1/2 inch thick) of these potatoes over the bottom of a large well-buttered ovenware dish. Bake in a hot oven (425º) for about 40 minutes or until crisp and golden. Turn out of the dish onto a warmed serving platter.

PREPARATION: 30 min. BAKING: 40 min.

POMMES DARPHIN (POTATO PANCAKE)

1 *lb. potatoes*
1 1/4 *cups butter*
Salt, pepper

These potatoes are prepared on the same principle as *Pommes Maxim's*, the only difference being that they are cut in strips instead of slices and are cooked on top of the stove in a large frying pan. Season beforehand.

The layer of potatoes should be over 1 inch thick. When the underside is golden (after about 15 minutes over a low flame), turn it over and brown the other side.

PREPARATION: 15 min. BROWNING: 25 min.

POMMES SURPRISE (STUFFED BAKED POTATOES)

6 *medium potatoes*
1/2 *cup diced cooked ham*
1/2 *cup cubed Gruyère cheese*
1/2 *cup grated Gruyère cheese*
2 *tbsp. heavy whipping cream*
3/4 *cup butter*
Salt, pepper

Wash the potatoes and bake them in a medium oven (350º) for about 1 hour, or until done. Remove from the oven and cut them in half horizontally. Scoop out the pulp, being careful not to break the skins. Place the potato pulp, ham, small cheese cubes, cream, and butter in a saucepan over a low flame and mix thoroughly with a fork. Season to taste.

Stuff the potato skins with this mixture, sprinkle with grated cheese, and brown in a hot oven (425º) for 4 or 5 minutes.

PREPARATION: 1 hr. COOKING: 10 min.

TOMATES FARCIES CARMÉLITE (STUFFED TOMATOES)

6 *large firm tomatoes*
6 *eggs*
1 *cup Sauce Béchamel*
or 1 1/2 *cups heavy whipping cream*
1/2 *cup grated Gruyère cheese*
1/2 *cup melted butter*
Salt, pepper

Slice the tops off the tomatoes and hollow them out carefully. Salt the interiors lightly. Hard-boil the eggs, cool, and cut into fairly thick slices. Bind with the *Sauce Béchamel* or the cream, heated and reduced by one-third. Season with salt and pepper.

Stuff the tomatoes with this preparation and sprinkle with grated cheese. Place the tomatoes in an ovenware dish, pour over the melted butter, and brown in a hot oven (425º).

PREPARATION: 5 min. COOKING: 15 min.

POMMES MAXIM'S

ANANAS A LA CRÉOLE (PINEAPPLE-RICE DESSERT)

1 fresh pineapple
1 1/2 cups granulated sugar
1/2 cup Kirsch
Riz à l'Impératrice
3/4 cup apricot jam
Candied angelica

Peel the pineapple, cut it in half lengthwise, and core it. Boil the sugar with 2 cups of water for 10 minutes. Add 1/4 cup of Kirsch, and cook the pineapple in this syrup for 20 minutes. Let cool in the syrup; once cooled, cut each half of the pineapple in thin even semi-circular slices. Keep the syrup for later use.

Prepare the *Riz à l'Impératrice*. Line a dome-shaped mold with overlapping slices of pineapple. Pour in the *Riz à l'Impératrice* and chill in the refrigerator for at least 2 hours. Turn out onto a cold platter and decorate with strips of angelica. Mix the apricot jam with a little of the cooking syrup and the remaining 1/4 cup of Kirsch. Spread this mixture around the rim.

PREPARATION: 45 min. (plus chilling). COOKING: 25 min.

PÊCHES FLAMBÉES (PEACHES FLAMBÉES)

6 large ripe peaches
3/4 cup Kirsch
1 1/2 cups granulated sugar

Plunge the peaches in a large pan of boiling water. Remove immediately, rinse in cold water and peel. If the peaches are very ripe, they should peel easily without this operation.

Bring the sugar and 2 cups of water to a boil. Add 1/4 cup of Kirsch and poach the peaches gently in this syrup until just soft. Drain. Remove the stones carefully as you would core an apple, and place the peaches in a warm serving dish. Reduce the syrup and pour some of it over the fruit. Just before serving, heat the remaining Kirsch. Pour over this Kirsch at the table and light a match to it.

* Be careful not to overcook the peaches or they will fall apart. They should be tender but still fairly firm. Check by pricking with a knitting needle.

PREPARATION: 5 min. COOKING: 8-10 min.

POMMES IRÈNE (STUFFED BAKED APPLES)

6 large ripe eating apples
1 cup prunes
1/2 pt. vanilla ice cream
2 egg whites
3 cups granulated sugar
1 oz. Kirsch
Vanilla

Soak the prunes for 3 hours in warm water. Drain, stone, and poach them with 1 cup of water, 1/2 cup of sugar and a drop of vanilla for 20 minutes. Drain and press through a strainer, making a fine purée. Peel the apples neatly and poach them in 2 cups of water and 1 1/4 cups of sugar for about 10 minutes. The flesh should remain quite firm. Let cool in the syrup. Then scoop out the inner pulp, leaving a thin shell. Press the pulp through a strainer, add 1/4 cup of sugar and a drop of vanilla and mix thoroughly. Spread a layer of this mixture in the bottom of each apple shell. Mix the vanilla ice cream with the prune purée and fill the apples to the top. Place in an ovenware serving dish just large enough to hold them. Beat the egg whites very stiff, add the Kirsch and the remaining cup of sugar, and top each apple with this meringue. Place in a slow oven (300°) until light golden and serve immediately.

PREPARATION: 30 min. COOKING: 20 min.

ANANAS MONTPENSIER (PINEAPPLE-CREAM DESSERT)

12 slices cooked or canned pineapple
3 cups Crème Pâtissière
1/2 cup heavy whipping cream
1 1/2 cups granulated sugar
Kirsch or rum

Make a caramel syrup by dissolving the sugar in 2 cups of water and bringing to a boil. Let cool. Whip the *Crème Pâtissière* and cream together lightly with an egg-beater. Flavor to taste with the Kirsch or rum. Arrange some of the pineapple slices in a circle on a round serving dish. Place the cream in a mound in the center, lay the remaining pineapple on top, and pour over the cooled caramel syrup.

PREPARATION: 10 min. (plus *Crème Pâtissière*). COOKING: 8 min.

BEIGNETS DE FRAISES (STRAWBERRY FRITTERS)

50 *large strawberries*
1/2 *cup granulated sugar*
1/2 *cup powdered sugar*
1/2 *cup Kirsch*
2 *cups frying batter*
Oil for deep frying

Wash and clean the strawberries. Dry with absorbent paper and place in a bowl with the Kirsch and the granulated sugar. Mix carefully and chill for one half hour to macerate. Prepare the frying batter (See *Grenouilles à l'Aurore*, page 67) and heat the oil.

Drain the strawberries, dip them one by one in batter, and drop them in the oil a few at a time.

As soon as they are crisp and golden, remove and drain on absorbent paper. Arrange in a pyramid on a warm dish, sprinkle with powdered sugar, and serve at once.

* For best results make the batter well ahead of time. Standing makes it lose any elasticity which might be produced in mixing the ingredients. If the batter is to be used at once, mix the ingredients by turning them gingerly with a spoon. Too much elasticity prevents the batter from sticking.

PREPARATION: 45 min. (plus batter). COOKING: 15 min.

RIZ A L'IMPÉRATRICE (RICE WITH CANDIED FRUIT)

1 *cup rice*
3/4 *cup mixed chopped candied fruits*
6 *egg yolks*
1/2 *cup butter*
1 *qt. milk*
1 1/2 *cups whipped cream*
5/8 *cup sugar*
1 *orange*
1 *leaf gelatin*
1 *cup* Crème Anglaise
3/4 *cup red currant jelly*
1 *vanilla bean*
Salt

Scrape off the rind of the orange in tiny surface strips. Blanch for 2 minutes in boiling water. Rinse the rice several times in cold water, blanch it 1 minute in boiling water, rinse in cold water, and drain. Boil almost all the milk in a saucepan with the vanilla bean, the blanched orange rind, and a pinch of salt. Add the rice, cover, and put in a moderate oven (350º) for 20 to 25 minutes, without stirring. In the meantime, prepare a *Crème Anglaise*. While still warm, add the leaf of gelatin (dissolved in cold water) and the whipped cream, and mix well.

When the rice is done, carefully stir in the sugar, the egg yolks which have been beaten with 2 tablespoons of milk, and 1/4 cup of softened butter. Be careful not to break the grains of rice. Let cool. When the rice is almost cool, remove the vanilla bean and orange rind. Stir in the remaining butter, the candied fruits, and the *Crème Anglaise*.

Line a deep mold with red currant jelly and spoon in the rice. Chill in the refrigerator. Just before serving, unmold on a serving dish.

* Decorate with candied angelica, if you can get it.

PREPARATION: 40 min. (plus chilling). COOKING: 20 min.

CROUTES AUX FRUITS (FRUIT CUP DESSERT)

12 *thin slices homemade-type white bread*
12 *thin slices pineapple*
3 *lb. assorted fruit*
1/4 *lb. dried apricots*
Granulated sugar
Maraschino liqueur

Soak the apricots overnight in 1 cup of water. Prepare an apricot sauce by adding 1/3 cup sugar to the fruit and water and cooking until the fruit is very soft. Mash through a strainer, let cool and, just before using, stir in as much water as necessary for the consistency desired.

Slice a loaf of homemade-type, solid-texture white bread as thin as possible. It will probably slice more easily if one day old. Place the slices on a baking sheet, sprinkle with sugar, and put under the broiler to dry out the bread and crystallize the sugar.

If using apples and pears, peel and core them, cut in quarters, and poach them in a little sugar and water. Line a round deep mold-type dish with alternating overlapping slices of bread and pineapple. Fill the center with the stewed apples and pears, orange and peach slices, thick slices of banana, stoned cherries, strawberries or any other fruit in season. Add a little Maraschino liqueur to the apricot sauce, and pour over the dessert. Serve immediately.

PREPARATION: 15 min. (plus soaking). COOKING: 15 min.

RIZ A L'IMPERATRICE

CRÊPES (PAPER-THIN PANCAKES)

2 *cups sifted flour*
4 *eggs*
1 /2 *cup sugar*
2 *cups milk*
1 /4 *cup melted butter*
Vanilla
Salt

Mix the flour, sugar, and a pinch of salt together in a bowl. Stir in the eggs one by one, a drop of vanilla, and the warmed milk, stirring constantly with a wooden spatula. The batter should be smooth and just thick enough to coat the spatula. If too thick, add a little more milk. Finally, add the melted butter and stir until homogeneous. Cover and chill for at least 1 hour before use.

Cook the *crêpes* in a large moderately heated buttered pan, putting in just enough batter to cover the bottom. Brown lightly, shake to loosen, turn, and brown the other side very lightly. Keep warm in a moderate oven (350º). Regrease the pan between each *crêpe*.

*This is a classic recipe for *crêpes*. For the extra-light *crêpes* used in Maxim's desserts, separate the eggs and stir the yolks alone into the dry ingredients. Beat the whites stiff in another dish and add them at the very end, after the melted butter.

In preparing the *Crêpes Veuve Joyeuse*, add 1 /4 cup Cognac to the batter in addition to the warm milk. As well as having a delicate flavor all its own, Cognac is known for bringing out or blending together other flavors present in a dish. Another delicious and very simple way to serve these *crêpes* is to fold them, sprinkle with sugar, and flambé with warm Cognac.

PREPARATION : 10 min. COOKING: 1 min.

CRÊPES VEUVE JOYEUSE (LEMON SOUFFLÉ CRÊPES)

12 *large* crêpes
12 *tbsp. granulated sugar*

Soufflé au Citron :
(*12 heaping tablespoons*)
4 *egg whites, 3 egg yolks*
1 *lemon, 1 /2 cup milk*
3 /4 *cup granulated sugar*
1 *tbsp. flour*
1 1 /2 *tbsp. butter*
1 /2 *tsp. vanilla*

Prepare the *crêpes* and keep warm. Prepare the filling in the following manner : peel off the rind of the lemon in tiny surface strips. Blanch for 2 minutes in boiling water and macerate in 1 cup of water and 1 /2 cup of sugar which have been boiled together for 15 minutes. Make a thick white sauce by heating the butter, flour, milk, sugar, and vanilla together. Remove from the fire and beat in the egg yolks and lemon rind. Finally, fold in the stiffly beaten egg whites.

Place a heaping tablespoon of lemon filling on half of each *crêpe*, fold over, and place in a hot oven (400º). As the soufflé cooks, the *crêpes* should swell and open. They should be done in about 15 minutes. Remove, sprinkle with sugar, and brown rapidly under the broiler. Serve at once.

PREPARATION: 45 min. COOKING: 15 min.

CRÊPES MADAME DE... (PINEAPPLE CREAM CRÊPES)

24 *large* crêpes
1 /2 *cup diced candied pineapple*
1 *cup* Crème Patissière
1 /2 *cup butter*
3 /4 *cup heavy whipping cream*
1 /4 *cup Cointreau liqueur*
1 *cup granulated sugar*
Salt

Soak the pineapple in Cointreau for at least one half hour. Drain and set the liqueur aside. Prepare the *Crème Pâtissière*. Whip the cream and mix it with the *Crème Pâtissière*, at the same time adding the drained pineapple. Make the 24 thin *crêpes* and stuff them with this mixture.

Heat an ovenware dish, butter it lightly, sprinkle with sugar, caramelize to a light golden color, and add a few drops of Cointreau. Put in the *crêpes*, sprinkle generously with sugar, and brown rapidly under the broiler. Warm the remaining Cointreau.

Bring to the table, pour over the Cointreau, and flambé.

**Madame de...* is the title of one of Louise de Vilmorin's best novels, published in 1956. It evokes the voluptuous, intrigue-ridden end of the last century. The heroines of these intrigues reveled in the sensual pleasures of life, one of which was undoubtedly good food.

PREPARATION: 1 hr. 30 min. (soaking included). COOKING: 20 min.

130

DESSERT DU CLUB (RASPBERRY SHERBET CRÊPES)

24 crêpes

Sorbet aux framboises:
5 *egg yolks*
2 *cups scalded milk*
1 1/4 *cups granulated sugar*
1 *cup raspberry purée*

Make the sherbet in the following manner: beat up the egg yolks and sugar. When the mixture reaches a ribbon consistency, add the scalded milk. Heat gradually, stirring constantly, and being careful that the mixture does not boil. When it is of custard consistency, remove from the fire, pour in a bowl, and cool. Once cool, incorporate the purée made by crushing raspberries through a strainer. Chill until firm.

Make the *crêpes* and while they are still warm, place a large spoonful of sherbet in the center of each. Roll up or fold over and serve immediately.

* This recipe comes from the Club des Cent, the most famous club of gastronomes in the world ever since its creation in 1923. Highly secretive about their recipes and the restaurants they consider worthy of their patronage, they are in a way the "Skull and Bones" Society of the gastronomic world.

PREPARATION: 1 hr. 30 min. COOKING: 15 min.

CROQUEMBOUCHE (CREAM-PUFF PYRAMID)

2 *cups* Pâte à Choux
1 *cup* Pâte Brisée
1 *pt. sweetened whipped cream*
1 1/3 *cups granulated sugar*
1 *egg*

Crème Bachique:
2 *cups granulated sugar*
6 *egg yolks*
1 1/4 *cups dry white wine*
1 /2 *cup Grand Marnier liqueur*

Prepare the *Crème Bachique* in the following manner: beat the sugar and egg yolk with a wooden spatula in the top of a double-boiler off the fire. When the mixture is white and of ribbon-like consistency, add the wine and place over simmering water, beating constantly, until it is thick, frothy, and cream-like. Remove from the fire and continue to beat until completely cooled. Stir in the Grand Marnier and chill.

With a pastry bag or spoon, drop the *Pâte à Choux* on a large buttered pastry sheet in small mounds less than 1 inch in diameter and 1/2 inch high. Brush with beaten egg and put in a preheated hot oven (425°) for about 20 minutes or until they are twice their original size, crisp and brown. Remove from the oven and pierce with a knife to let steam escape. Return to the turned-off oven for 10 minutes, leaving the door ajar. Remove and cool.

Line a 10-inch pie tin with *Pâte Brisée*, cover with dried beans or raw rice, and put in a hot oven (400°) for about 10 minutes. Remove the beans, prick with a fork, and return to the oven until crisp and golden (about 10 minutes). Cool.

Boil the sugar with 2/3 cup of water over a medium flame until the syrup turns light brown. Dip the cream puffs in this caramel syrup and make a circle just inside the rim of the pie crust. Top with a smaller circle, and continue to place smaller circle on circle until you have a pyramid. The caramel should make the puffs stick. Before putting the last puff in place, pour the whipped cream in the center. Serve the *Crème Bachique* on the side.

* The term *croquembouche* is used for any kind of pyramid made up of small pastries or fruit glazed with cooked sugar, making them crisp and crunchy.

PREPARATION: 1 hr. 30 min. BAKING: 50 min.

PUITS D'AMOUR (PASTRY CREAM PIE)

1 1/4 *cups* Pâte Feuilletée
5 /8 *cup* Pâte à Choux
1 1/4 *cups* Crème Pâtissière
1 *egg*
1 /2 *cup granulated sugar*

Prepare your 2 pastry doughs in advance. Finally prepare your *Crème Pâtissière*. Roll out a 1/4-inch layer of *Pâte Feuilletée* and, with a 10-inch pie tin, cut out a disk of dough. Place this disk on a baking sheet sprinkled with water; prick it in several places with a fork to avoid bubbles. Fill a pastry tube (with a nozzle about 1/2 inch in diameter) with *Pâte à Choux* and squeeze a rim around the outer edge of your pastry disk. Brush the rim with beaten egg and place in a hot oven (425°) for about 20 minutes or until golden. Cool and fill the center of the pie with a thick layer of *Crème Pâtissière*. Sprinkle generously with sugar and caramelize directly under a red hot broiler.

PREPARATION: 2 hrs. BAKING: 20 min.

132

DESSERT DU CLUB

POIRES HÉLÈNE (STUFFED PEARS)

6 large ripe pears
1/4 cup butter
1/2 cup powdered almonds
1 cup granulated sugar
4 oz. cooking chocolate
1 pt. vanilla ice cream
Vanilla
1 tsp. lemon juice
6 marzipan leaves

Peel the pears and remove the cores from below with an apple corer. Poach them gently in 1/2 cup of sugar and 1 cup of water, a drop of vanilla and the lemon juice for about 10 minutes, or until tender but still fairly firm. Let cool in the syrup.

Make a chocolate sauce by melting the chocolate with 4 cups of water and 2 tablespoons of sugar. Bring to a boil and remove from the fire. Mix the butter with the powdered almonds and 1/4 cup of sugar to make a butter cream. Fill the pears with this mixture.

Line a crystal bowl with vanilla ice cream. Stand the pears upright on the ice cream. Pour over the chocolate sauce and decorate each pear with a marzipan leaf.

PREPARATION: 1 hr. 30 min. COOKING: 20 min.

POIRES BOURDALOUE (PEAR AND ALMOND PIE)

6 large ripe pears
2 cups Pâte Brisée
2 cups Crème Frangipane
4 macaroons
1 1/2 tbsp. melted butter
1/2 cup granulated sugar
Vanilla
1 tsp. lemon juice

Peel the pears and remove the cores from below with an apple corer. Poach them gently in 1/2 cup of sugar and 1 cup of water, a drop of vanilla and the lemon juice for about 10 minutes, or until tender but still fairly firm. Let cool in the syrup.

Prepare the *Pâte Brisée*. Line a buttered 12-inch pan with this pastry dough, pricking with a fork in several places to avoid bubbles. Line with wax paper and spread with dried beans or uncooked rice so the crust will keep its shape. Bake in a hot oven (425°) until a light golden color, remove the paper and vegetables, and return to the oven for a few more minutes.

Line the baked pastry crust with a 1-inch-thick layer of *Crème Frangipane* (see *Tarte Hollandaise*, p. 142), mixed with the crumbs of 3 crushed macaroons. Cut the pears in half, arrange them on the bed of cream, pour over the remaining *Crème Frangipane*, and sprinkle with the 1 remaining crushed macaroon. Pour over the melted butter and brown rapidly under the broiler.

PREPARATION: 30 min. COOKING: 35 min.

TARTE TATIN (APPLE UPSIDE-DOWN PIE)

5 lb. eating apples
1/2 cup Pâte Brisée
1 cup sweet butter
1 cup granulated sugar

The best kind of baking tin for this pie is one in copper lined with tin, about 2 1/2 inches deep and 8-10 inches in diameter. Coat the bottom and sides with a thick layer of butter topped by 1/2 inch of sugar. Peel, core, and quarter the apples and fill up the pan with them. Cover with the remaining butter and all the sugar except 1/8 cup.

Prepare the *Pâte Brisée*, rolling it out no more than 1/8 inch thick. Place this on top of the apples. Bake in a hot oven (425°) for 20-30 minutes. Lift the pastry crust occasionally to make sure the apples are not cooking too quickly. They should gradually become a golden brown and the sugar and butter should caramelize.

Place a serving dish face down on top of the pie. Turn over so the crust is on the bottom, the apples on top. If the pie is done and the sugar caramelized, it should keep its shape. Sprinkle with sugar and caramelize directly under a red hot broiler. Serve warm.

* This delicious and unusual pie has an amusing story behind it, a spy story. My wife Maggie and I discovered it completely by accident in a tiny provincial hotel run by three old maids, the Tatin sisters. We liked it so much that we asked the owners to give us the recipe, but the ladies refused. It was a jealously guarded family secret handed down from generation to generation. As soon as we returned to Paris, we sent one of Maxim's cooks on a special mission. He went to the Tatin sisters, got himself hired as an assistant gardener and, while raking the flowerbeds, he succeeded in raking in the formula for the pie! You can see just how far we gourmets will go!

PREPARATION: 15 min. BAKING: 30 min.

TARTE HOLLANDAISE

The Home Cooking
of France

● **POTAGE PARMENTIER (CREAM OF LEEK AND POTATO SOUP)**

2 cups milk
3 leeks
5 medium potatoes
3 tbsp. butter
1 egg yolk
Chopped parsley
Croûtons
Salt, freshly ground pepper

Chop the white part of the leeks quite fine and sauté them until golden in a saucepan with 1 tablespoon of butter. Add the pared and quartered potatoes, cover with water, season with salt and pepper, and simmer until the potatoes are cooked. Mash the leeks and potatoes through a strainer or in a blender. Add the heated milk and enough water to reach the consistency of a cream soup. Simmer 4 minutes, stirring constantly. Remove from the fire. Pour a little of the soup into a bowl, add the egg yolk, beat together, and pour back into the soup; reheat but do not boil. Season to taste. Garnish with chopped parsley and croûtons.

* It was Antoine-Augustin Parmentier who brought the potato to French tables in the eighteenth century. This soup is the ancestor of the New-York-born Vichyssoise.

PREPARATION: 20 min. COOKING: 25 min.

● **POTAGE AURORE AUX ŒUFS (CREAM OF TOMATO SOUP WITH EGGS)**

1 qt. milk
4 eggs
4 tbsp. tomato paste
1 tbsp. butter
2 tbsp. cornstarch
Salt

Boil the eggs for 6 minutes, plunge them for a moment in cold water, peel carefully, and put aside in luke-warm water.

In a saucepan away from the fire, mix the cornstarch with 3 tablespoons of cold water, and stir in the tomato paste. Heat the milk and when it is boiling, pour it into the tomato mixture. Stir well. Return to the fire for 3-4 minutes, season to taste, and add the butter. Drain the eggs, put one in each soup plate and pour the soup over them.

PREPARATION: 10 min. COOKING: 10 min.

● **SOUPE A L'OIGNON AU FROMAGE (ONION SOUP WITH CHEESE)**

1 qt. water
3 large onions
2 tbsp. butter
2 tbsp. flour
5 tbsp. grated Swiss cheese
French bread
Salt, pepper

Cut the onions in thin strips and sauté them in butter until golden. Sprinkle with flour, continue cooking until lightly browned, add the water, season with salt and pepper, and simmer for 10 minutes. Cut the bread into thin slices and place in a deep ovenware casserole dish. Pour the soup over the bread, sprinkle with cheese, and bake in the oven or under a hot broiler until a golden crust has formed.

* As Alexandre Dumas said in his *Grand Dictionnaire de Cuisine*, large white onions are very nourishing and "therefore chosen to make soup for huntsmen and drunkards, two classes of people who require fast recuperation."

PREPARATION: 10 min. COOKING: 20 min.

SOUPE A L'OIGNON AU FROMAGE

POTAGE AUX ARTICHAUTS (CREAM OF ARTICHOKE SOUP)

2 *cups* Fond de Cuisson
3 *cups milk*
6 *artichokes*
2 *tbsp. flour*
1/2 *cup butter*
1/2 *cup heavy whipping cream*
Croûtons
Salt, pepper

Wash the artichokes and cook them in boiling water for 20-30 minutes, or until tender. While the artichokes are cooking, make a cream sauce with the flour, 2 tablespoons of butter, the *Fond de Cuisson*, and 2 cups of milk. When the artichokes are done, strip them of their leaves and choke, leaving only the hearts. Cut these into thin strips and simmer gently in the cream sauce for one half hour. Take from the fire, remove the hearts, mash them through a fine strainer (or in a blender), and incorporate this purée back into the cream sauce.

Heat the remaining 1 cup of milk in a saucepan. Reheat the soup, add the warmed milk, and mix thoroughly. Finally add the heavy cream, stirring constantly, and the rest of the butter. Heat to the boiling point, but do not boil. Season to taste. Serve with croûtons. *(Mapie de Toulouse-Lautrec).*

* If artichokes are not in season, this soup can be made with canned artichoke hearts. In this case, replace part of the veal stock by the liquid in the can.

Today, a *potage* is usually thicker than a *soupe*, the former made with a purée of vegetables and sometimes thickened by the addition of cream or an egg yolk. When adding an egg yolk to a sauce or soup for thickening purposes, beat the yolk in a separate dish and add the hot liquid bit by bit, stirring constantly. When you have mixed a reasonable amount in this manner, return to the saucepan and stir into the remaining liquid. Adding the cold, raw yolk directly to the hot soup or sauce would risk curdling the latter.

PREPARATION: 30 min. COOKING: 1 hr. 15 min.

POTAGE AUX CONCOMBRES (COLD CREAM OF CUCUMBER SOUP)

3 *lb. cucumbers*
1 *cup heavy whipping cream*
2 *tsp. chopped tarragon*
Salt, pepper, paprika

Peel the cucumbers. Make about 20 small balls with a melon-ball cutter. Cook the balls and the rest of the sliced cucumbers in 2 separate saucepans of salted boiling water for 15 minutes. Drain; set aside the balls. Mash the rest of the cooked cucumber through a fine strainer or in a blender. Add the chopped tarragon, cream, and the cucumber balls. Refrigerate for several hours. Just before serving, sprinkle lightly with paprika. *(Mapie de Toulouse-Lautrec).*

* If you have no melon-ball cutter, make small cucumber cubes instead.

PREPARATION: 30 min. CHILLING: 2 hrs.

SOUPE AU POTIRON (CREAM OF PUMPKIN SOUP)

6 *cups milk*
2 *cups cooked or canned pumpkin*
2 *tsp. sugar*
2 *tbsp. butter*
French bread
Salt, pepper

Make a purée by mashing the pumpkin through a strainer (or in a blender). Scald the milk, cool it, and add it to the purée, beating with an egg-beater until smooth. Bring slowly to a boil and season to taste with sugar, salt and pepper. Add two or three 3/4-inch slices of French bread and simmer for 10 minutes. Stir in the butter; as soon as it is melted, remove from the fire and serve immediately. *(Mapie de Toulouse-Lautrec).*

* To cook a pumpkin, cut it in half, remove the seeds, and place it, the cut side down, in a baking dish. Bake in a moderate oven (350°) for an hour or until tender, at which time the pulp may be scraped from the skin.

Originally, the word *soupe* meant a piece of bread which was boiled in a bouillon or porridge. The medieval meaning, slightly changed in spelling, still exists in the English *sop*. In French, the word evolved through various stages, meaning first the boiled bread, then the boiled meat, and finally the bouillon itself. Today, a *soupe* is usually a rather thin liquid, garnished with bread slices or fried croûtons.

PREPARATION: 20 min. COOKING: 20 min.

SOUPE A L'AIL (GARLIC SOUP)

5 cups water or Bouillon Blanc
5 or 6 garlic cloves
1 sprig thyme
2 tsp. cornstarch
6 slices white bread
1 tbsp. olive oil
Salt, pepper

Boil the whole peeled garlic cloves and the thyme in slightly salted water or bouillon for 15 minutes. Meanwhile toast the bread, brush with olive oil and cut into small cubes. Strain the soup through a strainer, mashing the garlic through (or use a blender), and return to the saucepan. Mix the cornstarch with a bit of cold water in a dish and stir into the soup. Return to the fire for 2 minutes; season with salt and pepper.

Place a few toasted cubes in the bottom of each soup plate and pour the boiling soup over them. *(Mapie de Toulouse-Lautrec).*

* Garlic is never served at a dinner party, but there's nothing to keep you from serving this soup *dans l'intimité*; in the country, for instance. This is a recipe from Provences where garlic is almost a staple!

PREPARATION: 10 min. COOKING: 20 min.

GARBURE BASQUAISE (BASQUE VEGETABLE SOUP)

2 qt. water
1 smoked ham bone (some meat attached)
1 1/2 cups pea beans or small dried limas
3 shallots, 4 potatoes
4 turnips, 4 carrots, 2 onions
3 stalks celery
1/4 head firm white cabbage
1 cup grated Swiss cheese
Croûtons
Salt

Soak the beans overnight. Peel and chop the other vegetables. Shred the cabbage coarsely. Place the beans, ham bone, and all the vegetables (except the potatoes), in a large pot. Pour in enough water to cover the ingredients amply. Add a little salt. Bring to a boil, skim, lower the heat, and simmer for 2 hours 30 minutes. Add the potatoes and cook for another one half hour. Remove the ham bone and potatoes and keep hot. Pour the soup into an ovenware casserole dish, sprinkle generously with grated cheese, and brown in a hot oven. Place the croûtons on top and serve at once.

* This soup is generally served in two plates: one with the meat and potatoes, the other with the soup itself. Moreover, almost any ingredients can be used in a *Garbure*, as nearly every province in France has its own variation of this hearty soup. Some add roasted chestnuts or pickled goose, or a few tablespoons of red wine just before serving. This dish is aptly named, as the word *Garbure* is thought by some to come from the Spanish *garbias* or stew. Others contest, however, that the name comes from *garbe*, meaning a bunch (of vegetables). Whatever its etymological significance, the *Garbure* is a meal in itself.

PREPARATION: 15 min. COOKING: 3 hrs.

AIGO CORSE (CORSICAN VEGETABLE SOUP WITH EGGS)

5 cups Bouillon Blanc
1 large onion
2 leeks
2 garlic cloves
2 tomatoes
4 potatoes
2 tbsp. olive oil
4 eggs
1 bouquet garni
1 branch fennel
Dried orange peel
Saffron, chopped parsley
Salt, pepper

Peel and chop the onion and the white part of the leeks. Heat the olive oil and brown them in it. Meanwhile, heat the bouillon, peel the tomatoes, and crush the garlic. Tie the fennel and the dried peel of 1/4 orange to the *bouquet garni*. Quarter the peeled potatoes. When the onions and leeks are lightly browned, add the tomatoes, garlic and *bouquet garni* and stir with a wooden spoon until hot. Add the potatoes, a pinch of saffron, and the boiling bouillon. Season to taste.

Boil uncovered for about 20 minutes, or until the potatoes are cooked. Remove the *bouquet garni* and the potatoes. Keep the latter hot on a separate plate. Slow the boil to a simmer. Poach the eggs in the soup for 2 1/2 minutes. Drain and place them on top of the potatoes. Sprinkle with parsley.

Serve the soup by placing some potatoes and 1 egg in each dish and ladling the soup over them. This soup, followed by salad, cheese, and fruit, makes an excellent Sunday supper. *(Mapie de Toulouse-Lautrec).*

* The eggs will hold together better if you break them into a saucer, one at a time, and then gently slip them into the soup. This will be easy if your pot is almost filled with soup.

PREPARATION: 25 min. COOKING: 35 min.

GARBURE BASQUAISE

SOUPE AUX POISSONS

SOUPE AUX POISSONS (FISH SOUP)

3 cups water
2 lb. assorted white fish
1 cup oil
1 cup dry white wine
Grated Parmesan or Swiss cheese
1 garlic clove
1 tsp. powdered saffron
1 bay leaf
Croûtons
Salt, pepper

Clean the fish and cut them up if necessary to fit into the pot. Heat the oil and put in the fish. Cook 15 minutes but do not brown. Salt and pepper generously, add the bay leaf, the finely chopped garlic, white wine and water, and boil for 1 hour. Take out the fish heads and large bones and mash the flesh through a strainer (or in a blender), straining through the juice at the same time. Add saffron and bring to a boil once more.

Serve bubbling hot with croûtons and grated cheese. *(Mapie de Toulouse-Lautrec)*.

* Use whiting, halibut, carp, flounder, pike, turbot, or any other white fish.
Do not worry about getting out all the bones; they will be taken care of by the strainer or blender.

PREPARATION: 15 min. COOKING: 1 hr. 30 min.

154

BISQUE DE CREVETTES (SHRIMP BISQUE)

2 cups water
3 cups Fond de Cuisson
1 lb. fresh shrimp
1 onion
1 carrot
4 slices stale bread
2 tbsp. Madeira wine
1 1/2 tbsp. butter
1 bouquet garni
Salt, black pepper

Mince the carrot and onion, cover with 2 cups of water, and add salt, pepper, and the *bouquet garni*. Bring to a good boil and add the shrimp. Reduce the heat and simmer 15 minutes. Strain off the liquid and reserve. When the shrimp are cool enough to handle, shell them. Force the shells through the finest blade of a meat chopper, then pound to a purée. Mix the purée with 1 cup of the cooking liquid and simmer 5 minutes. Strain and return to the fire. Add the *Fond de Cuisson* and the stale bread; stir until the bread is virtually dissolved. Add the Madeira and the rest of the cooking liquid and bring to the boiling point, stirring constantly. Just before serving, put in the shrimp and add the butter.

Serve immediately, with croûtons if desired.

PREPARATION: 45 min. COOKING: 1 hr.

SALADE CÉVENOLE (CHESTNUT SALAD)

8 large chestnuts
2 large apples
3 medium dill pickles
4 large raw mushrooms
4 walnuts
4 hard-boiled eggs
15 ripe olives
1 1/2 tbsp. capers
4 tbsp. olive oil
2 tbsp. vinegar
2/3 cup Sauce Mayonnaise
Salt, pepper

Slit the chestnuts all around and heat them in the oven until the shells pop open. Remove the outer shell, boil for one half hour in salted water and carefully remove the inner peel.

Mix together oil and vinegar, season with salt and pepper. Chop the mushrooms, cut the apples into thin slices, dice the pickles, wash and stone the olives, shell and chop the nuts. Mix all of these with the capers in a bowl, pour over the oil and vinegar dressing, and let stand for 15 minutes. Add the sliced chesnuts, mix carefully, and let stand 15 minutes more. Just before serving, drain and transfer to a salad bowl. Cover with *Sauce Mayonnaise* and garnish with the quartered hard-boiled eggs.

* The easiest way to stone olives is to peel them in a spiral right down to the stone, being careful that the spiral does not break. Once the stone is gone, the olive will spring back into its original shape.

PREPARATION: 30 min. COOKING: 30 min. (chestnuts).

SALADE A L'INDIENNE (RICE SALAD)

2 cups cooked rice
4 small tomatoes
1 large green pepper
6 tbsp. oil
2 1/2 tbsp. vinegar
1 tbsp. strong mustard
Salt, pepper

Peel the tomatoes and cut them in fine slices. Cut open the pepper, remove the seeds and filaments, and cut into thin strips.

Dilute the mustard with 1/4 teaspoon of cold water, mix with the oil and vinegar, season with a little salt and pepper. Place the peppers, tomatoes, and rice in this sauce, mix well, and let stand in the refrigerator for at least 2 hours.

* It is much easier to peel tomatoes if they have been plunged momentarily in boiling water.

PREPARATION: 15 min. CHILLING: 2 hrs.

SALADE NIÇOISE (OLIVE AND ANCHOVY SALAD)

2 large tomatoes
2 green peppers
1 /2 lb. fresh string beans
5 oz. anchovies
8 ripe olives
3 eggs
1 medium onion
1 medium can tuna fish
3 tbsp. olive oil
1 tbsp. wine vinegar
Salt, pepper

Wash and clean the beans and cook them for 20 minutes in rapidly boiling salted water. When tender, drain and cool. Hard-boil the eggs, then hold for an instant under cold running water. Peel and quarter 2 of them, cut the third in slices. Wash the peppers, remove the seeds and filaments, and cut into thin strips. Peel and slice the onion; slice the tomatoes; stone the olives. Hold the anchovies under cold running water for 10 minutes to remove excess salt. Drain.

Pile the vegetables, quartered eggs, anchovies, and the tuna in small chunks, into a salad bowl. Pour over an oil and vinegar dressing seasoned with pepper and salt. Toss lightly, decorate with slices of egg, and serve.

* To keep beans green, put them bit by bit into the boiling pot so that the water never stops boiling. Do not cover.

PREPARATION: 20 min. COOKING: 20 min.

OIGNONS A LA GRECQUE (PICKLED ONION SALAD)

1 lb. tiny button onions
1/2 cup sultana raisins
1 cup dry white wine
1 garlic clove
1 bouquet garni
1/2 lemon
Salt, pepper

Peel the onions and place them, the raisins, the *bouquet garni*, and the crushed garlic, in a small pan. Pour in the white wine. Add enough water to cover. Season with salt and pepper. Cover and cook gently for 15 to 20 minutes or until the onions are tender. Remove the pan from the fire and add the juice of 1/2 lemon. Place in a serving dish and chill until serving time.

PREPARATION: 10 min. COOKING: 15-20 min.

SALADE NIÇOISE

SALADE DE SCAROLE AUX RAISINS (GREEN SALAD WITH RAISINS)

1 *curly endive or chicory*
1 *tbsp. white raisins*
1 *egg*
1 /2 *cup salad dressing*

Soak the raisins for at least 1 hour in warm water. Rinse thoroughly. Wash and pick over the salad greens and cut in fairly small pieces. Hard-boil the egg, chop it up very fine, and add to the salad dressing.

Put the salad greens in a salad bowl, add the raisins, and pour over the dressing.

PREPARATION: 15 min. (plus soaking).

SALADE AU LARD (BACON SALAD)

1 /2 *lb. young watercress, chicory*
or romaine
4 *oz. bacon*
2 *tbsp. white vinegar*
Salt, pepper

Pick over, wash, and dry the salad greens. Put them in a deep ceramic salad bowl and place in a slightly preheated oven. Dice and fry the bacon and when it is done, pour it and the hot fat over the salad greens. Pour the vinegar quickly into the same pan, stir, heating slightly, and pour over the salad. Season with pepper and a little salt, toss, and serve.

PREPARATION: 15 min. COOKING: 10 min.

SALADE POMONE (CHEESE AND APPLE SALAD)

1 *large curly chicory*
1 *large fairly tart apple*
2 *tbsp. grated Swiss cheese*
2 *tbsp. vinegar*
6 *tbsp. oil*
1 *tsp. strong mustard*

Pick over, wash, and dry the chicory. Mix together the oil, vinegar, and mustard, and pour into a salad bowl. Add the cored apple cut in thin strips. Sprinkle with cheese. Just before serving, add the chicory and toss well.

* Salad greens should aways be thoroughly dried in a special basket or tea towel, to avoid diluting the dressing.

PREPARATION: 20 min.

ENDIVES A L'ORANGE (COOKED ENDIVE SALAD)

3 *lb. endive*
2 *oranges*
3 *tbsp. oil*
Salt, pepper

Wash the endive and boil them in boiling salted water for one half hour. Drain and set aside to cool. Prepare a salad dressing using oil, salt, pepper, and substituting orange juice for vinegar. *(Mapie de Toulouse-Lautrec).*

PREPARATION: 10 min. COOKING: 30 min.

CŒURS DE CÉLERI (CELERY HEART SALAD)

4 *large celery hearts*
1 *cup tomato ketchup*
1 *cup sour cream*
6 *drops Worcestershire Sauce*
3 *drops A-1 Sauce*
2 *drops Tabasco Sauce*
1 *lemon*
Salt, pepper
Parsley sprigs

Place the celery hearts in boiling salted water and cook for one half hour or until just tender. Remove at once, drain the celery, and let cool.

Mix all the other ingredients thoroughly together and pour this sauce over the celery on a serving dish. Decorate with lemon quarters and parsley.

* As the above recipes illustrate, there are innumerable ways of preparing salads, depending on the season and one's tastes and imagination. Besides those ingredients mentioned, one can use beets, raw or cooked cauliflower, red cabbage, cucumbers, cold chicken, cold fish.... The list could go on indefinitely.

Dressings can be varied too. The usual proportions of oil to vinegar are 3 to 1. Oil can be replaced by heavy cream, vinegar by lemon juice... a pleasing variation for sliced cucumbers. Heavy cream and a dash of mustard is perfect for a beet salad. Mayonnaise complements meat and fish.

PREPARATION: 10 min. COOKING: 30 min.

ŒUFS MAGDA (SPICY SCRAMBLED EGGS)

8 fresh eggs
2 1/2 tsp. finely chopped chives
2 1/2 tsp. grated Gruyère cheese
1 1/3 tsp. French mustard
2 tbsp. butter
Croûtons
Salt, pepper

Scramble the eggs in a well-buttered pan. Season to taste. When still fairly liquid, incorporate the chives, cheese, and mustard. Mix all together and empty the scrambled eggs into a hot serving dish. Arrange the hot, crisp croûtons around the outer rim. Serve at once.

* For best results, cook scrambled eggs in a double-boiler, stirring continually with a wooden spatula. Scrambled eggs should have the consistency of thick heavy cream.

PREPARATION: 10 min. COOKING: 10 min.

SOUFFLÉ AU FROMAGE (CHEESE SOUFFLÉ)

4 fresh eggs
4 tbsp. butter
1/2 cup flour
2 cups milk
2/3 cup grated Swiss cheese
Salt, pepper

Melt the butter and stir in the flour. Cook for a few moments without browning, add the scalded, cooled milk, and season with salt and pepper. Stir over a low flame until the mixture thickens. Remove from the fire and cool. Separate the eggs, beat the yolks with 1 teaspoon of water, and add to the sauce; stir in the cheese. Beat the egg whites very stiff and fold in carefully. Butter a deep straight-sided soufflé dish, pour in the mixture, and bake 20 minutes in a preheated moderate oven (375º).
Serve *immediately*. A soufflé cannot wait. A fine family supper is a soufflé baked around a cauliflower which has been previously cooked until about three-quarters done. *(Mapie de Toulouse-Lautrec)*.

* Egg whites can be beaten stiff more easily when they are at room temperature and have had a pinch of salt added.

PREPARATION: 20 min. BAKING: 20 min.

ŒUFS AU PLAT MIRABEAU (SHIRRED EGGS WITH ANCHOVIES)

8 fresh eggs
8 large green olives
8 tarragon leaves
8 anchovy fillets
2 tbsp. tarragon butter
4 tbsp. anchovy butter
Salt, pepper

Spread 1 tablespoon of anchovy butter* in each of 4 individual ramekins and cook 2 eggs in each in a moderate oven (350º). The eggs should be shirred, not fried.
Take the dishes from the oven, place a large olive stuffed with tarragon butter* on either side of the 2 eggs, and decorate each yolk with a leaf of tarragon. Arrange 2 anchovy fillets around the 2 eggs in each dish.

* Anchovy butter: Mash 1/4 cup fillets of anchovies with 6 tbsp. butter and press through a strainer. Tarragon butter: Pound 4 tbsp. blanched tarragon leaves with 4 tbsp. butter and press through a strainer.

PREPARATION: 20 min. COOKING: 5 min.

ŒUFS FROIDS MOUSSE DE TOMATES (COLD EGGS WITH TOMATO MOUSSE)

8 fresh eggs
2 lb. ripe tomatoes
3 small new onions
2 stalks celery
1 sweet pimento
1/2 cup vinegar
1 cup gelatin
1 small bunch fresh tarragon
Powdered thyme, bay leaf
Sugar, salt, pepper

Cut the tomatoes in quarters and put them in a saucepan with the celery, onions, pimento, tarragon, 1 small bay leaf, a pinch of thyme, salt and pepper. Add 1/2 cup of water and the vinegar, bring to a boil, and simmer for about 1 hour 30 minutes. The liquid should evaporate almost completely. Mash through a strainer or in a blender, taste the resulting purée, and add a pinch of sugar if it seems too acid. Spread evenly over the bottom of 8 small cups.
Poach the eggs in boiling water with a little vinegar but no salt. After 4 minutes, drain the eggs, set in cold water to cool, drain thoroughly, and place 1 egg in each cup. Cover with half-set gelatin and chill.

PREPARATION: 1 hr. 45 min. CHILLING: at least 2 hrs.

162

SOUFFLÉ AU FROMAGE

TARTE AUX OIGNONS (ONION PIE)

1 *cup* Pâte Brisée
or 1 *unbaked pie crust*
10 *oz. large sweet onions*
3 1/2 *oz. thick bacon*
3 *tbsp. butter*
3 *eggs*
1 *cup scalded milk*
Salt, pepper

Cut the onions into fine strips, plunge for 10 minutes in briskly boiling water, drain, and rinse in cold water. Dry in a tea towel. Cut the bacon into 1/2-inch cubes, place in a saucepan with cold water to cover, and bring to a boil. Simmer 10 minutes. Strain, rinse in cold water, drain, and dry.

Melt the butter in a large saucepan, sauté the bacon cubes lightly on all sides, turn the flame down as low as possible, add the onions, and simmer gently, without browning, for 30 minutes. Remove from the fire. Beat the eggs and milk together and pour into the saucepan with the onions and bacon; stir well, season generously with pepper; taste before adding salt.

Prick the unbaked pie crust to avoid bubbles. Pour in this filling and bake on a lower shelf in a hot oven (400º) as the crust will need more heat than the filling. Bake for 15-20 minutes. When crust and filling are golden brown, serve immediately. The same filling can be used for small individual tarts. *(Mapie de Toulouse-Lautrec).*

* There are two ways of serving the three baked specialties on this page. The first is in small portions as an hors-d'œuvre, followed by meat and vegetables, cheese and fruit. The second is in larger portions (individual tarts, 2 or 3 slices of toast per person), accompanied by a tossed salad and followed by a fruit dessert, as the *plat de résistance* on a light luncheon or supper menu.

PREPARATION: 1 hr. 15 min. BAKING: 15-20 min.

CROUTES AUX CHAMPIGNONS (BAKED MUSHROOMS ON TOAST)

6 *oz. mushrooms*
8 *slices plain white bread*
1 *cup thick* Sauce Béchamel
5 *tbsp. butter*
Salt, pepper

Prepare the *Sauce Béchamel*. Clean the mushrooms, cutting off the earthy part of the stems, and wash them only if really necessary; chop them coarsely and stir into the hot sauce. Taste and season if necessary.

Toast the bread, lay the slices on a cookie sheet or in an ovenware dish, and spread each one with the mushroom sauce. Place a generous dab of butter on each slice and bake 15 minutes in a hot oven (425º). Serve piping hot and bubbly.

* All of the recipes on this page are delicious with a fairly dry white wine.

PREPARATION: 15 min. (plus *Sauce Béchamel*). BAKING: 15 min.

QUICHE AU SAUMON FRAIS (FRESH SALMON PIE)

1 *baked pie crust*
5 *oz. fresh salmon*
3 *eggs*
1 *cup cream*
2 *tbsp. oil*
1 *tbsp. lemon juice*
1/2 *sprig thyme*
1/2 *bay leaf*
Salt, pepper

Cut the salmon into thin strips and marinate it for 2 hours in a solution of lemon juice, oil, thyme, 1/2 bay leaf and pepper. Drain well, place on a heated broiler rack and broil both sides under a hot flame for 5 minutes. Cool. Arrange the cooled bits of salmon in the bottom of the baked pie crust, beat the eggs and cream together, season with salt and pepper, and pour this mixture over the salmon; try not to disturb the arrangement you have made.

Bake in a moderately hot oven (375-400º) for about 20 minutes or until set. Serve hot or lukewarm, as an hors-d'œuvre or a light luncheon dish.

* Instead of cream, you may use rich milk boiled down to reduce it by half or more; to keep milk from boiling over, place a small saucer upside-down in the bottom of the saucepan. This recipe comes from the Touraine region, famous in France for its trout and salmon. The traditional French *quiche* originally came from Lorraine and Alsace, and each region of these provinces has its own version. The most classic is identical to the one above except that the salmon is replaced by sautéd lean bacon cubes.

PREPARATION: 2 hrs. 45 min. (marinating included). BAKING: 20-25 min.

166

WATERZOI DE POISSONS A LA FLAMANDE (FLEMISH FISH STEW)

2 *lb. assorted fresh-water fish*	1 *stalk celery*
1 bouquet garni	4 *slices white bread*
4 *tbsp. butter*	*Salt, pepper, sage*
1/4 *cup cracker or dry breadcrumbs*	

Cut the fish into 1-inch slices and place in a heavy stewpan with almost enough water to cover. Add the *bouquet garni*, a pinch of sage and the celery chopped in small pieces; dot with butter. Season with salt and pepper. Cover, but leave a space for the steam to escape.

Boil rapidly for 30 minutes. There should be only about 1 inch of liquid in the bottom of the pan when the fish is done. If necessary, continue to boil rapidly, uncovered, until the liquid is reduced. Stir in the crumbs to thicken it, remove the *bouquet garni*, and pour the stew over thick slices of buttered white bread.

* The *waterzoï* is usually made with pike, carp, river eel, etc. but can also be made with salt-water fish. This fish stew is considered by some the Flemish equivalent of the French Provençal *bouillabaisse*. A meal in itself, the *waterzoï* is best accompanied by beer.

PREPARATION: 20 min. COOKING: 30-40 min.

TRUITES DE RIVIÈRE AU BLEU (BLUE BROOK TROUT)

4 *live trout*	1 *lemon*
2 *cups vinegar*	1 bouquet garni
1/2 *cup butter*	4 *peppercorns*

Boil the vinegar, the *bouquet garni* and the peppercorns in 2 quarts of water for 20 minutes. Kill the trout by striking their heads against the edge of a table, clean them as quickly as possible but do not scale. It is the scales that give these trout their distinctive blue color. Wash them rapidly.

Throw the trout into the seasoned boiling water, lower the heat and simmer for 7 to 8 minutes depending on their size. Take out carefully with a skimming ladle and arrange on a heated platter with a little of the cooking liquor.

Serve hot with lemon quarters and melted butter.

* For this recipe the trout must be alive. Even a few hours' waiting is too much. To handle them more easily, grasp them with a towel. Connoisseurs consider this the only way to eat fresh trout as there is nothing to detract from the superb flavor of the fish itself. Boiled potatoes with a little melted butter and chopped parsley are usually recommended with fish. A highly seasoned vegetable would destroy the full appreciation of its delicate savor.

PREPARATION: 25 min. COOKING: 7-8 min.

WATERZOI DE POISSONS A LA FLAMANDE

DORADE AU FOUR (BAKED SEA-BREAM OR SHAD)

A 2-lb. sea-bream or shad
2 medium onions
3 tomatoes
1/2 cup dry white wine
3 slices stale bread
1/2 cup milk
5 tbsp. butter
1 tbsp. chopped parsley, thyme,
and basil
Salt, pepper

Clean and scale the fish, and wash it thoroughly. Chop the onions and prepare a stuffing of onions, bread soaked in milk and squeezed dry, herbs, salt and pepper. Mix well and stuff the fish.

Slice the tomatoes and lay them on the bottom of a flat buttered ovenware dish, place the fish on top, pour over the wine, and dot with butter. Bake 20 minutes in a very hot oven (450-475º). Towards the end, check to make sure the fish does not burn.

* Do not forget the basil which gives this dish its distinctive flavor.

PREPARATION: 20 min. COOKING: 20 min.

BRANDADE DE MORUE (SALT COD CASSEROLE)

1 lb. boneless salt cod
1 1/2 cups olive oil
2 garlic cloves
1 cup scalded milk
Croûtons
Chopped parsley
Salt, freshly ground pepper

Soak the cod for 24 hours, changing the water 2 or 3 times. Put it in a saucepan, cover with cold water, and bring slowly to a boil. Cover, turn the heat as low as possible, and barely simmer for 15 minutes. Drain and shred, picking the fish over carefully. Place the cod in a mixing bowl with 1/2 cup of very hot olive oil. Mix vigorously with a wooden spatula or an electric beater until completely crushed. Mince and add the garlic and, alternately, the remaining heated oil and the hot milk, beating constantly. The result should have the consistency of finely mashed potatoes. Season generously with pepper; taste before adding salt.

Place the mixture in an ovenware dish, reheat quickly in the oven, and serve sprinkled with chopped parsley and small croûtons.

* Green beans go well with this simple and excellent fish dish. Perfect for Sunday night suppers.

PREPARATION: 50 min. COOKING: 10 min.

MAQUEREAU A LA FLAMANDE (BAKED MACKEREL FLEMISH STYLE)

A 2 1/2-lb. mackerel
2 tbsp. butter
2 chopped shallots
1/2 lemon
2 tbsp. chopped parsley
1 tbsp. chopped chives
Parsley sprigs
Salt, pepper

Clean and scale a fresh mackerel, leaving the head and tail intact. Make a long incision along the belly of the fish.

Soften the butter and mix it with the chopped parsley, chives, shallots, salt, pepper, and 1 teaspoon of lemon juice. Stuff the fish with this mixture.

Roll the mackerel in oiled brown paper and tie carefully at both ends. Bake for 45 minutes in a moderate oven (350º). Carefully cut open the paper and transfer the fish to a heated platter; pour over the melted butter sauce. Sprinkle with the remaining lemon juice, garnish with parsley sprigs, and serve with boiled or steamed potatoes.

* To soften butter, take it out of the refrigerator well ahead of time and cream it in a bowl that has been rinsed out with hot water and dried.

PREPARATION: 30 min. COOKING: 45 min.

BROCHET AU VIN BLANC (BAKED PIKE IN WHITE WINE)

A 3-lb. pike
2/3 cup butter
1 1/2 cups dry white wine
1 1/2 tbsp. flour
5 oz. fresh larding pork
Salt, pepper

Cut the larding pork into strips and insert them in slits in the cleaned, scaled, and washed fish. Dot a flat baking dish with 1/3 of the butter. Lay the pike on it. Season with salt and pepper. Bake for 25 minutes in a hot oven (400º). Carefully transfer the fish to a heated serving platter and keep hot. Pour the wine into the baking dish, scrape the sides and bottom, and cook 3 to 4 minutes.

Melt the remaining butter in a saucepan, stir in the flour, cook for a moment or two, and add the hot wine. Simmer 5 minutes and pour over the fish. *(Mapie de Toulouse-Lautrec)*.

PREPARATION: 20 min. COOKING: 40 min.

CHAUD-FROID DE SOLES (COLD FILLETS OF SOLE IN CREAM SAUCE)

4 medium sole or flounder
5 tbsp. butter
1 cup dry white wine
5 tbsp. heavy cream
4 sprigs fresh tarragon
Salt, pepper

Clean and fillet the fish, saving the heads, bones and skin. Dot the bottom of a large ovenware dish with half the butter. Roll up the fillets and place them on the pieces of butter. Cover with the heads, bones and skin; dot with the remaining butter and pour over the wine. Bake in a moderate oven (350°) for 15 minutes. Take the fillets out carefully with a spatula, drain, and arrange on a serving platter. Return the bones to the oven and continue to bake. After 25 minutes, add the cream to the baking dish and bring to a boil; then lower the flame. Strain the sauce; add salt and pepper to taste.

Pour the sauce over the fillets, let cool, and place in the refrigerator. When the sauce begins to set, decorate with leaves of tarragon. Serve chilled. *(Mapie de Toulouse-Lautrec)*.

* Be very careful when removing the fillets from the baking dish as they will be very soft and risk falling apart.

PREPARATION: 40 min. COOKING: 1 hr.

SOLES AUX CREVETTES (FILLETS OF SOLE WITH SHRIMP)

3 medium sole or flounder
7 oz. shelled cooked pink shrimp
3 cups dry white wine
3/4 cup butter
2 tbsp. flour
2 tbsp. heavy whipping cream
3 egg yolks
1 carrot
2 shallots
Powdered thyme, 2 bay leaves
Salt, pepper

Bone and trim the fish (or have your fish dealer do it) and set aside the fillets. Cook the bones and trimmings in a saucepan with 2 cups of wine, a pinch of thyme, the bay leaves, salt, pepper, and a cut-up carrot. When it comes to a boil, skim and simmer 30 minutes without covering. Strain and set the liquid aside.

Put the fillets in a shallow saucepan, add the remaining wine, chopped shallots, and enough water to cover them. Simmer over a low flame for 5 to 6 minutes (until they are just firm to the touch). Take out the fillets and place in a shallow ovenware serving dish.

Melt the butter in a saucepan, add the flour, and cook gently for several minutes without browning. Stir in the cooking liquid from the fish bones and cook 5 minutes, stirring constantly. Remove from the fire and stir in the egg yolks and the lightly-beaten cream. Add the shrimp and pour the sauce over the fish. Bake for 10 minutes in a very hot oven (425°) until the top just begins to brown. Serve piping hot. *(Mapie de Toulouse-Lautrec)*.

* The sole is a European flat fish, considered the most delicate of white fish. As it is not found in American waters, it is rarely seen in American markets. Good American substitutes are flounder or whiting. Serve with French bread and a dry white wine.

PREPARATION: 45 min. COOKING: 15-20 min.

MATELOTE DE MERLANS (BRETON WHITING STEW)

4 whitings
1/2 cup flour
2 tbsp. oil
1 medium onion
3 tbsp. tomato purée
2 cups red wine
1 bouquet garni
Croûtons
Salt, pepper

Clean the whitings, remove the heads and tails, and cut the fish into 1-inch slices. Dredge them thoroughly in flour and brown quickly in 1 tablespoon of oil. Remove the fish.

Mince the onion and brown it in the same pan. Add a second tablespoon of oil and continue cooking for a few minutes, stirring constantly. Add the wine and 1 cup of boiling water, the *bouquet garni*, salt and pepper, and stir in the tomato purée. Simmer a few minutes until the sauce has thickened slightly. Add the fish, cover, and cook gently for 10-15 minutes. Serve very hot with croûtons.

* A *matelote* is a fish stew made with white or red wine. Most *matelotes* are made with fresh-water fish garnished with onions and mushrooms which have been cooked with the fish and most are served with small croûtons. The most well-known *matelote* is made with eel and probably originated in the Ile-de-France region.

PREPARATION: 15 min. COOKING: 35-40 min.

MOULES A LA MARINIÈRE (MUSSELS IN WHITE WINE)

3 qt. mussels
1 onion
3/4 cup dry white wine
1 shallot
5 tbsp. butter
1 lemon
2 sprigs parsley
1 sprig thyme
1/2 bay leaf
Pepper

Scrape and scrub the mussels. Pile them into a large stewpan with the chopped onion and shallot, parsley, thyme, bay leaf, pepper, white wine, and butter, cover tightly, and place over a high flame. After 3 minutes, stir well so that the mussels on top go to the bottom and vice versa. Continue shaking often during the cooking time of about 10 minutes. When all the mussels are open they are done.

Take the mussels from the pot, remove the top shell of each, pile onto a hot platter and strain the cooking liquid over them.

Serve with lemon quarters and crisp French bread with sweet butter.

* This is the elegant method of serving them; at informal fishermen's places, the whole kettle is brought to the table and mussels and sauce are ladled into deep soup plates. No utensils are used; deft fingers and one double mussel shell used as tongs suffice. Followed by salad, cheese, and dessert, and accompanied by a dry white wine, you have an excellent, simple, and unusual meal in itself.

PREPARATION: 40 min. COOKING: 10 min.

COQUILLES SAINT-JACQUES A LA PARISIENNE (CREAMED SCALLOPS)

12 scallops
1 cup white wine
1 medium onion
1 shallot
6 tbsp. butter
3 tbsp. flour
4 oz. small mushrooms
3 tbsp. milk
4 tbsp. grated Swiss cheese
1 bouquet garni
Breadcrumbs
Salt, pepper

Wash the scallops thoroughly; open them by setting in a hot oven for 5 minutes. Cut the meat from the shells and reserve the deeper shell. Wash the meat several times and cut out the black part.

Cook the white wine, chopped onion and shallot, *bouquet garni*, salt and pepper for 10 minutes. Add the scallops and cook 10 minutes longer. Meanwhile sauté the mushrooms in a little butter for 3 minutes. Remove the mushrooms, add and melt the rest of the butter, stir in the flour, and cook without browning for 5 minutes. Strain the cooking liquid from the scallops into the flour-butter mixture; add the milk and simmer, stirring constantly, for 5 minutes.

Cut the scallops and mushrooms into small pieces, add to the sauce, and season with salt and pepper. Simmer for 5 minutes, stirring continually. Stir in 3 tablespoons of cheese.

Fill the washed and dried shells with this mixture, sprinkle with breadcrumbs and cheese, and broil until golden. Serve immediately.

* When a recipe contains the phrase *à la Parisienne*, you can almost be certain it contains a white cream sauce.

PREPARATION: 30 min. COOKING: 35 min.

CROQUETTES DE CREVETTES (SHRIMP CROQUETTES)

7 oz. cooked shrimp
4 tbsp. chopped walnut meats
3 slices stale white bread
3 egg yolks
4 tbsp. butter
Breadcrumbs
Salt, pepper, curry

Soak the bread in milk, squeeze dry, and mash or put in the blender with the chopped shrimp, nuts, egg yolks, butter, and a pinch of curry. Blend 2 minutes, taste, and add salt if necessary.

Form the resulting purée into small patties, dredge them in breadcrumbs, and sauté them in butter until nicely browned on all sides.

Serve, if desired, with a *Sauce Béchamel* or *Sauce Aurore*.

* If you have no blender, mash up the mixture with a fork, making it as smooth as possible.

This is an excellent recipe, quick and easy, perfect for a light luncheon or supper menu. For a more substantial meal, serve small croquettes as an hors-d'œuvre, or, as a main course, accompanied by *Riz à l'Indienne* and a sauce.

PREPARATION: 10 min. COOKING: 10 min.

TOURNEDOS HENRI IV (STEAK WITH BÉARNAISE SAUCE)

4 tenderloin steaks
2 tbsp. butter
4 round croûtons
Salt, pepper

Sauce Béarnaise:
3 tbsp. wine vinegar
1 shallot
3 egg yolks
4 tbsp. butter
2 tsp. chopped parsley
1 tsp. chopped tarragon
Salt, freshly ground pepper

Prepare the *Sauce Béarnaise* first. Simmer the vinegar, 2 tablespoons of water, the chopped shallot, 1 teaspoon of parsley and a good dash of pepper for 5 minutes. Melt the butter in the top of a double boiler, stir in the egg yolks and continue stirring over hot but not boiling water until the mixture thickens. Slowly strain in the hot vinegar, beating constantly. Season with salt. Keep hot.

Heat the butter in a frying pan until sizzling hot. Sauté the steaks 3 to 4 minutes on each side; season with salt and pepper.

Arrange the croûtons on a heated platter and place a steak on each one. Add the tarragon and remaining parsley to the sauce and pour over the steaks. Serve immediately with crisp French-fried potatoes.

* Instead of serving the steaks with a *Sauce Béarnaise* you may wish to try another traditional French recipe, *Beurre Maître d'Hôtel*, or highly seasoned butter; For 4 servings, mash together 7 tbsp. butter, 1/2 tbsp. chopped parsley, 1 tsp. lemon juice, 1 tsp. very good strong mustard and season with salt and pepper. Keep at room temperature while cooking the steaks, then put a quarter of the mixture on each one. Traditionally the steaks should be garnished with generous sprigs of watercress and served with French-fried potatoes.

PREPARATION: 20 min. COOKING: 6-8 min.

DAUBE PROVENÇALE (PROVENÇAL BEEF STEW)

2 lbs. shoulder of beef
1 tbsp. lard
1 tbsp. olive oil
2 oz. thick bacon
2 oz. salt pork
1/2 calf's foot
2 shallots. 2 onions
1 garlic clove
2 tomatoes, 2 carrots
1 stalk celery
1 celery root (celeriac)
1 cup dry red wine
1 sprig thyme, 1 bay leaf
2 cloves, peel of 1/2 orange
Powdered cinnamon and ginger
Salt, black peppercorns

Dice the salt pork and heat it in a stewpan with the lard and olive oil. Dice the bacon and put it in to brown. Peel the onions. Cut one into quarters and stick the other with the cloves. Slice the carrots. When the bacon is browned, add the carrots, onions and the half calf's foot to the pot.

Cut the beef into 2 1/2-inch pieces and put them in to brown. Toss in 1 crushed sprig of thyme, 1 crushed bay leaf and the cut-up garlic clove. Turn the meat often to brown it on all sides. Quarter the tomatoes, cut up the shallots as well as the celery stalk and root and add these to the meat. Add the wine, a pinch of powdered cinnamon, and one of ginger, 1/2 teaspoon of peppercorns, the orange peel and 1/2 teaspoon of salt. Bring to a boil.

Cover, lower the flame, and simmer for at least 6 hours. Serve with boiled potatoes. *(Mapie de Toulouse-Lautrec)*.

* This highly seasoned stew is typical of the region of Provence. Serve with a full-bodied red wine.

PREPARATION: 45 min. COOKING: 6 hrs.

STEAK AU POIVRE (STEAK WITH PEPPER SAUCE)

1 thick sirloin or porterhouse steak
1 tsp. white peppercorns
3 tbsp. butter
2 tbsp. fine cooking oil
2 tbsp. Jus Brun
1 tbsp. Cognac
1/2 tsp. cornstarch
Salt

Crush the peppercorns with a fork; with your fingers, press the crushed bits evenly into the steak on both sides.

Heat the butter and oil in a heavy frying pan; when very hot but not brown put in the steak. If you like it rare, count about 2-3 minutes per side. Season both sides with salt after cooking and place on a heated platter. Keep hot.

Mix the cornstarch into the *Jus Brun* and stir into the hot fat in the frying pan. Stir in the Cognac, scraping all drippings on the sides and bottom of the pan into the sauce. Taste and add salt if necessary. Simmer the sauce for 5 minutes, stirring from time to time, pour over the steak, strain, and serve immediately. *(Mapie de Toulouse-Lautrec)*.

* The butter and oil must be *very* hot when you put in the steak in order to sear the surface immediately and make the pepper stick.

PREPARATION: 10 min. COOKING: 12 min.

TENDRONS DE VEAU AU CÉLERI (VEAL AND CELERY RAGOUT)

1 3/4 lb. good stewing veal
1 bunch celery
5 tbsp. butter
1 1/2 cups dry white wine
3 tbsp. lemon juice
Salt, pepper

Trim and wash the celery, cut away the leaves, and cut the stalks into 1-inch slices. Boil for 10 minutes in just enough salted water to cover them; drain.

Cut the meat into rather large chunks and season well with salt and pepper. Melt 4 tablespoons of butter in a heavy stewpan; brown the meat on all sides. Add the celery and half the wine and stir well; cover the pan tightly and continue cooking in a medium oven (350°) for 1 hour 30 minutes.

Remove the cooked meat and celery to a heated serving dish and keep warm. Pour the remaining wine into the stewpan, scrape in the drippings from the sides and bottom, and add the remaining butter and the lemon juice. Cook over a high flame for 5 minutes, stirring occasionally. Pour over the meat and celery, and serve immediately with buttered noodles. (*Mapie de Toulouse-Lautrec*).

PREPARATION: 30 min. COOKING: 1 hr. 40 min.

COTELETTES AU CHASSEUR (VEAL CHOPS IN TOMATO SAUCE)

4 veal chops
4 tbsp. butter
6 oz. mushrooms
1 tbsp. olive oil
1 shallot
1/4 cup dry, white wine
1/4 cup Jus Brun
2 tbsp. Sauce Aurore
1 tbsp. chopped parsley
Salt, freshly ground pepper

Sauté the chops in butter until brown on both sides; lower the flame and continue cooking for 20 minutes. Transfer to a hot serving plate and keep warm.

Clean and chop the mushrooms and sauté them in the same hot butter. Add the oil and the chopped shallot and brown lightly. Pour in the wine and *Jus Brun*, simmer, reducing the sauce by half, stir in the *Sauce Aurore*, taste, and add salt and pepper if necessary.

Pour the sauce over the chops, sprinkle with chopped parsley, and serve with potatoes browned in butter.

PREPARATION: 10 min. COOKING: 30 min.

VEAU BRAISÉ AUX TOMATES (VEAL BRAISED WITH TOMATOES)

A 2-lb. boneless roast of veal
3/4 cup Bouillon Blanc
2 garlic cloves
4 tbsp. olive oil or lard
12 medium tomatoes
12 small onions
2 shallots
1 sprig rosemary
1 bouquet garni
Salt, pepper

Quarter the garlic cloves lengthwise and stick them into the meat; rub the whole roast with salt and pepper. Melt the oil or lard in a heavy stewpan; when it is hot, sear the meat on all sides.

Lower the flame, add the peeled whole onions, the whole tomatoes, the minced shallots, rosemary, and the *bouquet garni*. Cover tightly and simmer for about 1 hour 30 minutes. Check from time to time to make sure there is enough juice; add a little hot *Bouillon Blanc* if necessary.

Before serving, remove the *bouquet garni* and rosemary. Serve the meat on a bed of onions surrounded by tomatoes.

PREPARATION: 20 min. COOKING: 1 hr. 30 min.

MIGNONS DE VEAU MOUTARDIER (VEAL WITH MUSTARD SAUCE)

4 veal tenderloin steaks
1/4 cup mustard
1/2 cup heavy whipping cream
1/2 cup butter
2 egg yolks
1/2 cup Sherry wine
Salt, pepper

Sauté the veal steaks in butter in a shallow pan over a high flame, about 5 minutes per side. Set them on a serving dish and keep hot.

Drain off the butter from the pan, put in the mustard and half the cream and bring to a boil, stirring constantly. Lower the flame and simmer slowly.

Mix the egg yolks, the remaining cream, and the Sherry in a bowl. Remove the pan from the fire and stir in the Sherry mixture, beating vigorously. Reheat if necessary, but do not boil. Pour over the veal and serve immediately.

PREPARATION: 5 min. COOKING: 20 min.

GIGOT BRETONNE (ROAST LAMB WITH WHITE KIDNEY BEANS)

A 3-lb. leg of lamb
3/4 lb. dried white kidney beans
1 tsp. baking soda
1 carrot
1 onion
1 garlic clove
1/2 cup heavy whipping cream
1/2 cup butter
1/4 lb. thick bacon
1 clove
1 bouquet garni
Breadcrumbs
Salt, pepper

Soak the kidney beans overnight and cook in lightly salted water with a carrot, the *bouquet garni*, the coarsely chopped onion, and a clove, until the beans are tender. Drain, remove the carrot, clove, and *bouquet garni*, and set the beans aside.

Prepare the lamb for roasting by making 2 or 3 small incisions near the bone and slipping a sliver of garlic in each one, then smearing the meat lightly with butter. Roast in a shallow pan in a hot oven (400°) for 25 minutes for the first 2 pounds and 15 minutes for each additional pound, basting occasionally. At the same time, dice and brown the bacon in a pan and cook until transparent; mix into the beans, reheat, and add the cream and 3 tablespoons of butter. Spread the bean mixture in a flat ovenware serving dish, sprinkle lightly with breadcrumbs, dot with butter, and brown in a hot oven (400°) for about 20 minutes.

Place the roast lamb on top of the beans and serve. Serve the drippings from the lamb separately. *(Mapie de Toulouse-Lautrec)*.

* A teaspoon of baking soda in the water in which you soak the beans will make them more tender. Choose good quality, medium-sized beans; they cook more quickly than the tiny ones.

PREPARATION: 15 min. COOKING: about 2 hrs. 30 min. (beans) 40 min. (lamb).

ÉPAULE DE MOUTON FARCIE BONNE FEMME (STUFFED SHOULDER OF MUTTON)

A 2-lb. boned shoulder of mutton
1/2 lb. fine sausage meat
2 medium onions
4 slices stale bread
3 tbsp. Jus Brun
1 egg
2 tbsp. lard
4 cups fresh lima beans
1 1/2 lb. carrots
1 tbsp. chopped parsley
Salt, pepper

Soak the bread in the *Jus Brun* and squeeze it out with your fingers. Mix the bread pulp with the sausage meat, the chopped onions, parsley, and the beaten egg; season with a little pepper. Spread this stuffing on the meat and roll up into a round or oblong form, depending on your stewpan. Bind tightly with a sturdy string.

Spread half the lard in the bottom of the pan, place the stuffed shoulder on it and smear with the rest of the lard. Brown on all sides over a high flame. Cover and continue cooking over a medium flame or in a moderate oven (350°) for a little over an hour. Turn several times.

Cut the carrots in quarters and cook them in a little water; cook the beans separately in salted water. When the carrots and beans are three-quarters done, drain them. Twenty minutes before serving time, put the vegetables in with the meat and continue cooking together. Baste often. Serve with boiled potatoes as an added vegetable.

* Encircling the lamb with alternate mounds of lima beans, carrots, and quartered potatoes sprinkled with parsley is an attractive way of presenting this dish.

PREPARATION: 50 min. COOKING: 1 hr. 15 min.

RAGOUT D'AGNEAU (LAMB RAGOUT)

2 lb. stewing lamb
3 large tomatoes
1 cup rice
1 1/2 cups Jus Brun
10 small onions
1 garlic clove
1/3 cup olive oil
1 sprig thyme, 2 bay leaves
1 lemon
Salt, pepper

Cut the meat into 2-inch cubes. Peel the tomatoes, onions, and garlic. Cut four 1/4-inch strips of peel from the lemon.

Heat the oil in a stewpan; when it is very hot, put in the meat and onions and brown them lightly on all sides. Heat and pour in the *Jus Brun*; simmer for 5 minutes. Add the peeled, quartered tomatoes, the whole garlic clove, bay leaves and thyme, lemon peel, a good pinch of salt, and a healthy dash of pepper. Cook, uncovered, for 10 minutes; then cover and simmer over a low flame for 45 to 50 minutes. Twenty minutes before serving, stir in the uncooked rice, cover the pan again, and finish cooking. Serve piping hot.

PREPARATION: 20 min. COOKING: at least 1 hr.

GIGOT BRETONNE

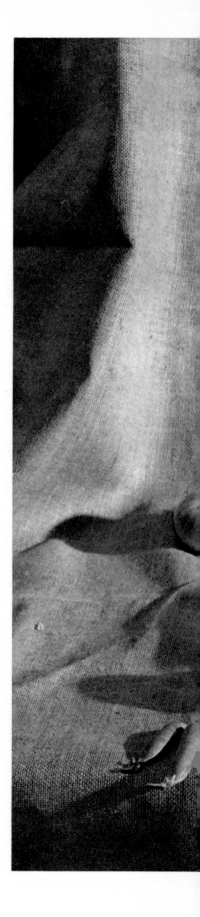

● **CERVELLE AU BEURRE NOIR (BRAINS IN BROWN BUTTER)**

2 *pairs calf's or lamb's brains*	3 *tbsp. wine vinegar*
1 /2 *cup butter*	*Salt, pepper*

Soak the brains in cold water for at least 2 hours, changing the water once or twice. Drain, carefully remove as much of the skin and membranes as possible, place in a saucepan, cover with cold water and add 1 1/2 tablespoons of vinegar and 1/2 teaspoon of salt. Bring to a boil and simmer gently for 15 minutes. Drain, rinse in cold water, and drain again.

Heat 2 tablespoons of butter in a frying pan, brown the brains on both sides and transfer them to a hot platter. Keep warm. Add the rest of the butter to the pan, heat until nut-brown but not burned, remove from the fire, and stir in the remaining vinegar. Season with salt and pepper, pour over the brains, and serve immediately with boiled potatoes.

* In France, brains are considered not only a delicacy but good for children because of their digestibility. They must be soaked ahead of time to clean off all blood and facilitate the removal of the membrane.

PREPARATION: 2 hrs. 30 min. COOKING: 25 min.

● **RIS DE VEAU AUX PETITS POIS (SWEETBREADS WITH PEAS)**

1 *large calf's sweetbread*	1 *tbsp. butter*
1 *tbsp. white vinegar*	2 *cups* Bouillon Blanc
1 *thick slice salt pork*	2 *cups shelled peas*
2 *medium onions*	1 /2 *tsp. cornstarch*
2 *carrots*	*Salt, pepper*

Soak the sweetbread for 1 hour in luke-warm water, drain, and plunge into boiling salted water to which has been added 1 tablespoon of vinegar. Boil for 3 minutes, drain, rinse in cold water, and wipe dry. Cut the salt pork in slivers, make small incisions in the sweetbread with a sharp knife, and insert the pork.

Sauté the chopped onions and carrots in the butter for 5 minutes without browning; spread over the bottom of a baking dish. Lay the sweetbread on top. Add enough *Bouillon Blanc* to half cover the meat, sprinkle with salt and pepper, and bake for 40 minutes in a moderate oven (350º), basting frequently.

Cook the fresh peas (or heat up canned French peas) so that they will be done at the same time as the sweetbread. Slice the sweetbread, arrange on a heated platter, and strain the sauce into a saucepan; skim off as much fat as possible. Boil until reduced by half and thicken with the cornstarch. Season to taste, pour over the sweetbread, and serve surrounded by peas.

* For 2 cups of shelled peas you will need about 2 pounds of fresh peas in their pods. Either cook them with a few moist lettuce leaves in the top of a double-boiler for about 45 minutes, or until tender, or put them in a saucepan with boiling water to cover and boil for 10 minutes, then lower the flame and simmer until tender. Canned or frozen peas, which are quicker, may of course be substituted.

PREPARATION: 1 hr. 45 min. COOKING: about 50 min.

RIS DE VEAU AUX PETITS POIS

NOISETTES DE PORC AUX PRUNEAUX (PORK CUTLETS WITH PRUNES)

4 boned pork cutlets
16 prunes
1 1/2 cups Vouvray wine
2 tbsp. butter
1 tbsp. red currant jelly
2 tbsp. heavy cream
1 cup flour
Salt, pepper

Soak the prunes overnight in just enough wine to cover them. Melt the butter in a frying pan until it is very hot, flour the cutlets lightly, brown in the butter, add salt and pepper, and cook, uncovered, over a very low flame for about 30 minutes. Meanwhile, simmer the prunes in the wine in which they have soaked. Drain but reserve the sauce. When the cutlets are cooked, arrange them on a heated platter, encircle with prunes, and keep hot. Pour the wine into the frying pan in which you cooked the cutlets and, stirring and scraping the pan, reduce the sauce by about half. Add the red currant jelly and cook gently until it has melted, stir in the cream, heat just to the boiling point, but do not boil as this could easily curdle the cream.

Pour the sauce over the cutlets and serve immediately.

* This is a recipe from Vouvray, where the white wine was appreciated in the sixteenth century by Rabelais and is still appreciated today as the best in all Touraine. The excellence of the *cuisine* of this region is also widely recognized and the prunes from Tours itself are appreciated all over France.

PREPARATION: 15

PORC AUX CHOUX ROUGES (PORK WITH RED CABBAGE)

A 2-lb. loin of pork
1 firm red cabbage
2 tbsp. sugar
4 tbsp. butter
1 cup red wine
Salt, pepper

Cut away the core of the red cabbage, remove any wilted leaves and the largest, toughest veins. Cut the cabbage in quarters and then into thin strips as for slaw. Wash the strips, blanch for 5 minutes in boiling salted water, and drain thoroughly.

Melt the butter in a large stewpan and brown the pork on all sides. Pile in the red cabbage around the pork, season well with salt and pepper, add the sugar, pour over the heated wine, and cover tightly. Simmer slowly for 2 hours, then remove the meat, slice it, and arrange on a large, heated serving platter with the cabbage around it. Serve with boiled potatoes. *(Mapie de Toulouse-Lautrec)*.

* An excellent recipe from Lorraine which will appeal even to those members of your family who are not red cabbage lovers. Serve with the same wine that was used in the preparation of the dish: a dry red wine.

PREPARATION: 30 min. COOKING: 2 hrs.

SAUTÉ DE PORC COMME A CANNES (PORK STEWED WITH VEGETABLES)

3 lb. shoulder of fairly
lean pork
1 tbsp. olive oil
1 tbsp. flour
1 cup dry white wine
1/2 lb. small new carrots
1 cup shelled green peas
4 oz. black olives
1 or 2 red peppers
3 shallots
1 large onion
2 garlic cloves
1 sprig thyme. 1 bay leaf
1/4 tsp. allspice
1 tsp. sweet paprika
Salt, pepper

Cut the meat into 2-inch cubes and brown them in olive oil in a heavy stewpan; season with salt and pepper. Chop the shallots, onion, garlic and thyme, and add to the meat together with the bay leaf, allspice and paprika. Sauté gently until the onions are golden. Sprinkle with 1 tablespoon of flour, stir until lightly browned and add the wine. Boil quickly, stirring constantly, for a few moments or until the sauce has thickened; then lower the flame and cover.

Simmer gently for 1 hour. Forty minutes before serving, add the peas, 10 minutes later the carrots, 10 minutes later the peppers, seeded and chopped. Ten minutes before serving, stir in the olives. Taste, adjust the seasoning. and serve piping hot.

* Allspice is the familiar name for Jamaica pepper, a very aromatic spice. It is surprising to find a stew as simple as this in a city as cosmopolitan as Cannes!

PREPARATION: 35 min. COOKING: 1 hr.

PORC AUX CHOUX ROUGES

POULET BOURBONNAIS (CHICKEN IN RED WINE)

A 5-lb. dressed roasting chicken
5 oz. thick lean bacon
15 small onions
1 cup Bouillon Blanc
2 cups red wine
1/4 cup butter
1 tbsp. flour
1 egg yolk
1 bouquet garni
Salt, pepper

Dice the bacon, cut the chicken into pieces and peel the onions. Brown the chicken and bacon in the melted butter in a heavy iron pot. When golden brown, remove the meat and set it aside. Add the flour to the remaining melted butter to make a smooth paste. Then stir in the bouillon a little at a time and add 1 cup of red wine.

Put back the chicken and bacon and add the rest of the wine. The chicken should be almost covered by the liquid. Add the peeled whole onions and the *bouquet garni*. Season lightly with salt and pepper. Cover tightly and simmer over a low flame for at least 1 hour, or until the chicken is tender.

Put the chicken on a serving platter and keep hot. Boil the sauce, reducing it by half; remove the *bouquet garni*. Beat the egg yolk separately with 1/4 cup of the sauce: then return to the pan.

Pour a little of the sauce over the chicken and serve the rest separately in a heated gravy boat.

PREPARATION: 30 min. COOKING: about 1 hr. 30 min.

POULET A L'ESTRAGON (CHICKEN WITH TARRAGON SAUCE)

A 3-lb. dressed roasting chicken
(with giblets)
2 tbsp. butter
2 oz. salt pork
2 onions
2 carrots
3 cups chicken bouillon
1 tbsp. Madeira wine
1 tsp. cornstarch
3 large sprigs tarragon
Salt, pepper

Mince together the salt pork, chicken livers and the leaves of 1 large sprig of tarragon: season with salt and pepper and use to stuff the dressed and drawn chicken. Truss.

Melt the butter in a heavy stewpan, mince the carrots and onions, place them in the butter and lay the chicken on top; cover and simmer over a very low flame for 20 minutes. Then add the hot bouillon, season with salt and pepper, cover tightly, and place in a moderate oven (375°) for 50 minutes.

Remove the chicken, place on a serving platter and keep hot. Strain the cooking juices into a small saucepan and add the rest of the chopped tarragon and the Madeira. Boil briskly without covering until reduced by half. Thicken with the cornstarch.

Pour a little of the sauce over the chicken and serve the rest separately in a heated gravy boat.

* If possible, make your own bouillon from chicken feet, head, a piece of veal, veal bones, and soup greens.

PREPARATION: 25 min. COOKING: 1 hr. 30 min.

POULET AU BLANC (CHICKEN WITH CREAM SAUCE)

A 3-lb. dressed tender chicken
1 strip fresh larding pork
2 1/2 qt. chicken bouillon
1/2 lb. small white mushrooms
1/2 cup butter
2 tbsp. lemon juice
3 tbsp. flour
2 egg yolks
1/3 cup heavy whipping cream
Salt, pepper

Tie the strip of larding pork over the breast of the chicken, and truss as though for roasting. Place in a stewpan just large enough for the chicken, and pour enough bouillon around the chicken to cover it by about 1/2 inch. Slowly bring to a boil, skimming off any surface scum. Cover, but leave an opening for the steam to espace. Simmer for 1 hour. Meanwhile, cut away the earthy part of the mushroom stems, scrape them and peel the heads. Put the lemon juice and 1/4 cup chicken bouillon into a small saucepan and add the mushrooms. Add 2 tablespoons of butter, cover, and bring quickly to a boil. Simmer 5 minutes, remove from the fire, and keep hot.

Meanwhile, melt 3 tablespoons of butter in a small saucepan, stir in the flour and cook slowly, stirring constantly, over a low flame for 5 minutes. Slowly pour in 2 cups of strained chicken broth and continue stirring until the sauce is boiling. Beat the egg yolks with the cream, then add a little of the hot sauce; pour this mixture back into the rest of the sauce. Beat hard, and reheat over a low flame. Stir in the mushrooms and their cooking liquor.

When the chicken is cooked, remove from the broth, drain, and quickly cut into pieces for serving. Arrange on a heated serving platter. Scatter the mushrooms over the chicken. Pour over a little of the sauce and serve the rest in a heated gravy boat. Excellent with *Riz à l'Indienne*.

PREPARATION: 10 min. COOKING: 1 hr. 15 min.

POULE FARCIE (STUFFED CHICKEN IN THE POT)

A 3 1/2-lb. dressed stewing chicken
3 oz. boiled ham
2 boned pork chops
1 cup soft white bread
1 egg
2 tbsp. milk
1 shallot
1/2 lb. leeks, 1/2 lb. carrots
1/2 lb. turnips
Several large cabbage leaves
1 tbsp. chopped parsley
Salt, pepper

Clean the chicken and prepare it for stuffing. Soak the bread in milk and squeeze it dry. Chop up the ham and pork chops and mix them with the bread, the finely chopped shallot, egg, parsley, salt and pepper. Stuff the fowl with about half this mixture, sew it up and truss for cooking. Put the chicken in a deep pot, cover with cold salted water and bring slowly to a boil. Skim off all surface scum. Add the carrots, turnips and leeks, all cleaned and sliced. Make a ball of the remaining stuffing, wrap in cabbage leaves and tie securely with a string. Wrap again in a piece of cheesecloth and drop into the pot with the fowl. Simmer 2 hours to 2 hours 30 minutes or until done.

When ready to serve, place the fowl on a large platter and remove the string. Arrange the vegetables around it and decorate with wedges of the cabbage-wrapped stuffing.

* Serve with a light red or dry white wine.

PREPARATION: 50 min. COOKING: 2 hrs. 30 min.

CHAUD-FROID DE POULET (CHICKEN IN CHILLED CREAM SAUCE)

A 3-lb. dressed roasting chicken
1 calf's foot
2 carrots
1 tbsp. flour
5 tbsp. butter
2 cups heavy whipping cream
2 egg yolks
1 sprig thyme
1 bay leaf
Salt, pepper

Truss the chicken as for roasting, place it in a pan with 2 quarts of cold water as well as the carrots cut in slices, thyme, bay leaf, salt, pepper, and split calf's foot. Slowly bring to a boil and cook for 1 hour to 1 hour 30 minutes. Remove the chicken. Cool and cut into pieces for serving.

Melt the butter in a saucepan, stir in the flour, and add 6 tablespoons of the hot chicken bouillon. Cook until thickened, or about 10 minutes. Remove from the fire, add the cream and the 2 egg yolks beaten with 1 teaspoon of water. Let cool.

Dip each piece of chicken into the sauce twice and let drip dry on a rack between each dipping. Arrange on a serving platter, decorate each piece with a slice of truffle, a bit of tomato, or a few leaves of watercress. Serve well chilled. (Mapie de Toulouse-Lautrec).

* To make the sauce, reheat the cold bouillon and strain off the quantity required.

PREPARATION: 45 min. COOKING: 1 hr. 30 min.

POULET EN GELÉE (CHICKEN IN ASPIC)

A 3-lb. dressed roasting chicken
1 lb. boneless boiling beef plus
beef or poultry bones
1/2 veal knuckle sawed through
1 calf's or pig's foot
1 onion
1 carrot
1 leek
3 egg whites
1/2 cup Port wine
1 tbsp. chopped parsley
1 sprig thyme
1 bay leaf
1 clove
Salt, pepper

Roast the chicken, cool, cut into pieces for serving, and set aside; combine all the remaining ingredients except the egg whites and Port in a large stewpan. Add 3 quarts of water and bring slowly to a boil; skim off any surface scum. Cover, leaving a small space for the steam to escape, and simmer 3 hours. Strain the liquid and cool completely, preferably overnight. Skim every bit of fat from the surface.

Beat the egg whites with the Port until frothy, add to the broth and bring to a boil. As soon as the first large bubbles appear, remove from the heat and strain through a double thickness of fine cheesecloth into a pyrex or pottery bowl; cool. Before the aspic thickens, spoon a layer over the chicken arranged on a serving platter.

Garnish each piece with a few leaves of tarragon or watercress, or a slice of truffle, stuffed olive or pimento. Cool. Spoon over another layer of aspic and chill thoroughly before serving. Two hours in a refrigerator should suffice.

* Sticking the clove in the onion is a good way not to lose it.

PREPARATION: about 5 hrs. (preliminary cooking included which must be done the day before). COOKING: 45 min.

POULET EN GELÉE

OIE A LA PÉRIGOURDINE (STUFFED ROAST GOOSE)

(serves 10)

An 8-lb. dressed young goose	1 *lb.* pâté de foie gras
4-5 slices stale white bread	1 1/2 *cups Madeira wine*
4 medium truffles or	1 *cup* Bouillon Blanc
1 medium can truffle scraps	*Salt, pepper*

Soak the bread in the bouillon for at least 15 minutes and squeeze dry. Mix with the *pâté de foie gras* and 1 finely-chopped truffle.

Prepare the goose for roasting, stuff about three-quarters full with the stuffing, and truss. If any stuffing remains, place it in a small buttered pan and bake separately with the goose for the last 1 hour 30 minutes.

Place the goose in an open roasting pan with a little bouillon. If very fat, prick through the skin around the wings and legs. Roast in a moderate oven (about 325º), counting 25 minutes per pound. Remove the fat as it accumulates. Turn the goose, browning it on all sides, and baste occasionally. When done, remove the goose from the pan, season, and keep hot.

Pour almost all the fat out of the pan, add the Madeira, and stir in the truffles cut in slivers. Cook, stirring and scraping all the pan drippings into the sauce, for about 10 minutes. Season with salt and pepper and serve this sauce separately in a heated gravy boat. If you wish to serve a vegetable, a good choice might be fried cauliflower.

PREPARATION: 45 min. COOKING: 3 hrs. 30 min.

CANARD AU VIN (DUCK IN WINE SAUCE)

A 4-lb. dressed roasting duck	1/2 *lb. small onions*
3 cups dry red wine	1/2 *lb. mushrooms*
1/4 lb. thick lean bacon	1/4 *cup Cognac*
6 tbsp. butter	*1 bouquet garni*
1 tbsp. flour	*Salt, pepper, sugar*

Truss the duck as for roasting. Melt half the butter in a heavy stewpan with a lid, and lightly brown the diced lean bacon. Put in the duck, brown it on all sides, then sprinkle it with flour, salt and pepper. Pour over the heated red wine, add 1 teaspoon of sugar, and the *bouquet garni*. Cover and simmer for 1 hour.

Melt the remaining 3 tablespoons of butter in a frying pan with 1 more teaspoon of sugar and brown the peeled, whole onions. Add the onions to the duck for the last half hour of cooking. Ten minutes before serving, add the sliced mushrooms; 5 minutes later, taste and adjust the seasoning, take out the *bouquet garni*, arrange the duck on a platter, pour the warmed Cognac over it and light a match to it. Arrange the onions around the duck and serve the sauce in a heated gravy boat.

PREPARATION: 30 min. COOKING: about 1 hr.

CANARD AU VIN

PIGEONS AUX PETITS POIS (SQUAB WITH PEAS AND BACON)

4 small or 2 large squab
3 tbsp. butter
1/4 lb. thick lean bacon
3 tbsp. flour
2 cups chicken bouillon
1 bouquet garni
3 cups shelled peas
Salt, pepper

Dress and truss the birds. Melt the butter in a heavy stewpan and brown them 5 minutes on each side. Remove, keep hot, and brown the diced bacon in the same butter ; remove. Stir in the flour, cook until lightly browned, add the bouillon, season with salt and pepper, and add the *bouquet garni*. Cook 2 or 3 minutes, stirring constantly. Put the bacon back in as well as the fresh peas. Cook half an hour, put the squab back in and continue cooking another 20-30 minutes or until the latter are tender.

Place the squab on a heated platter. Remove the *bouquet garni* and pour the peas and sauce around the squab. This is a good way of preparing birds of unknown age. Serve with fresh, soft new potatoes.

* If you wish to use frozen peas, put them in at the same time as the squab. For 3 cups of shelled fresh peas, you must start with 3 pounds of peas in their pods.

PREPARATION: 25 min. COOKING: 50-60 min.

PIGEONS FARCIS AUX HERBES (SQUAB WITH HERB STUFFING)

4 very young squab
2 small eggs
4 slices stale white bread
2 oz. fat salt pork
2 tbsp. butter
1/2 cup mixed chopped chives,
thyme, parsley, marjoram, chervil
3/4 cup chicken bouillon
Salt, pepper

Trim the crusts off the bread and soak in warm bouillon for a few minutes. Squeeze dry with your fingers and crumble it. Chop the herbs and the salt pork finely together and mix with the bread and the eggs. Season with salt and pepper and blend thoroughly with a fork. Stuff the birds with this mixture and sew them up with string.

Melt about 2 tablespoons of butter in a wide, shallow pan and roast the squabs in a preheated hot oven (400°) for 35-40 minutes. Sprinkle with salt and place on a warmed platter. Pour 3 or 4 tablespoons of boiling water into the roasting pan and swish around, lightly scraping sides and bottom to get all the drippings. Serve this light sauce with the birds.

Do not try this recipe except with very young squab. For more mature birds (or birds of doubtful vintage) use the above recipe for *Pigeons aux Petits Pois*.

* Do not add salt until the squab are completely cooked or they may toughen.

PREPARATION: 25 min. COOKING: 35-40 min.

DINDONNEAU AUX MARRONS (TURKEY WITH CHESTNUT STUFFING)

(serves 8-10)
An 8-lb. dressed young turkey
3/4 lb. sausage meat
1 1/2 lb. chestnuts
1 qt. Fond de Cuisson
2 stalks celery
5-6 strips larding pork
Salt, pepper

Slash the chestnuts (after removing the outer shell) and toss them into the boiling *Fond de Cuisson* with the cut-up celery. Cook for 20-25 minutes; peel while still hot. Mash them with the sausage meat and pile this stuffing into the cavity of the dressed young turkey. Do not pack too tightly; any extra stuffing can be baked separately in a buttered ramekin.

Sew up the turkey and truss for roasting; tie the strips of salt pork over the breast.

Place on a rack in an open pan and pour 1/2 cup of water in the bottom of the pan. Season this with salt and a little pepper and use it to baste the turkey from time to time. Roast in a moderate oven (350°), counting 25 minutes per pound.

* It is never a bad idea to stuff a fowl a day ahead of time and let it stand overnight. In this way the bird becomes impregnated with the flavor of the stuffing.

This recipe yields a greater number of servings as it is really dinner-party fare.

PREPARATION: 45 min. COOKING: about 3 hrs. 30 min.

196

PIGEONS FARCIS AUX HERBES

CAILLES AU CHASSEUR (QUAIL WITH WINE AND HERBS)

4 quail
2 tbsp. butter
1 1/2 tbsp. flour
1/2 cup white wine
1/2 lemon
2 chopped shallots
1 bay leaf, 1 sprig thyme
1 tbsp. chopped parsley
Croûtons
Salt, pepper

Dress and truss the quail. Melt the butter in a heavy stewpan, put in the quail as well as the parsley, shallots, bay leaf and thyme, season with salt and pepper, and brown the birds on all sides. Sprinkle with the flour, add the heated wine and 1/2 cup salted water. Cover and simmer gently for half an hour.

Arrange the quail on a heated serving platter with the croûtons fried in butter, add the juice of 1/2 lemon to the sauce, taste, adjust the seasoning, and strain over the birds.

* The quail, unlike the pheasant (see below), should be eaten as soon after killing as possible. Usually a dish which is prepared with wine is served with the same wine at the dinner table – in this case, a dry white wine.

PREPARATION: 20 min. COOKING: 45 min.

FAISAN ROTI (ROAST PHEASANT)

1 pheasant
2 tbsp. sweet butter
1 tbsp. Madeira wine
8 small slices stale bread
2 lemons

Dress the pheasant, smear it thoroughly with butter, and roast on a rack in an open pan in a hot oven (400°) for 45 minutes. At the end of the first 15 minutes add the Madeira to the juice in the pan and baste with this mixture every 10 minutes. Ten minutes before the end of the roasting time, place the slices of bread in the sauce. They will absorb the juice and roast at the same time.

Serve the pheasant surrounded by the roasted bread and slices of lemon. If you wish, decorate the bird with the neck and tail feathers saved at the time of plucking.

* French connoisseurs advise that a pheasant be hung for at least three days before cooking to allow the meat to begin to decompose. Furthermore, it should be hung unplucked. There are two theories behind this latter principle: one is that the air robs a plucked bird of some of its flavor; the other is that the oil in the feathers brings out the flavor of the flesh.

PREPARATION: 15 min. COOKING: 45 min.

PERDRIX AUX CHOUX (PARTRIDGE WITH CABBAGE)

1 large or 2 small partridge
2 tbsp. butter
1/4 lb. lean bacon
4 Chipolata sausages
2 tbsp. flour
1 cup chicken bouillon
1 large carrot
1 medium cabbage
1 sprig thyme
2 cloves
Salt, pepper, nutmeg

Clean the partridge and cut in halves or quarters according to size. Cut the bacon into fairly small, thin slices. Heat the butter in a heavy stewpan and brown the partridge together with the bacon and sliced sausages. When browned on all sides remove all 3 ingredients from the pan and stir the flour into the butter; cook until brown and then add the bouillon, thyme, cloves, a dash of nutmeg, and the thinly sliced carrot; season with salt and pepper.

Quarter the cabbage and blanch it 10 minutes in boiling salted water; drain. Put the partridge, bacon, and sausages back in the sauce with the cabbage quarters around them, cover, and simmer gently for 2 hours. Arrange the partridge, sausages, bacon, and cabbage on a heated platter; skim the fat off the sauce and strain over the platter. Serve with boiled potatoes or potato dumplings.

* This is a recipe which can be used with either young or old birds. Simmering with the cabbage leaves imparts the flavor of the fowl to the cabbage. Serve with a full-bodied red wine.

Young partridges may be broiled in the oven for 20 to 40 minutes and served with potatoes and a green vegetable, but this is not recommended for birds of over 15 months of age.

PREPARATION: 30 min. COOKING: 2 hrs. 15 min.

FONDS D'ARTICHAUTS FARCIS (STUFFED ARTICHOKE HEARTS)

12 small artichoke hearts (canned
or freshly cooked)
5 oz. lean ham
1 cup butter
2 slices white bread
1/2 cup milk
1 egg
1 shallot, 1 garlic clove
2 sprigs parsley
Salt, pepper

Chop together the ham, shallot, garlic and parsley. Sauté the mixture in 1 tablespoon of butter. Cut off the crusts and soak the bread in a little milk; squeeze dry and mix in small pieces into the stuffing. Season with salt and pepper and stir in the whole egg.

Drain the artichoke hearts thoroughly and place them in a buttered ovenware dish. Cover each one with stuffing and a small dab of butter. Bake in a hot oven (425°) until brown. Serve immediately with a gravy boat of melted butter.

* Arabic by origin, and brought back to France by the Crusaders, artichokes were a great favorite of Catherine de Medici, who consumed so many of them at a wedding banquet one day that she thought she would die from the experience.

Artichoke hearts can be served hot or cold with countless stuffings. Asparagus tips and truffles mixed with a Sauce Béchamel, chopped onion and sausage meat covered with a Sauce Béchamel, and vegetable purées are only some of the unlimited possibilities of hot stuffed artichoke hearts. All of these should be sprinkled with grated cheese and melted butter and browned in the oven before serving. Cold suggestions include chopped asparagus tips, chicken, lobster, or shrimp, in a cold Sauce Mayonnaise and garnished with chopped hard-boiled egg and parsley.

PREPARATION: 20 min. BAKING: 10-15 min.

HARICOTS VERTS A LA FRANÇAISE (FRENCH STRING BEANS)

2 lb. tender string beans
1/2 lb. small onions
1 head Boston lettuce
6 tbsp. butter
1 tsp. sugar
2 sprigs parsley
1 sprig chervil
Salt

Choose the smallest, youngest, tenderest beans you can find. Cut off the ends, remove any strings, wash thoroughly, and cut lengthwise in 2 or 3 pieces, depending on their size. Peel the onions but do not cut them up. Remove the outer leaves of the lettuce, wash thoroughly, and tie with string to keep the head intact.

Melt all but 1 tablespoon of butter in a large saucepan and put in the beans, onions, lettuce, sugar, and 1 teaspoon of salt; tie the parsley and chervil together and add to the vegetables. Stir, add 1/2 cup of cold water, bring to a boil, cover, and let cook over a very low flame for about 40 minutes, or until the beans are done.

Remove the parsley and chervil and the string from the lettuce, add the remaining tablespoon of butter and serve. (Mapie de Toulouse-Lautrec).

* In cleaning the lettuce, leave only the heart and tender inner leaves. Peas can be cooked in the same way.

PREPARATION: 30 min. COOKING: 40 min.

PAPETON D'AUBERGINES (EGGPLANT CASSEROLE)

10 medium eggplant
6 tbsp. olive oil
1 tbsp. heavy whipping cream
3 eggs
2 cups Sauce Aurore
2 garlic cloves
3 shallots
1 sprig thyme
1 bay leaf
Salt, pepper

Peel the eggplant, cut them in slices, sprinkle liberally with salt, and let stand for one half hour; drain. Heat the olive oil in a saucepan, put in the eggplant, garlic, shallots, thyme, bay leaf, salt and pepper; cover and simmer 15 minutes, or until done. Mash through a strainer or in a blender and stir in the cream. Beat the eggs and stir them into the eggplant purée. Pour into a greased mold, set the mold in a dish of hot water, and bake in a moderate oven (375°) for 20-25 minutes. Near the end of the baking time, test with a knife; it should come out clean, but the eggplant should not be hard.

Meanwhile, heat the Sauce Aurore. When the eggplant is cooked, unmold it onto a hot serving platter and either pour the sauce over it or decorate it with stripes, as on the photograph.

PREPARATION: 30 min. BAKING: about 25 min.

202

ENDIVES GLACÉES AU JUS (BRAISED ENDIVE)

12 small heads Belgian endive
1 tsp. sugar
2 tbsp. butter
1 tsp. cornstarch or arrowroot
3/4 cup Bouillon Blanc
Salt, pepper, nutmeg

Wash and trim the endive. Melt the butter in a heavy skillet and lay the endive side by side in the butter. Season with salt, pepper, a dash of nutmeg, and sugar, and add 1/2 cup of bouillon. Cover tightly and simmer over the lowest possible flame for 1 hour. Turn the endive once after one half hour.

When they are done, arrange on a heated platter, mix the cornstarch or arrowroot with the remaining 1/4 cup of bouillon, add to the juice in pan, cook 2 or 3 more minutes, and pour over the endive.

* One of the few vegetables available in the wintertime, endive are appreciated in Europe for their delicate, slightly bitter taste.
Particularly good with pork, rabbit, or game.

PREPARATION: 5 min. COOKING: 1 hr. 15 min.

BULBES DE FENOUIL PERSILLÉS (FENNEL WITH PARSLEY)

1 1/2 lb. fennel bulbs
2 1/2 tbsp. butter
2 tsp. chopped parsley
1 lemon

Peel the fennel, cut off the stalk ends, and remove any green leaves which may remain; wash well. Bring to a boil enough salted water to cover them, throw in the fennel, and cook over a medium flame for about 30 minutes. Test with a fork for tenderness. Drain well, melt the butter in a saucepan, put the bulbs in side by side and sauté them very lightly.

Serve in a heated dish, sprinkle with chopped parsley, and garnish with lemon quarters or slices.

* Fennel is a very aromatic vegetable. Long ago it was put in closets to scent fine linens. Cooked, it lends its flavor admirably to fish.
If fennel is not available at your neighbourhood grocer's, try an Italian grocer.

PREPARATION: 15 min. COOKING: 45 min.

LAITUE AU JUS (BRAISED LETTUCE)

4 firm heads Boston lettuce
or romaine
2 tbsp. butter
1 tbsp. flour
1/2 cup Bouillon Blanc
1/2 tsp. Glace de Viande
1 bouquet garni
Salt, pepper

Remove the outer leaves of the lettuce and wash the heads carefully; drain and tie each one with a string. Blanch in boiling salted water for 5 minutes, drain, plunge the heads in cold water, drain again, and dry well with a cloth. Melt the butter in a heavy stewpan, stir in the flour, and cook until lightly browned. Add the bouillon, the *Glace de Viande* and *bouquet garni*, and season with salt and pepper, stirring constantly. Add the lettuce, cover tightly, and simmer for 35 minutes, basting often. Place the lettuce in a deep serving dish, remove the *bouquet garni*, and pour over the sauce.

PREPARATION: 15 min. COOKING: 40 min.

CÉLERIS BRAISÉS MOELLE (CELERY WITH MARROW)

12 bunches celery
5/8 lb. fresh beef marrow
3/4 cup butter
1 qt. Fond de Cuisson

Soak the marrow in cold water. Cut off the celery 6 to 8 inches from the base. Clean, trim, and wash the hearts thoroughly but do not separate them. Blanch for 15 minutes in boiling water, rinse in cold water, and drain.

Place the celery in a buttered shallow ovenware dish and pour over the *Fond de Cuisson*. Cover and place in a slow oven (300º) for 1 hour to 1 hour 30 minutes. Remove the celery, cut in half lengthwise, and fold over. Place in a deep casserole dish with the slices of marrow on top. Boil the cooking liquid for 10 minutes, reducing it by half. Stir in the butter and pour this sauce over the celery and marrow. Return to the oven for 5 minutes, or until the marrow is done.

PREPARATION: 25 min. COOKING: 1 hr. 30 min.

PRIMEURS A LA NIVERNAISE (MIXED SPRING VEGETABLES)

2 cups shelled peas
1/2 lb. small new carrots
15 small white onions
4 hearts Boston lettuce
2 1/2 tbsp. butter
1/2 cup heavy whipping cream
1/2 tsp. sugar
Salt, pepper

Scrub but do not peel the carrots. Peel the onions; wash and drain the lettuce hearts. Melt the butter in a heavy stewpan, put in the onions and carrots, and simmer them over a medium flame, shaking the pan often. After 10 minutes of cooking, add the lettuce hearts, and 5 minutes later the peas and 2/3 cup of water. Season with salt and pepper. Cover the stewpan with a saucer of cold water and bring to a boil. Adjust the flame to keep a light boil, not a simmer, for 25-30 minutes.

After this time, sprinkle in the sugar, shake the pan, and mix. Pour over the cream, shake again, and heat just long enough to heat the cream. Transfer the vegetables to a heated serving dish and serve immediately.

PREPARATION: 30 min. COOKING: 50 min.

SOUFFLÉ AUX ÉPINARDS (SPINACH SOUFFLÉ)

2 lb. fresh spinach
1/2 cup butter
1/2 cup sour cream
5 eggs
1/4 lb. grated Parmesan cheese
Salt, pepper

Cut off the stems and wash the spinach, being careful to remove all sand. Put in about 3 quarts of boiling salted water for 10 to 15 minutes. Drain, press out all liquid with your fingers, and mash through a strainer or in a blender. Place over a low flame and add the butter. While the butter is melting, beat the egg whites until stiff, and beat the yolks lightly in a separate dish. Remove the spinach from the fire and stir in the sour cream, grated cheese, and egg yolks; season to taste. Then carefully incorporate the whites into the mixture.

Butter a deep straight-sided soufflé dish and fill with the spinach mixture. Bake in a moderate oven (375°) for 10 minutes, then raise the heat to 425-450° for 15 minutes more. Serve immediately. A soufflé cannot wait. (Mapie de Toulouse-Lautrec).

* If you prefer, use frozen chopped spinach; 1 package is enough for this recipe (4 servings).

PREPARATION: 45-50 min. BAKING: 25 min.

RATATOUILLE NIÇOISE (SAUTÉD MIXED VEGETABLES)

1 lb. eggplant
2 lb. tomatoes
2 medium zucchini
3 green peppers
1/2 cup olive oil
1 garlic clove
Salt, pepper

Cut all the vegetables in fairly thin slices; do not peel them. Heat the oil and garlic in a large, deep frying pan. When the oil is hot, brown the vegetables rapidly in 4 or 5 successive batches, transferring them when cooked into a deep, round pot. When all the vegetables are browned, pour the oil over them in the pot, season generously, cover, and cook over a low flame for at least 1 hour. Serve in a heated vegetable dish. (Mapie de Toulouse-Lautrec).

PREPARATION: 40 min. COOKING: 1 hr.

SOUFFLÉ DE MAIS (CORN SOUFFLÉ)

6 ears fresh corn
2 tsp. chopped onions
3/4 cup butter
2 tbsp. heavy whipping cream
4 eggs
Salt, pepper, paprika

Drop the shucked corn, ear by ear, into 1 inch of boiling water. Cover and boil until tender (about 5 to 10 minutes). Meanwhile, soften the onions in a little butter. Cut the corn from the cob and put corn and onions in a blender, or mash through a strainer. Put this purée in a saucepan with the butter and reheat rapidly, preventing sticking by stirring with a wooden spatula. Evaporate any excess moisture. Remove from the fire and stir in the cream and a generous pinch of paprika.

Beat the egg yolks and add them to the mixture. Beat the egg whites until stiff and fold them in carefully. Butter a deep straight-sided soufflé dish and pour in the mixture. Bake in a fairly hot oven (400°) for about 15 minutes. Serve immediately.

PREPARATION: 25 min. BAKING: 15 min.

RATATOUILLE NIÇOISE

GRATIN DAUPHINOIS

GRATIN DAUPHINOIS (SCALLOPED POTATOES)

2 lb. waxy potatoes
3 tbsp. butter
2 tbsp. heavy whipping cream
3 tbsp. grated Swiss cheese
2/3 cup milk
Salt, pepper. nutmeg

Peel, wash, and cut the potatoes in thin slices. Scald the milk. Butter an ovenware dish and make a neat layer of about half the potatoes in it. Melt the remaining 2 tablespoons of butter, pour over the potatoes, and spread with a layer of cream. Sprinkle with grated cheese; season generously with salt and pepper. Make a second layer of potatoes, pour over the milk, and sprinkle with salt, pepper and nutmeg.

Bake in a hot oven (400°), checking occasionally to make sure the top does not brown too quickly; in this case, cover with a piece of wax or aluminum paper. After 45 minutes, test the potatoes with a fork for doneness; this is one dish a little extra cooking cannot hurt.

Serve piping hot directly from the baking dish. *(M. de Toulouse-Lautrec).*

PREPARATION: 30 minutes. BAKING: 50 minutes.

210

POMMES DUCHESSE (POTATO PATTIES)

8 *medium potatoes*
1 *egg*
2 *tbsp. butter*
1 *tbsp. chopped parsley*
Salt, pepper

Boil the peeled and quartered potatoes in salted water until tender. Mash through a fine strainer or in a blender. Return to the fire for a few minutes to dry them out, stirring constantly with a wooden spatula to keep from scorching. Remove from the fire and stir in the unbeaten egg, parsley, salt and pepper. Cool.

Fry small cakes of these potatoes in sizzling butter until golden brown on both sides. Salt and serve very hot, garnished with parsley.

* *Pommes Duchesse* may also be forced through a pastry tube to form spirals or other decorations on a platter and then browned in the oven. Very attractive around a roast.

PREPARATION: 50 min. COOKING: 10-15 min.

POMMES FLAMBÉES (APPLES FLAMBÉES)

8 medium tart apples
1 cup granulated sugar
1/4 tsp. cinnamon
1/4 cup rum

Bring the cinnamon, sugar, and 2 cups of water to a boil. Wash the apples, remove the cores, and poach them in the syrup until just tender. Arrange them in a pyramid on a heated platter or in a chafing dish. Reduce the syrup by boiling it over a high flame until thickened; at the same time heat the rum. Pour the syrup over the apples and carry them and the rum to the table.

Pour over the hot rum and light a match to it.

* Be careful not to overcook the apples or they will fall apart. They should still be fairly firm when pricked with a fork or knitting needle.

PREPARATION: 5 min. COOKING: 25 min.

ORANGES AU COINTREAU (ORANGES BAKED IN COINTREAU)

4 fine seedless oranges
2 eggs
2 egg yolks
1/3 cup heavy whipping cream
1/2 cup granulated sugar
3 tbsp. Cointreau liqueur

Peel the oranges carefully, scraping away all the white skin; divide them into sections and arrange in an ovenware serving dish with half the sugar. Sprinkle with Cointreau and let stand at least 6 hours, overnight if possible.

About three quarters of an hour before serving, heat the oranges in their dish either in the oven or on the stove. As soon as the juice comes to a boil, remove from the heat. Drain off the hot juice, leaving the oranges in the dish. Let both orange sections and juice cool slightly. Beat up the eggs, yolks, and cream, add the remaining sugar, stir in the juice, and pour the mixture back over the orange sections. Bake in a hot oven (400°) just long enough to thicken the sauce. Serve immediately.

PREPARATION: 45 min. (plus standing). COOKING: 15-20 min.

CLAFOUTIS LIMOUSIN (CHERRY CUSTARD)

1 lb. cherries
1 1/2 cups milk
3 eggs
1 egg yolk
6 tbsp. granulated sugar
1 cup flour
1 tsp. butter

Butter a deep baking dish. Remove the stems from the cherries but do not stone them, and place them in the bottom of the dish. Beat up the milk, eggs, egg yolk, flour, and all but 1 tablespoon of sugar. Pour over the cherries and bake in a hot oven (400-425°) for 25-30 minutes. At the end of 20 minutes, sprinkle the remaining tablespoon of sugar on top. Cool and unmold before serving.

* In the wintertime, use canned cherries or pears or apple slices.

PREPARATION: 15 min. COOKING: 25-30 min.

MELON MERVEILLE (MELON CUP WITH MERINGUE)

2 medium cantaloupes
1 pt. fresh strawberries
3 pears
1/2 cup Cointreau liqueur
2 egg whites
2 tbsp. granulated sugar

Cut the melons in half and scoop out the seeds and part of the flesh. Wash and clean the strawberries and peel and cut the pears in small pieces. Put a mixture of this fruit in each melon cup, pour over the liqueur, and chill in the refrigerator for at least 1 hour.

Beat the egg whites until stiff and stir in the sugar carefully. Cover each chilled melon cup with this meringue and place in a preheated hot oven (400°) for about 5 minutes or until golden. Serve hot or cold.

* Ideally the melon should be quite cold, the meringue hot out of the oven.

PREPARATION: 1 hr. 20 min. (chilling included). COOKING: 5 min.

CLAFOUTIS LIMOUSIN

FRAMBOISES A L'ORANGE (RASPBERRIES WITH ORANGES)

2 navel oranges
1 lb. fresh ripe raspberries
1/3 cup granulated sugar
3 tbsp. Maraschino liqueur

Cut the oranges in thin horizontal slices without peeling them. Sprinkle with half the sugar and half the liqueur and let stand for at least 2 hours. Pick over the raspberries and sprinkle them with the remaining sugar and liqueur.

Arrange the orange slices on the bottom and around the edge of a serving dish and heap the raspberries in the center. Serve well chilled.

* The orange slices may be replaced by pineapple slices in this dessert.

PREPARATION: 30 min. (plus standing). CHILLING: at least 2 hrs.

MOUSSELINE DE FRUITS CONFITS (CANDIED FRUIT MOUSSE)

6 egg whites
2 cups granulated sugar
1 1/2 cups mixed chopped candied fruits
2 tbsp. Cointreau liqueur

Sauce:
1 lb. cooking apples
1 1/3 cups granulated sugar
1 tbsp. lemon juice
3 tbsp. heavy whipping cream
3 tbsp. Cointreau liqueur

Sprinkle the Cointreau over the candied fruits and let stand for at least 2 hours. Melt 6 tablespoons of sugar with a little water in a large, deep mold and cook until a light caramel. Tip the mold to coat the whole inner surface and let cool. Beat the egg whites stiff and little by little stir in the remaining sugar, the candied fruits, and their juice. Pour into the mold, filling it only halfway, and bake in a water bath for 20 minutes in a moderate oven (350°). Remove from the oven and leave the mold in the water bath for another 5 minutes. Do not unmold until just before serving.

Cut the pared apples in thin slices and place them in a deep heavy saucepan with the sugar, lemon juice and 2 tablespoons of water. Simmer gently for 20 minutes but do not brown. Mash them through a fine strainer or in a blender, the result being a rather thin, clear sauce. If the purée is too thick, add a little cold water; cool. Just before serving, stir in the cream and Cointreau, unmold the mousse onto a flat serving dish, and pour over the sauce.

* The first *fruits confits* or candied fruits were introduced in France in the Middle Ages. Probably of oriental origin, they were eaten at the end of a meal "to aid the digestion and perfume the breath" and were known by the name of " *épices de chambre* " or " *chamber spices* ". Nougat and sugar-covered almonds *(dragées)* were served in the same manner.

PREPARATION: 1 hr. 30 min. (plus standing). BAKING: 20 min.

HÉRISSON DE FRAISES (FRENCH STRAWBERRY SHORTCAKE)

1 1/2 qt. strawberries
8 eggs
2 cups granulated sugar
1/2 cup flour
9 oz. potato starch
1 pint whipped cream
3 tbsp. Kirsch (or cherry brandy)
1/2 lemon
Salt

Separate the egg whites from the yolks. Beat the yolks with the sugar and a pinch of salt in a large mixing bowl until a smooth cream is obtained. Add the potato starch and the juice of 1/2 lemon. Mix well.

Beat the egg whites until stiff and fold them into the batter. Blend with a cutting motion.

Butter a deep round metal cake mold and sprinkle it with flour. Pour in the batter, filling it only two-thirds full to allow the cake to rise. Bake in a moderately hot oven (375°) for 45 minutes. Test with a knife for doneness. Cool and cut in 3 horizontal layers.

Sprinkle the first layer with a tablespoon of Kirsch. Cover with a layer of strawberries followed by whipped cream. Then a second layer: cake, Kirsch, strawberries, whipped cream. For the third layer, sprinkle with Kirsch, cover the sides and top generously with cream, and cover the whole cake with strawberries. Refrigerate for an hour or so before serving. *(Mapie de Toulouse-Lautrec).*

* The literal translation of the picturesque name of this dessert is "Strawberry Hedgehog."

The whipped cream must be thick enough to hold the outside coat of strawberries or "quills" in place.

PREPARATION: 1 hr. COOKING: 45 min.

216

PROFITEROLES AU CHOCOLAT (CREAM PUFFS WITH HOT FUDGE)

3/4 cup butter
1 cup flour
1 3/4 cups granulated sugar
4 eggs
2 1/2 cups heavy whipping cream
4 oz. cooking chocolate
2 tsp. Cognac

Melt 1/2 cup of butter, add 1 cup of water, and bring to a boil. Remove from the stove, add the sifted flour all at once, and stir vigorously until blended. Stir in 1 teaspoon of sugar and put back over a very low flame, stirring constantly, until the mixture is dry and leaves small traces of dried dough on the bottom of the saucepan. Take off the fire; add the eggs one by one, beating after each one, until the mixture is smooth. Drop this cream puff pastry by teaspoons onto a buttered and lightly floured baking sheet. Bake 35-40 minutes in a moderate oven (350°) until a light golden color. Remove from the oven and cool.

Whip 1 1/2 cups of cream until thick but not dry, and stir in 2 tablespoons of sugar. Make a small hole in the bottom of each puff and force in the whipped cream with the help of a pastry tube.

Make a pyramid of cream puffs on a dessert platter. Melt the chocolate with the remaining sugar and butter in the top of a double boiler; stir in the remaining cup of cream and the Cognac. Pour the hot fudge sauce over the cream puff pyramid and serve hot.

* The word *profiteroles* is used for any number of small cream puff variations. *Profiteroles* filled with cheese are excellent as small hors d'œuvres; *profiteroles* filled with a meat purée make an unusual garnish for soups and consommés. These tiny cream puffs may also be filled with a variety of sweet pastry creams or fruit preserves.

PREPARATION: 1 hr. 15 min. BAKING: 40 min.

SOUFFLÉ AU CHOCOLAT (CHOCOLATE SOUFFLÉ)

2 tbsp. butter
2 tbsp. flour
3/4 cup milk
2 oz. cooking chocolate
6 tbsp. granulated sugar
2 tbsp. powdered sugar
3 eggs
1/2 tsp. vanilla extract

Melt the butter in a saucepan and stir in the sifted flour; add the warm milk and continue stirring until well blended. Melt the chocolate very slowly with 2 tablespoons of water in the top of a double boiler; add the granulated sugar, stirring until smooth. Pour into the batter and mix well. Separate the eggs and beat the yolks until smooth; stir them and the vanilla into the batter. Beat the egg whites very stiff and fold in carefully.

Pour immediately into a buttered deep straight-sided soufflé dish. Set in a pan of hot water and bake for 20-25 minutes in a preheated moderate oven (350°). Sprinkle with powdered sugar and serve *immediately*. *(Mapie de Toulouse-Lautrec).*

* The principle of the water-bath for baking is the same as that of the double boiler and is often used for soufflés and similar dishes. It insures a gradual and even distribution of heat.

PREPARATION: 35 min. BAKING: 20-25 min.

CRÈME MARBRÉE AU CARAMEL (CARAMEL MARBLE CUSTARD)

4 egg yolks
5 tbsp. flour
1/2 cup granulated sugar
5 lumps sugar
2 cups milk
1/2 lemon

Mix the sifted flour, granulated sugar, and 4 egg yolks in a bowl. Stir in the milk, mix well, and strain through a fine strainer into a saucepan. Heat over a low flame, stirring constantly with a wooden spatula until the cream thickens; do not boil unless an unusually thick custard is desired. Remove from the fire and mix in the grated peel of 1/2 lemon. Cool slightly, stir, and pour again through a fine strainer into a deep serving bowl. Set aside to cool.

Make a caramel sauce by melting the lumps of sugar (or 2 1/2 tablespoons more of granulated sugar) in a little water. Do not stir. Cook until nicely browned; be careful that the caramel does not harden.

Trickle the caramel over the surface of the cream, leaving a little space between the drops. With the fine point of a small knife, mix the caramel carefully into the cream until you have a marbled design all over the surface.

PREPARATION: 15 min. COOKING: 35 min.

PROFITEROLES AU CHOCOLAT

GATEAU DE MARRONS AU CHOCOLAT (CHESTNUT FUDGE CAKE)

1 1/2 lb. chestnuts
8 oz. cooking chocolate
3/4 cup granulated sugar
1/4 lb. sweet butter
1/2 cup whipped cream

Chill a metal cake mold. Slit the chestnuts all around; heat them in the oven until the shells pop open. Remove the outer shell, boil for one half hour or more in salted water, and drain carefully of all juice. Press through a fine strainer, add the sugar and melted butter, and mix well.

Melt the chocolate slowly in a double-boiler, stirring with a wooden spatula. Stir the melted chocolate into the chestnut purée. Spoon into the chilled mold and refrigerate for several hours.

Unmold just before serving by dipping the mold in hot water for a few seconds, placing a serving dish over the mold, and turning over quickly. Shake several times if necessary to free the cake. Decorate with whipped cream and serve. *(Mapie de Toulouse-Lautrec)*.

* It is absolutely essential that the cake be refrigerated so it can "set" and take on the consistency of thick rich fudge. On the photograph, the cake has been shaped by squeezing the partly cooled purée through a pastry tube. For a very elegant dessert, decorate with candied chestnuts.

PREPARATION: 1 hr. 15 min. CHILLING: at least 3 hrs.

GATEAU ISABELLE (CHOCOLATE-ALMOND ICEBOX CAKE)

8 oz. cooking chocolate
7 oz. toasted almonds
1 1/2 cups granulated sugar
3/4 cup sweet butter
2 tbsp. milk
1/2 cup heavy whipping cream

Crush the almonds with 1/2 cup of sugar. Cream the butter with the remaining cup of sugar, adding the butter to the sugar a little at a time and beating vigorously with a wooden spatula or in a blender. Break the chocolate into small pieces and melt them with the milk over a low flame or in the top of a double boiler. Add the almond-sugar and butter-sugar mixtures. Stir in the heavy cream and mix well.

Pour into a mold and refrigerate for several hours. Unmold just before serving by dipping the mold in hot water. Very good with a *Crème Anglaise*. *(Mapie de Toulouse-Lautrec)*.

* According to Alexander Dumas, chocolate was first discovered in Mexico and was brought to Spain in the seventeenth century. It crossed the Pyrenees into France with Anne of Austria and immediately became very fashionable as a hot beverage. The famous gastronome Brillat-Savarin stated that it was "a tonic, a stomachic, and a digestive"!

When making chocolate cakes, always be sure that every bit of chocolate is completely melted; otherwise there will be lumps. This is a long but very important step. If you cannot find toasted almonds, spread blanched almonds on a baking sheet and place them in a medium oven (350°) for about 10 minutes, stirring frequently so they do not burn.

PREPARATION: 40 min. CHILLING: 3-4 hrs.

GATEAU MOKA (MOCHA CAKE)

1 cup sweet butter
1 cup granulated sugar
4 egg yolks
1 cup very strong black coffee
Lady fingers

Cream the butter and sugar, then beat in the egg yolks and, little by little, the coffee.

Line the bottom and sides of a buttered mold with lady fingers, packing them in tightly side by side. Spread them with a thick layer of cream filling. Continue making alternate layers of lady fingers and mocha cream until the latter is used up. Cover with a piece of buttered wax paper, then place a plate or a tray over the mold and weight down heavily. Let stand overnight in a cool place. Unmold by dipping the mold in hot water and serve quite chilled.

* The exact number of lady fingers will depend on both the size and shape of your mold. As these three desserts are all quite rich, they are perfect for an otherwise light meal.

PREPARATION: 30 min. COOLING: overnight.

222

An Expert's Advice

In France, six million people or twelve per cent of the population are more or less directly connected with the wine world. More wine is drunk in France than in any other country in the world; statistics show that thirty-five gallons a year are consumed per inhabitant. This figure is not an overstatement: the alcohol content involved corresponds to one dry Martini per day per person. For every Frenchman, wine is an integral part of his daily diet and, as expressed by a popular advertising slogan, "A meal without wine is a day without sunshine".

France is also the country where people do the most talking about wine. It is a topic of conversation at all social levels. To own a reputed cellar is a sign of great distinction; it makes one almost as famous as owning a large yacht. But interest in wine is not a social prerogative. The renown of a good wine can make the reputation of a neighborhood *bistrot*. Everywhere in France the man who knows how to talk about wine is esteemed and envied, for he is considered able to judge the mysterious workings of nature.

Becoming a connoisseur

For the beginner, however, wine presents many problems: how should it be drunk and when? Should one prefer white wine or red wine? Bordeaux or Burgundy? And many other questions. Those who do not know the answer to these questions often feel intimidated by wine.

But enjoying wine need not be a complicated matter.

If somebody asks you to express an opinion on a work of art—painting, tapestry, furniture—the style of which you do not understand, the only thing you can say is "I like it" or "I do not like it". This holds true for wine as well. There is no point pretending to be competent when you are not; choose your wine according to your own taste and your inclination will surely lead you to the best.

Later, you may become interested in the subject and wish to learn more about it. Little by little you will begin to judge a wine by comparison and memory. You will say "I like this wine because it reminds me of another". You will also be able to distinguish the different qualities of a wine: its consistency and its fragrance. This is the first step in learning about wine; you are on your way to becoming a connoisseur. If your passion for learning (I did not say your passion for wine) takes you one step further, your thirst... for knowledge...will lead you to delve deeper into the subject. You will be able to identify a wine according to its origin; you will be able to guess the name of the vineyard and the date of the vintage by holding the wine between your tongue and your palate. And at this rate, you will soon be an expert.

This brings us to the root of the matter. I do not want to present here

on French Wines

by Louis Vaudable of Maxim's

a technical or documentary treatise on wine. I simply want to repeat certain basic facts and, above all, give a few of my personal ideas. In doing so, I am thinking neither of the professionals nor of the initiated but of the beginners and of all those who would like to learn but who may be discouraged by the apparent complexity of this science, which in reality is a very simple art because it is a natural one.

The geography of French wine

The French wine-producing regions are spread throughout the country with no apparent reason for their location. However, one can remark that white wines are of better quality in the north while red wines dominate in the south.

The biggest French wine regions are the Bordelais, or the region around Bordeaux; Burgundy, or the area south of Dijon; and Champagne, or the region around Rheims.

There are also the vineyards in Alsace, the Loire valley, the Rhône valley and Provence. The region around Montpellier produces a wine of average quality called *Vin du Midi* or "Southern Wine" which is not exported to the United States.

The vineyards of Bordeaux

The choice Bordeaux wines—those which interest us here—are, for the most part, red wines. The Bordeaux region has a very old wine tradition and, owing to the fact that it is near a seaport, its wines were exported by sea long before overland trading routes were established. For this reason it has long been a wealthy region and, as of two or three centuries ago, its vineyards have been exploited by individual châteaux. A château is both a residence and an estate on which a particular vine is cultivated. These vineyards generally produce a high quality wine which is named after the château. A respectable château produces approximately 2,000 cases of wine per year. There are about 3,000 châteaux in the Bordelais, but the names of only about thirty are known to the general public, the most famous of these being Haut-Brion, Margaux, Latour, Lafite, Mouton, Cheval-Blanc and Ausone.

The vineyards of Bordeaux are not limited to wine production by châteaux however. There are other wines produced by other vineyards and bearing the name (known as the *appellation générique*) of the community or region in which they are cultivated. Médoc, Margaux (which produces a lower quality wine than Château Margaux because the vineyards are on the town land and not on the château estate). Saint-Julien, Pauliac, Saint-Estèphe and Saint-Emilion and Pomerol are the best known if these wines.

All of these wines, both of château and regional nomenclature, belong to the vast family of red Bordeaux wines. Wines from the Médoc region are generally light; those from Saint-Emilion are more full-bodied. They have a subtle, discreet taste which makes them suitable for almost any occasion and of which one does not easily tire. These famous vineyards produce wines of the highest quality.

The Bordeaux region also produces white wines. These are generally sweet-tasting, occasionally even liqueur-like. Flowery whites generally come from the Graves district and sweet whites from Sauternes and Barsac. Like the red wines, the whites are divided between châteaux and *appellations génériques*. The best-known white château wine is Château d'Yquem.

The vineyards of Burgundy

The name of Burgundy applies to the vineyards situated on a narrow range of hills that extend from the southern edge of Dijon to about twenty-five miles south of the city. Here the vine is cultivated on a much smaller scale than in Bordeaux. There are no châteaux, but small, individual vineyards cultivated by the loving care and hard work of the same family from generation to generation.

The hills of Burgundy are divided into two parts. The northernmost region, known as the Côte de Nuits, produces almost exclusively red wines: Chambertin, Musigny, Clos de Vougeot, Richebourg, Romanée and the most famous of them all, Romanée-Conti, which yields an average of 7,000 bottles a year. And what wine!...

About six miles further south lies the second region, the Côte de Beaune, which produces mostly red wines but also some excellent whites. The most famous among the red wines of this region are Corton, Beaune, Pommard and Volnay. The greatest names among the white wines include Montrachet, with its offspring Chassagne-Montrachet and Bâtard-Montrachet, and Meursault, with its numerous secondary vineyards such as Perrières and Goutte d'Or. Corton also occasionally produces some excellent white wines, known as Corton Charlemagne.

Red Burgundies are always full-bodied and generally supple and fragrant. They are considered "generous" wines because they have a pronounced and obvious taste—they divulge all their secrets in the first swallow. The white Burgundies are dry wines. Full-bodied, yet with a very subtle taste, they are considered the best white wines in France.

About sixty-five miles north of Burgundy there is a little village called Chablis. Here a dry white wine is produced that is reputed for its delicate and fruity flavor.

At about the same distance to the south of Burgundy exists another wine-producing region: the Beaujolais. This region produces a very popular red wine of fair quality that is known simply as Beaujolais, sometimes referred to by the name of the village where it was cultivated: Saint-Amour, Fleurie, etc., and sometimes by a name given the wine: Moulin à Vent. This area also produces a dry white wine known as Pouilly, or, to be exact, Pouilly-Fuissé, named after the small village of Fuissé around which the vineyards are located. These two wines—Beaujolais and Pouilly—are never very expensive and have a very pleasant taste. For these reasons, they are very popular in France.

Bordeaux or Burgundy

One of the questions that bothers beginners is the difference between a Bordeaux and a Burgundy. The first obvious difference is in the shape of the bottle: a Bordeaux bottle has straight shoulders, a Burgundy bottle does not. And now, after this small tribute to candor, let us say that red Burgundy is usually stronger than red Bordeaux. It has a more pronounced flavor, that is, it gives a taste sensation that is more direct, more mellow and more ample. Bordeaux is more discreet, more subtle, more refined. The sensation it produces lasts longer and has more resonance; it comes in waves, each of which seems to carry a distinct flavor.

Does this seem very complicated? Do not be misled; it is much simpler in practice than in theory.

One of the famous Vineyards of Burgundy

People often ask me whether Bordeaux are better than Burgundies or vice versa. This is a touchy question and one which reflects a certain naïveté. It is like asking "Are Camels better than Chesterfields?" There are as many unshakeable partisans of the one as of the other. Burgundy is usually preferred by people with strong constitutions, those who might be referred to as "Jupiterians". Others of milder temperament, older people as well, prefer Bordeaux because it is easier to digest and does not go to one's head as quickly. As André Simon said in his *Encyclopedia of Gastronomy*: "Bordeaux is the most natural of wines. No other wine has such a variety of styles and types, such perfect balance and harmony in everything that a wine has to offer: color, *bouquet*, taste and savor".

I must admit that at Maxim's a great deal more red Bordeaux is ordered than red Burgundy.

The vineyards of Champagne

One hundred and twenty-five miles northeast of Paris lies the city of Rheims and the Champagne vineyards. Here, the vintages bear the names of the villages, but these names are known only to the professionals. The public knows Champagne by the names of the firms that buy the wine from the wine-growers or co-operatives and transform it into Champagne. This process has been described in many books and, as it is purely technical, I shall not go into it here.

The commercial aspect of the production of Champagne has brought about a greater centralization than exists elsewhere as well as an amassing of immense stocks which is very impressive to see. Some cellars, such as those of Moët & Chandon at Epernay, house as many as 24,000,000 bottles distributed along fifteen miles of underground galleries.

The Champagne vineyards are at the northernmost limit of the region suitable for wine-growing, and for this reason the wine is occasionally fragile and does not always have the optimum required quality. In this case, it becomes a non-vintage Champagne. When the year's harvest yields a top quality wine however, the Champagne made from it is labeled and sold with its vintage year. These choice wines are always *brut*, that is, extra-dry. If the label indicates *sec*, it means the Champagne is sweet, and *demi-sec* means very sweet. This terminology is particular to Champagne and does not apply to wines in general.

The French are great drinkers of Champagne, and the greater part of the non-vintage production is consumed in France. The majority of vintage bottles, however, is exported.

The other French wine-producing regions: Alsace, the Loire, the Rhône and Provence

There remain four groups of vineyards which, although smaller than those we have already mentioned, deserve our attention.

The Alsatian vineyards are located on the western slopes of the foothills of the Vosges mountains, overlooking the beautiful Rhine valley. These vineyards produce dry delicate-tasting white wines such as Sylvaner and Riesling, as well as more fragrant wines such as Traminer and Gewürz-traminer. It is believed that the type of vines from which the latter are made was introduced by the Spanish at the time that the route to their northern possessions in Flanders lay through the Rhine valley. We might also point out in passing that Alsatian wines, like German wines, come in flute-shaped bottles reminiscent of the single spire of the remarkable Strasbourg cathedral.

The Loire valley produces a white wine that is generally dry and very fruity. The best known are dry wines like Pouilly-Fumé or Blanc-Fumé and Sancerre, which resemble certain white Burgundies; very fruity wines like Muscadet, and others which can be sweet or sparkling like Vouvray. From the Rhône valley come strong and generous red wines—Hermitage and Châteauneuf du Pape—and the very good rosé wine: Tavel.

The vineyards of Provence produce mostly rosé wines. This rosé is very pleasant to drink in warm weather, for it is served chilled and can be drunk in fairly large quantities without harmful effects.

A few words now with regard to spirits. First let us look at Cognacs, the senior member of the family. Like Champagne wines, they bear the names of firms. They are what is known as a "choice product" and are divided, according to quality, into different groups: the first is Three Stars: then, VSOP (Very Special Old Pale). Sometimes, the names refer to the place of origin: "Fine Champagne" and "Grande Champagne", references which can be considered as authentic titles of nobility. Since the services involved keep records only up to seven years, Cognacs never bear the vintage year. In any case, Cognacs do not age in bottles but in barrels, and, as they are generally blended, dates are hard to verify.

As for Armagnacs, the conditions are even more difficult to determine. Here, one has to rely on the brand name.

Finally, there are the white fruit spirits from Alsace: Kirsch, Quetsch, Mirabelle, and the famous Framboise, in great demand and of which excellent

A view of Maxim's famous wine cellar.

quality is hard to find. These spirits have an enticing taste and flavor, assuring their success.

This has been a very rapid survey of the vineyards of France, but I think it as unavailing to describe each wine separately as would be an attempt to describe with mere words all the flowers in a garden. One must let the wine speak for itself.

The vintage years

Wine, as we have seen, is produced only in regions with a temperate climate. Apart from the influential factors of soil, type of plant, and knowledge of its care, the vine requires sunshine, for it is the sun that ripens the grape. During fermentation, the sugar turns into alcohol and gives the wine its constitution, a bit like the flesh and bones of a human being.

It must not be concluded, however, that the more sun the better the wine. Aside from alcohol, wine contains other elements which combine to give it its individual character, its physical features and moral qualities, so to speak.

In the colder temperate regions where the amount of sunshine is variable from one summer to the next, each year produces a wine of which the quality may vary from poor to excellent (as we have already seen with Champagne). These variations in quality gave rise to the notion of vintage years, as well as to the charts that are regularly published on this subject. These charts are widely distributed, so it is only in passing that I mention the best recent years for French wines: 1947, 1949, 1952, 1953, 1955, 1957, 1959 and 1961. For German wines this list is limited to 1949, 1953, 1959 and 1961. The sun was less generous there than in France!

The publicity given the great vintage years—1959, for example, creates a heavy demand and causes the prices to rise disproportionately. The inevitable result is that the intermediate years sell less well and sometimes even below their real value. Thus, a Bordeaux wine of 1959, such as Haut-Brion or Margaux, can be quoted in New York at about $ 8 a bottle whereas the same wines, but of 1956 or 1958, sell for only $ 4. I can assure you, however, that many of the 1956 and 1958 Bordeaux were wines of very good quality. They were pleasant, fruity and full-bodied. The same is true of 1954 and 1951 wines, both unjustly ignored.

Wine is a living thing and, like all living things, it develops according to certain general rules. But each individual, each group or generation of individuals—and each growth, each group or generation of growths—has its own personality which is often distinct from the production as a whole.

Wine and its age

This brings us to the question of the age of wine. It is very pleasant to be able to say, "I drank a 1911 Chambertin", but that does not necessarily imply "It was the best wine I've ever tasted". In 1953 I remember tasting an 1893 Chambertin, that is, a sixty-year-old wine. The bottle had been lying on its side all that time in a cellar in Burgundy; the cork had been changed once, but otherwise the bottle was untouched. The wine had retained all its strength and *bouquet*, and it still set off some very pretty fireworks. Nevertheless, I think the same wine would have been just as good, if not better, thirty years earlier at just half that age.

Age is therefore not synonymous with quality, at least in respect to wine. Generally speaking, one can formulate the following rule: dry white wines should be drunk when they are young, between three and ten years of age. Red wines should be older; they are at their best between five and twenty years after their date of vintage, depending on their origin.

But let us go one step further. In the case of white wines, the more they give a pleasant sensation of acidity and an impression of fruitiness and youth, the less aging is suitable for them. This is especially true of German wines (particularly those of Moselle), Alsatian wines, Champagne, Chablis, and the dry white wines of the Loire valley. The wines of Moselle and Alsace, for instance, can be drunk within eighteen months of their production.

The white Burgundies however, which have a higher alcohol content and are therefore more full-bodied, generally take five years to reach their peak and do not improve further after the tenth year. As for white Bordeaux, they are the exception that confirms the rule. Their alcohol and sugar content is preponderant in relation to their acid content, and these wines keep their savor for many many years.

The evolution of red wines is even more varied. Their oxidation or aging process can take place very quickly as in Beaujolais, which can be drunk as early as six months following its vintage and rarely beyond five years afterwards, or it can take a very long time as in the case of certain Bordeaux that require ten years or more before the first bottle can be opened. These latter are called "Gard" wines; they are a token of farsightedness and fondness for your grandchildren who will enjoy them years later.

Whether from Burgundy or Bordeaux, wines can be either "tough" or "tender", that is, their development is either rapid or slow. It is pleasanter from some points of view to drink wines that reach their peak quickly. This is often the case with wines of the intermediate years mentioned earlier.

Matching food and wine

If a detailed study of wine may appear to be long and difficult, the art of choosing a wine to accompany a meal is an easy matter that is based on a few simple principles.

To begin with let us say that to obtain a pleasing harmony between food and wine all one must do is match their respective tastes. Let us assume that foods can be classified according to the intensity of their taste, ranging from the most subtle to the most concentrated, that is, from oysters to venison through the successive ranks of fish, poultry, white meats, red meats and game.

For the more subtle flavors, a suitable wine is one that is also light and subtle, that is, a fine dry white wine that gives a fragrant but fleeting taste sensation. As the taste of the food becomes more pronounced, the appropriate wines will go from the full-bodied whites to the light reds and, finally, to the full-bodied red wines that give a deep and lasting taste sensation.

This principle should form the basis of your choice, but you should also take the following axioms into consideration:

1) Serve a white wine before a red wine;
2) Serve a dry wine before a sweet wine;
3) Serve a light wine before a full-bodied wine.

The following is a more detailed illustration of the principles explained above:

With oysters, clams and similar shellfish: A dry, very light white wine: Alsace (Riesling); or Burgundy (Chablis).

With lean fish: A dry white wine: Burgundy (Pouilly-Fuissé) or Loire-Valley (Blanc Fumé).

With fatty fish and crustacea: A full-bodied dry white wine: Burgundy (Montrachet, Meursault).

With poultry and white meats (veal, lamb, etc.): A light red wine: Bordeaux from the Médoc region (Château Cos d'Estournel).

With red meats (beef, mutton) and pork: A fairly full-bodied red wine: Bordeaux such as a Médoc or Graves (Château Haut-Brion) or Saint-Emilion or Pomerol ; Beaujolais (Moulin-à-Vent) ; Burgundy, Côte-de-Beaune (Pommard, Corton).

With game: A full-bodied red wine: Burgundy, Côte-de-Nuits (Clos de Vougeot, Chambertin); Côtes-du-Rhône (Châteauneuf-du-Pape).

With desserts: Champagne.

This enumeration may perplex the hostess and make her wonder if she must serve a different wine with every course. No, certainly not, for the rule is flexible.

Each wine can be moved one notch in either direction. In other words, one can serve a Pouilly-Fuissé with oysters and a light Alsatian wine with lean fish. With fatty fish, salmon for example, one can serve a light red wine. Likewise, poultry can be accompanied by either a full-bodied white wine or a fairly full-bodied red wine, but the ideal is a light red wine.

There are a few special cases which I purposely did not include. These are hors d'œuvres, eggs and cheese.

Since hors d'œuvres can be either fish or meat, either red or white wine is suitable. However, as the seasoning used on hors d'œuvres is almost always very acid, a choice wine should be excluded.

White or red wine is equally good with egg dishes.

As for cheese, it has the rare gift of bringing out the best in wine (especially red wine), just as make up can beautify a face. However, the cheese course never requires a special wine; one simply finishes the one chosen to accompany the preceding course.

A final remark is necessary concerning the sweet white Bordeaux wines which have been barely mentioned thus far. These wines used to be drunk at the end of the meal to accompany a sweet dessert. Desserts do not necessarily call for a special wine, but Champagne is always ideal for the end of a meal as it not only has a pleasant taste but also aids digestion. This alternative apart, it is customary at dessert to continue with the last wine served during the meal.

Is there a particularly appropriate wine for a particular dish?

This question arises on occasion, for we all like to be original. And, to a certain extent, we can be. Let me explain. A classic dish, such as a *Steack au Poivre* or a *Sauté de Veau*, calls for a classic wine like a Pommard or Saint-Estèphe. Certain regional dishes, however, such as a *Bouillabaisse*, Alsatian *Sauerkraut*, or *Poulet à la Basquaise* should be served with a wine from the same region, e.g. a Rosé de Provence, a Blanc d'Alsace, or a Saint-Emilion.

Lesser known wines are also worth exploring. I remember lunching at an inn near New York and discovering a Bourgueil 1959 which my friends are still raving about. This relatively little-known red wine comes exceptionally from Touraine in the Loire Valley. Wines from this region are inconsistent, but the good years are enchanting. The same is true of wines from Quincy (Blanc du Centre) and Crépy (Blanc de Savoie). White wines of Château de Médoc or Graves (Haut-Brion), although little-known, are fairly safe bets. And, if you are lucky enough to unearth a white Volnay regardless of the year, your friends will consider you a wizard of wines.

One type of originality to avoid is that of serving very ordinary and high quality wines at the same meal (Rosé de Provence coupled with Dom-Pérignon, for example, or Chambertin with sparkling Vouvray). Remember, harmony is an absolute premise to good taste.

In a restaurant, let the wine-steward be your guide. At Maxim's, he will show you a list of 850 wines from which to choose; you are likely to feel a bit lost in that maze of names and years! Although most of Maxim's customers are connoisseurs and know their wines like they know their alphabet, the others trust implicitly in the wine-steward who usually begins by asking them their menu, judges the tone of the occasion, and chooses the wines accordingly.

How many wines?

Today no one feels it necessary to serve three wines with every meal —white wine with the fish course, red wine with the meat course, Champagne with dessert—unless they are having a gala dinner. It is customary to serve two wines : a white and a red (the white wine can be Champagne), but it is also altogether acceptable to serve only one. Which one? The one that goes with the main course.

If the menu includes dishes at opposite extremes of the taste chart, there are several possibilities. If the meal is not one of gastronomic sophistication, then a dry white Graves is a choice that will meet with everyone's approval. This white Bordeaux is sufficiently full-bodied to accompany a red meat and sufficiently fruity to be served with fish. Or, during warm weather, a chilled light rosé is always welcome. And finally, a supreme solution and a supreme idea: Champagne, which goes well with almost everything except perhaps game. Besides, Champagne is an ideal drink. Anyone can drink it—between meals, or at any time during the day or evening.

After a good dinner, when the conversation becomes more intense, the guests might like a refreshing drink. There is no better solution than a mixture of half Champagne and half orange juice.

How much wine should you count on per person? In polite company one bottle will serve six. However people are inclined to drink more of the first wine served with a meal, and therefore it is safer to count on the first bottle serving five, or even four if all the guests are men. For more than six people two bottles are necessary, and, if appropriate to the meal, another wine can be served.

It is customary to serve more of a common wine, such as a Bordeaux *générique*, than of a choice wine. This is not out of stinginess, but because the former are wines that one drinks without thinking and that go down easily whereas a choice wine inspires a certain amount of concentration, if not "sublime wonder". One "tastes" more than one "drinks" a choice wine, and it would be too bad to serve such a wine to people who cannot appreciate it. As a general rule, the quality of the wine should correspond to the quality of the *cuisine*. One does not serve a choice Bordeaux with corned beef hash, but one can serve a good Burgundy with a broiled steak, provided the meat is of the best quality.

Wine glasses

Should each wine or category of wines be served in a different shaped glass? Yes and no. First of all, in order to taste a wine properly the glass should be of the thinnest, finest crystal. Try it yourself and you will see what I mean. As for the quantity, I must admit I like to see a table covered with glasses, especially if they are of crystal. The play of light on them lends gaiety to the table. But aside from decorative considerations, the series of glasses begins with at least two: a water glass and a wine glass. After that, in order of importance, come the Champagne glass, the hock glass (for Rhine and Alsatian wines), the Burgundy glass, and the brandy glass.

In any set of glasses, the water glass should be the first on the left, having a greater capacity than the others. Next comes the wine glass. It has no standard shape, but it is preferable that the two glasses be fairly similar in shape; unity of style should be respected. Personally, I prefer a slightly oval-shaped glass with no decoration and a thin stem which is even more elegant if cut in facets. This glass can be used for white wine, red wine, and even Champagne. It is known, however, as a Bordeaux glass; let us call it a "fine wine" glass.

A moderate degree of sophistication calls for serving a choice Burgundy in still another type of glass with a deeper bowl and a narrower opening. This shape facilitates swirling the wine in the glass with a precise gesture to aerate it and at the same time encloses the *bouquet* in a sort of chimney.

Ultra-sophistication is attained with very large wine glasses with enormous ballooned bowls. This type of glass is reserved for very old red wines that need to be abundantly aerated before they are drunk. The glass permits you to swirl the wine around as much as you like and also better enables you to judge its delicate rust color—a bit of an affectation, but one of which I approve.

As for Champagne, any type of glass is suitable except the *coupe* which is not only ugly in shape but also invites the wine to spill down your front. I am personally partial to a tulip-shaped glass for Champagne in which you can watch the irridescent, pearly bubbles rise in spirals towards the top where they burst, diffusing the subtle fragrance of the wine. The same is true of the flute-shaped glass.

Finally, it is customary to provide a special long-stemmed glass known as a hock glass for Rhine and Alsatian wines. Hock glasses used to be

From left to right: water glass, "fine wine" glass (or Bordeaux glass), Champagne glass.

made of red or green colored glass. Purists claim that this is a mistake because the color of the glass hides that of the wine, but I rather like the idea; these spots of color greatly brighten a table.

Cognac is served in a large balloon-bowled glass. If you watch connoisseurs, you will see them swirl it around while warming the glass in the palm of their hand. The purpose of this motion is to liberate the ethers or aroma for, while wine is tasted primarily in the mouth, Cognac is tasted three-quarters in the nose and only one-quarter in the mouth—which just confirms what your nose has already told you. Liqueurs in general should be served in the same sort of glass as cocktails, but of smaller size.

Wine serving temperatures

What is the proper temperature at which different wines should be served? On this subject tradition and experience have established the norms:

Champagne: between 41 and 46° F. Dry white wine: between 46 and 53° F. Red Burgundy: between 64 and 68° F. Red Bordeaux: between 68 and 72° F.

Champagne and white wines can quickly be brought to these temperatures in a refrigerator or ice-bucket. Red wines must be treated with a great deal more care. They should be left in a warm enough room to reach their ideal temperature slowly and gradually. This is what is known as *chambrer*, or to take the chill off a wine. Above all, never attempt to hasten the process by putting a bottle of wine next to a radiator.

Usually Burgundy and Bordeaux wines are served at room temperature, but Burgundy wines, which require a slightly lower temperature than Bordeaux wines, may simply be placed in the coolest room of the house.

Some precautions to take when serving wine

Certain very old wines, and particularly red wines, may have a deposit in the bottom of the bottle. This is not a sign of poor quality; it is the

Burgundy glass, old wine glass, Brandy snifter, liqueur glass (Baccarat).

result of the slow oxidation that has taken place in the bottle and the trans-
formation of the chemical elements in the wine. Nevertheless, this is not
an excuse to serve the deposit to your guests for dessert. On the contrary,
you must decant the wine, that is, transfer it slowly and carefully from the
bottle into a glass decanter or carafe and stop pouring as soon as the sediment
appears in the neck of the bottle. The decanting will be easier if you hold
a lighted candle behind the neck of the bottle; the transparency thus created
enables you to keep a constant check on the clarity of the wine.

The fear of a slight deposit in the bottom of a bottle has led to the adop-
tion of the pouring basket. The bottle placed in such a basket lies at an
angle, so that if there is a deposit it will slowly sink to the bottom. If you
pour carefully, the wine will come out clear and without sediment.

The use of pouring baskets has become so widespread today that you
will find them used in restaurants even for red wines of recent years which
could not possibly contain a deposit. A basket makes any wine of any
vintage appear choicer and more valuable.

One more piece of advice about red wine: if you are serving a choice
wine, uncork the bottle an hour before drinking it. This is what is called
"letting the wine breathe", that is, letting the first and generally bitter-
tasting ethers evaporate. This is not necessary, in fact it is even detrimental
in the case of white wines. The good ethers of white wines are more volatile
than those of red; they would evaporate along with the bitter ethers and the
wine would lose some of its *bouquet*.

Finally, I particularly recommend pouring the wine before, and not
after, the dish it is to accompany is served. This gives your guests the
opportunity to taste the wine at their leisure and over a longer period of time.

I might add that it is incorrect to fill a wine glass to the top; it should
be filled halfway when the wine is first poured and replenished to a third
full afterwards. For the host, this implies keeping an eye on his guests'
glasses and replenishing them as necessary except, of course, when the time

comes for a change of wine.

Should one, when serving Champagne, wrap the bottle in a white napkin? This custom is totally inept. The label dresses up the bottle far more than this borrowed finery and furthermore bears the name of the wine. The label should be visible to all who wish to read it.

"Listening" to wine

Now we know everything — or almost everything — about wine. We have seen where it comes from, what it looks like, what its date of birth means, how to match it with food, and how to serve it. Let us go one step further and try to establish communication with its soul; let us listen to it. The dialogue begins from the moment it enters your mouth and floods your taste buds. The sensations or impressions transmitted by your palate are as clear, as varied, and as colorful as those transmitted by your eyes or any other sense organ.

The first impression that strikes one is determined mostly by the alcohol content and constitutes, as we have seen, the body. Wine can give an impression of fullness or solidity, sometimes to such an extent that it seems as though one could chew it.

Next comes taste. The taste of wine is based on three of the four basic taste sensations: sweet, acid, and bitter (the salty taste is excluded). The blending of these three elements provides, as with colors, a palette of subtle, rich, and infinitely varied shades. A white Bordeaux, for example, has a sweet taste first, but immediately afterwards it divulges a slightly acid taste with a touch of bitterness. These three tastes form a pleasant mixture. Each enhances the other, either by counterbalancing or emphasizing it. Moreover, each taste is distinguishable on its own. The sensations return in successive waves, each of which strikes a different chord. The greater the quality of the wine, the more chords will echo against your palate and enchant you. The initiation of the palate to these mysterious sensory impressions differentiates the man of culture from the mere human being.

Then comes an impression of texture. It can be either coarse or fine. If the wine has but one taste which it presses upon you insistently, then it is a common wine. If, on the contrary, it is full of different suggestions of taste which it reveals slowly, like the different threads in a complicated fabric, it is a wine of elegance and distinction.

Finally comes the aroma. The aroma is a more or less pronounced fragrance reminiscent of fruit such as grapes, black currants or raspberries, flowers such as violets, and odors such as that of the truffle and many others. Developed to a certain degree, an aroma becomes a *bouquet*. This term, which immediately calls up images in every language when referring to wine, has been judiciously chosen. When tasting a wine, close your eyes and concentrate; if, at that moment, flowers appear before your "inner eyes" —lots of flowers of every shape, color and fragrance, near you and around you and at all distances from you—and if this image repeats itself in successive waves, then the wine you are drinking has *bouquet*. The *bouquet* constitutes the freshness and the charm of wine, and the greater the wine the more concentrated is its *bouquet*. When wine ages, the *bouquet* fades and disappears, for the acids in the wine oxidize from contact with the small amount of air in the bottle and are transformed into ethers which give the wine a different color and taste.

Thus, all its life wine presents us with a phenomenon of alchemy. Perhaps one day someone will discover a way to bring a newly-born wine to its ideal stage of maturity in a few minutes.

Talking about wine

If you like wine, you must know how to talk about it.

Wine is a living thing which has an external appearance as well as an internal personality. One talks about it as one would talk about a person.

The vocabulary used by connoisseurs in this connection is varied, and

Grape-picking in the Rhône valley

its epithets, it must be admitted, are sometimes whimsical. But this vocabulary is also made up of conventional terms that should be defined and explained. We have already seen that the qualities of a wine are dependent upon the chemical elements of which it is composed. A good method for reviewing the terms in this picturesque glossary consists, therefore, of connecting, as follows, the epithets or expressions to the element or group of elements that give the wine its individuality.

Alcohol: With a sufficient alcohol content a wine is "full-bodied", it has "volume" or "consistency". Too much alcohol makes the wine "coarse" and "ropy". If there is too little alcohol the wine is referred to as "light", "insignificant", and "thin".

Acids: Certain acids (fixed acids) give the wine its "bite" or "punch" and also insure its longevity. Other acids (volatile acids) give it its "*bouquet*". When both types are present one says that the wine "has *bouquet*", and that it is "fruity" or "tasty". If the wine has no *bouquet*, it is "mute" or "neutral". Too much acid gives the wine real acidity. In this case, the wine is "green", "sharp", or "like a knife-blade".

Sugar: The role of sugar is mainly to counterbalance the acidity. A wine lacking sugar therefore might have a predominantly acid taste. A perfect proportion of sugar makes the wine "tender" and "supple". Too much sugar makes red wines "velvety" and white wines "sweet and soft". Occasionally this velvety quality masks a high alcohol content in which case the wine is "heavy".

Tannin: Tannin gives the wine a slightly bitter taste. This occasionally counterbalances the sugar content and brings out the *bouquet*. It is a bit like the thorn on the rose. Tannin gives the wine its "vigor", its "nerve", and its "contrast" within itself. Too much tannin makes a wine "harsh", "raw", sometimes even "tart" and "astringent". If it lacks tannin, the wine is "dull", "flat", or "limp".

Gum and glycerin: These elements soften the action of the tannin and give the wine its "mellowness". In excess quantity they make a wine "unctuous".

Harmony: The quality of a wine is judged not by the quality of the elements of which it is composed but by the relationship between them. For example, if the alcohol and acids are in the proper proportion, the wine is "flowing" and "pleasant"; if not, the wine can be "common" or "coarse". If the ideal balance exists between the sugar content and the alcohol-acid content, the wine is "well-rounded" and "enveloped"; one can say it "has character". If all of these elements are well blended, the wine is "fine", "elegant", and "delicate". With the correct amount of tannin, the wine is "generous", "rich", "full", or "strong". Finally, if nature has endowed it with a sufficient amount of glycerin, there is perfect harmony. The wine will be referred to as "harmonious" and "complete" and, if it is a great wine, one can recite the litany from the beginning, saying that it has "body", "*bouquet*", "suppleness", "fullness", and "resonance", that it is a great lord of distinction, a worthy descendant of its forebears.

Buying wine

Everything we have said up to now concerns the act of drinking. But before wine can be drunk it must be bought. How shall you go about making a sure choice among so many names and years? Unless you are an expert or a connoisseur, the safest way is to ask the advice of a specialist. You do not have to look very far; usually the person who sells the wine is a specialist. And remember that the best store is the one that offers the widest choice, for this proves that the dealer is able to discriminate.

Place your confidence in those who sell wine. They are usually sincere, for wine never leaves anyone indifferent. If you live with it long enough, you cannot help becoming interested in it and even developing a passionate interest in its activities.

Do not forget either that for a Bordeaux the name of the château where it was made constitutes a guarantee. For Burgundy or the other French vineyards, this is not the case; the name of the wine is only an indication of its taste, and that alone cannot give you an assurance of quality. For each growth there are quality selections which only the renown of the local French shipper can guarantee. His name is, of course, on the label.

Below you will find my suggestions for a cellar of sixty bottles. This selection includes a large assortment of wines, but it can be easily reduced, for reasons of space or economy, to the essentials starred on the chart, a total of about thirty bottles.

A SAMPLE CELLAR OF SIXTY BOTTLES

RED WINES (30)

Burgundy :
6 Beaujolais Saint-Amour

Bordeaux régional :
* 2 Médoc
2 Saint-Julien
2 Saint-Emilion
1 Pomerol

Rhône :
1 Tavel
1 Hermitage

1 Châteauneuf-du-Pape

Burgundy-Côte de Beaune :
1 Beaume
* 1 Pommard
* 1 Corton

Burgundy-Châteaux :
* 1 Château Durfort
1 Château Palmer
1 Château Canon

* 1 Château Petit Village
* 1 Château Cos d'Estournel

Burgundy-Côte de Nuits :
2 Vosne Romanée
1 Clos de Vougeot
* 1 Chambertin

Bordeaux-Châteaux :
* 1 Château-Margaux
* 1 Château Haut-Brion

WHITE WINES (20)

Bordeaux (dry) :
2 Dry Graves

Bordeaux (sweet) :
1 Barsac
1 Sauternes

Loire :
1 Muscadet

1 Dry Vouvray
1 Pouilly-Fumé

Burgundy (Beaujolais) :
* 5 Pouilly-Fuissé

Alsace :
1 Sylvaner

* 1 Riesling
1 Traminer

Burgundy :
* 3 Chablis
* 1 Meursault
1 Montrachet

ROSÉ DE PROVENCE (5)

CHAMPAGNE (5)

In the columns of whites and reds, the wines are listed approximately according to price, from the least to the most expensive.

The bottles should be kept

1) lying down so that the cork is always moist and does not dry out, and so that air cannot enter.

2) away from daylight and, above all, from sharp differences in temperature.

Ideally, the temperature should not go below 50° F. during the winter nor above 60° F. during the summer.

3) away from vibration.

And now, " à votre bonne santé ! "

Cocktails, Canapés

Cocktails in France are an American importation which are very often —in my opinion quite advantageously—replaced by a dry white wine, Sherry or Port, an *apéritif* based on wine, a glass of Champagne, or a wine punch. These permutations of the cocktail are equally appropriate as simple before-dinner drinks as for a cocktail party.

Instead, then, of presenting another manual of cocktail recipes, here are a few of the more original French punches, "cups", and other variations, and, to complete the French flavor of your cocktail party, a number of suggestions for canapés and other small hors d'œuvres, what the French like to call *amuse-gueules*, or tongue-teasers, and what are known in America as appetizers.

COCKTAIL

● **KIR (KIR COCKTAIL)**

7 parts dry white wine   *1 part Black Currant cordial*

One of the rare authentic French cocktails, the *Kir*, is named in honor of Canon Kir, the priest and mayor of the city of Dijon in Burgundy, the home of superb wines and the best Black Currant cordial in France.

Mix the wine and cordial together, chill, and serve in tall glasses. Add ice if desired. The amount of cordial can be varied according to your taste.

COLD "CUPS" AND PUNCHES

● **EAU DE FRAISES (STRAWBERRY PUNCH)**

12 cups water   *1 qt. fine ripe strawberries*
1 cup Kirsch liqueur   *2 1/2 cups granulated sugar*

Rinse and clean the strawberries carefully. Remove even the slightest blemish. Heat the sugar and water slowly in a large aluminum, enamel, or stainless steel saucepan (avoid a tin lining which would discolor the fruit). The minute the syrup comes to a good boil, remove from the fire and add the strawberries immediately. Cover and let steep for 1 hour.

Line a strainer with a cheesecloth rinsed in cold water. Strain the strawberries and syrup through the cloth and let drip off without pressing. Chill the *Eau de Fraises* obtained for at least 2 hours in the refrigerator. Just before serving, add the Kirsch and mix well. Serve in chilled glasses.

and Appetizers

● **COUPE DE CHAMPAGNE (CHAMPAGNE CUP)**

1 bottle dry Champagne (brut)   *1 lemon*
1 bottle dry Alsatian white wine   *Raspberries or small strawberries*

Mix the Champagne, white wine, and the juice of 1 lemon in a punch bowl. Garnish with raspberries or small strawberries. Be sure all ingredients are ice-cold or place the bowl in a larger one full of crushed ice. Avoid diluting the *coupe* with melting ice which would spoil the proportions and flavor.

● **PUNCH AU CIDRE (CIDER PUNCH)**

2 qt. hard cider   *4 oz. Curaçao liqueur*
2 oz. Grand Marnier liqueur   *2 tbsp. granulated sugar*
2 oz. Cognac brandy   *2 oranges*

Mix the cider, Grand Marnier, Cognac, Curaçao, and granulated sugar in a punch bowl. Chill and serve in tall iced glasses garnished with slices of orange. The slightly melted ice dilutes this otherwise strong punch.

● **COUPE AUX PÊCHES (PEACH CUP)**

2 bottles dry white wine   *4 large freestone peaches*   *2 cups crushed ice*
2 oz. Grand Marnier liqueur   *2 tbsp. granulated sugar*

Peel and cut up the peaches over a large pitcher in order not to lose any juice. Stir in the sugar and crushed ice. Add the white wine and Grand Marnier. Stir again, wait until the mixture is frosty cold, and serve in tall glasses, garnishing each with several chunks of peach.

● **SOYER AU CHAMPAGNE (CHAMPAGNE FRAPPÉ)**

2 bottles Champagne   *3 oz. Curaçao liqueur*   *2 oranges*
4 oz. orange juice   *6 oz. Grenadine liqueur*
1 oz. Maraschino Cherry cordial *4 cups crushed ice*

Mix thoroughly the crushed ice, orange juice, Maraschino, Curaçao, Grenadine and Champagne. Serve in tall glasses with straws, garnished with orange slices. A very refreshing summer punch.

Chilled drinks may also be served in silver cups with handles.

HOT PUNCHES

● **PUNCH CHAUD AU VIN ROUGE (HOT RED WINE PUNCH)**

2 bottles good red wine	*2 lemons*	*1 stick cinnamon*
2 tbsp. sugar syrup	*2 cloves*	

Heat the wine with the sugar syrup (boil 1 1/2 tablespoons of sugar with 2 tablespoons of water), 2 thick slices of lemon each stuck with a clove, and the stick of cinnamon. Bring to a simmer, skimming off the white froth, but do not boil. Serve very hot in heated cups with peeled lemon slices.

● **PUNCH AU KIRSCH (KIRSCH PUNCH)**

2 qt. strong tea	*4 cups granulated sugar*
6 cups Kirsch liqueur	

Make 2 quarts of good strong tea. Place the sugar in a punch bowl and pour the tea over it through a strainer. Stir until the sugar is dissolved. Add the Kirsch and light a match to it. Serve in heated cups.

● **PUNCH AU RHUM (RUM PUNCH)**

2 qt. strong tea	*4 cups granulated sugar*
6 cups light or dark rum	*2 lemons*

Made exactly like the Kirsch Punch above, substituting light or dark rum for the Kirsch. Float a slice of lemon in each heated cup.

● **PUNCH DOUX (SWEET PUNCH)**

2 qt. weak tea	*1 cup brandy*	*2 lemons*
1 cup dark rum	*2 cups lump sugar*	*2 oranges*

Prepare 2 cups of lump sugar. Rub a few of these lumps over the rind of a lemon and an orange and place them with the rest in a large saucepan. Squeeze the lemons and oranges over a strainer into the same pan. Prepare 2 quarts of rather weak tea; strain and add to the sugar mixture. Add the rum and the brandy and heat but do not boil. Serve from a heated punch bowl in heated cups.

Hot punches are particularly appetizing served in small heavy ceramic mugs.

● **PUNCH MARQUISE PAULETTE (MARQUISE PAULETTE PUNCH)**

2 bottles good white wine	*1 1/3 cups granulated sugar*	*8 cloves*
1 1/2 cups Cognac	*4 lemons*	

Heat but do not boil the wine with the sugar, the peel of 2 lemons, and the cloves. Strain through a fine cheesecloth into a punch bowl. Lower into the punch a ladle containing 1 1/2 cups of flaming Cognac (the Cognac should be warmed beforehand). Serve in hot cups with slices of lemon.

HORS D'OEUVRES OR AMUSE-GUEULES

The French term *Amuse-Gueules*, meaning tongue-teasers, includes both canapés and miscellaneous bite-sized tidbits which are attractive to look at and easy to eat with one's fingers.

Many of the latter are simplicity itself, simplicity well-laced with imagination. Small cubes of Swiss or Cheddar cheese, salami, ham, and stuffed olives, stacked up on toothpicks spiked in a grapefruit or cabbage is hardly culinary wizardry, but a clever hostess can find countless variations on even such a simple theme.

Of course, there are appetizers which require no more preparation than a transfer from package to bowl—nuts and pretzels, salted crackers—but many French hostesses take pride in serving something completely original and different...a personal touch from a personal recipe. We are therefore including not only a selection of French canapés but several recipes for other hot and cold bite-sized morsels which are quick and easy to make and will delight and impress your friends.

● GALETTES AU SEL (SALTED CRACKERS)

| *(about 3 dozen)* | *2/3 cups softened butter* | *1 1/2 tsp. salt* |
| *2 1/2 cups sifted flour* | *1/2 cup milk* | |

Mix the flour, butter, and 1 teaspoon of salt together with your hands. Work quickly; if the dough is too sticky, flour your hands. Form a round ball and chill for at least 3 hours.

Roll out the dough as thin as possible on a floured board. Cut with a 2-inch round cookie-cutter. Prick each round twice with a fork (the traditional design is in the form of a cross), and place on a greased baking sheet. Brush with the milk in which you have dissolved the remaining 1/2 teaspoon of salt. Bake 5 minutes in a hot oven (450º). As the crackers come out, brush them again with salted milk. Serve plain or spread with unsalted butter.

PREPARATION: 40 min. (plus 3 hours chilling). BAKING: 5 min.

● ALLUMETTES AU FROMAGE (CHEESE STICKS)

(about 40)	*1/2 cup cold water*	*1 tsp. salt*
2 cups sifted flour	*1 1/2 cups grated Swiss cheese*	
3/4 cup softened butter	*1 egg yolk*	

Make a *Pâte Feuilletée* with the flour, butter, and water, kneading in 1 cup of cheese at the beginning. Before folding the dough each time, sprinkle with some of the remaining cheese. Chill 15 minutes before use.

Roll out the dough in a 1/8-inch thick layer. Cut into strips about 3 inches long and 1/2 inch wide. Place on a greased baking sheet on which you have sprinkled a little flour to prevent sticking; brush with the egg yolk beaten with 1 teaspoon of water, sprinkle with cheese, and bake until golden brown (about 7 minutes) in a very hot oven (450º).

PREPARATION: 1 hr. 30 min. BAKING: 7 min.

● BROCHETTES DE MOULES SURPRISE (LITTLE MUSSEL KABOBS)

(about 20)	*6 thick slices bacon*	*1 lemon*
1 qt. mussels	*1 egg*	*Fine breadcrumbs*
1/2 lb. lean ham	*3 tbsp. butter*	*Salt, pepper*

Scrape and wash the mussels and pile them in a heavy stewpan. Heat over a medium flame about 5 to 10 minutes or until they have all opened. Remove the mussels from their shells with a sharp knife. Cut the ham and bacon into chunks about the size of a mussel. Thread onto small skewers in alternating sequence: bacon, ham, mussel, ham, bacon, mussel, etc. Continue until all the ingredients are used up. Beat the egg with 1 teaspoon of water in a dish and fill another dish with breadcrumbs seasoned with salt and pepper. Dip the skewers into the egg, then roll in breadcrumbs.

Melt the butter in a frying pan. Put in the skewers over a low flame (so that the breadcrumb coating does not burn) and fry until the bacon is done on all sides. Sprinkle with lemon juice and serve immediately.

* The liquid in the bottom of the pan after the mussels have opened can be strained through cheesecloth and used as a base for soup.

PREPARATION: 45 to 50 min. COOKING: 10 min.

Many cold variations are possible on this theme of a skewered cocktail treat. The elements involved should be cut in small chunks or slices and threaded on skewers in alternating sequence. There is no need to point out that eye-appeal is particularly important. For example:

1) Maraschino cherry, banana marinated in lemon juice, olive.
2) Melon, raw smoked ham, Swiss or yellow cheese.
3) Cooked carrot, ham, pineapple, sausage.
4) Chicken, tomato, ham, orange, Swiss or Gouda cheese, green pepper.

● TARTELETTES AUX TRUFFES (TRUFFLE TARTS)

(about 12)	1 1/2 cups heavy whipping cream	Salt, pepper
2 1/2 cups flour	7 eggs	
1 cup butter	2 cans truffle slivers	

Pour the flour in a mixing bowl. Add 1 egg, the softened butter and a pinch of salt. Knead together quickly with your fingertips, adding cold water bit by bit. You will probably use about 1 1/2 cups water. Try to knead as little as possible so that the dough will not become hard and elastic. Roll into a ball, wrap in a cloth, and chill for at least 2 hours. The longer the dough waits the better.

Grease your small tart molds (about 2 inches in diameter), roll out your dough on a floured board, and line the molds with this pastry crust. Prick the bottoms in several places with the prongs of a fork to avoid bubbles. Put in a preheated moderate oven (375º) until golden, but not brown.

Beat the remaining 6 eggs in a mixing bowl. Add the cream, truffle slivers, salt, and pepper. Fill the pastry shells with this mixture and return to the oven for at least 10 minutes.

PREPARATION : 15 min. (plus 2 hours chilling). BAKING : 20 min.

● PETITES CROQUETTES DE POISSON (MINIATURE FISH BALLS)

(about 25-30)	1/2 medium onion	Deep frying fat
2 medium potatoes	2 egg yolks	Salt, pepper
1 1/2 cups fresh or salt cod or	1 tbsp. butter	
cooked or canned salmon	Fine breadcrumbs	

Peel and boil the potatoes until done. Drain and return to the stove for a few minutes to dry out thoroughly, shaking the pan constantly to prevent sticking and burning. Remove from the fire, mash, add butter and beat until smooth. Beat in the egg yolks one at a time. Mince the fish and onion together, using a sharp knife or even a blender. Stir into the potato mixture; season well with pepper, and lightly with salt (be especially careful if using salt cod).

Roll this mixture into tiny balls between the palms of your hands (less than 1 inch in diameter). Drop them into a dish of breadcrumbs, coating them completely, and then—a few at a time—into hot deep fat (375º). Fry until golden, a matter of 2 minutes at the most. Drain on absorbent paper and serve immediately with toothpicks.

PREPARATION: 30 min. COOKING: 2 min.

● BEIGNETS SOUFFLÉS AMANDINE (ALMOND FRITTERS)

(about 12)	4 1/2 tbsp. chopped cooked ham
1/2 cup Pâte à Choux	4 tbsp. chopped toasted almonds
2 tbsp. grated Swiss cheese	Deep frying fat

Make some *Pâte à Choux*. Mix in the ham (cut in thin strips), grated cheese, and almonds. Drop small walnut-size balls of this mixture into a pan of deep hot fat which is not yet boiling. It should reach the boiling point only after the *beignets* have been dropped in. When golden brown, remove, drain, and serve on a napkin to catch any surplus grease.

PREPARATION : 20 min. COOKING : 3-5 min.

CHAUSSONS AU JAMBON (HAM TURNOVERS)

(about 20)	2 cooked chicken livers	1/2 tsp. curry powder
2 cups Pâte Brisée	2 hard-boiled eggs	Deep frying fat
4 slices cooked ham	4 tbsp. chopped parsley	Salt, paprika

Chop the ham, chicken livers, and eggs together until very fine. Add the chopped parsley, curry powder, a pinch of paprika and one of salt, and mix thoroughly together.

Roll out a very thin layer of *Pâte Brisée*. Cut into 3-inch squares. Place 1 teaspoon of filling in the center of each square and fold over to form a triangle. Press the edges together with a fork. Fry in deep fat for 3 to 5 minutes or until golden. Drain and serve piping hot.

These turnovers can be made with a variety of fillings: chopped crab seasoned with French mustard, Worcestershire Sauce, or paprika; crushed smoked haddock with mustard; caviar, chopped onion and lemon juice; chopped chicken and turkey.

PREPARATION : 15 min. (plus *Pâte Brisée*). COOKING : 5 min.

CRÈME FRITE AU FROMAGE (HOT CHEESE LOZENGES)

(about 20)	3 eggs	Fine breadcrumbs
2 1/2 cups sifted flour	1 egg white	Deep frying fat
1 cup milk	1/2 cup finely grated Swiss cheese	Salt, pepper

Mix the sifted flour and 2 whole eggs plus 1 yolk, the salt and pepper, in a mixing bowl. Stir until you have a smooth batter. Heat the milk until it boils; transfer the batter to a saucepan and add the boiling milk. Cook for 5 minutes, stirring constantly. Remove from the fire. Add the finely grated cheese and mix well. Pour the mixture onto a buttered board, spreading it to a uniform 3/4-inch thickness. Let cool.

Cut into small lozenges, dip into the 2 remaining egg whites (lightly beaten), and coat with breadcrumbs. Fry in very hot deep fat (about 390°). Drain well on absorbent paper and serve with toothpicks.

*To test the fat without a thermometer, throw in a 1-inch cube of bread; it should turn brown immediately.

PREPARATION : 1 hr. (cooling included). COOKING : 20 min.

BOUCHÉES A LA REINE (SHRIMP CUPS)

(about 20)	1 egg	1 tsp. lemon juice
1 cup Pâte Feuilletée	1/4 cup cooked mushrooms	1 tsp. chopped parsley
1/2 cup Sauce Béchamel	1/2 cup cooked shrimp	Salt, pepper

Prepare the *Sauce Béchamel*. Chop up the mushrooms and shrimp and add them to the warm sauce. Mix thoroughly, stir in the lemon juice and parsley, season, and keep hot.

Roll out a 1/2-inch layer of pastry dough. Cut with a fluted pastry cutter 1 1/2 to 2 inches in diameter. Place the disks of pastry on a moistened pastry sheet and brush lightly with beaten egg. With a sharp knife, make a small circle on the upper surface which will be the cover. Make 3 knife-pricks all the way through each *bouchée* and bake in a hot oven (425°) for about 15 minutes or until brown, dry, and crisp. If the outer crusts are still soft, the *bouchées* risk falling once taken from the oven. Take off the covers and remove any uncooked pastry dough inside. Fill with creamed shrimp, replace the covers, and serve immediately.

These pastry shells may be served with a variety of fillings: creamed chicken, creamed ham, any kind of creamed seafood, chopped meat in a *Sauce Périgueux*, creamed and seasoned hard-boiled egg, even cream cheese and chopped chives. Whatever the filling, it should be of fairly creamy consistency. Although the principle is slightly different, another way of serving these pastry shells is to fill each one with a small hot cocktail sausage.

PREPARATION: 45 min. COOKING: 15 min.

CANAPES

Here are a few French ideas for successful and original small canapés and sandwiches as well as practical hints for making them.

When making canapés or little sandwiches:

1) Always use bread at least a day or two old. Very fresh bread cannot be cut into thin slices; moreover it will soak up the filling and become soggy immediately.

2) Whole wheat, graham, or dark rye bread is particularly good with caviar and other fish eggs; also with cream or cottage cheese and nut mixtures.

3) For some canapés, tiny pastry shells, crackers, toast, or small squares, rounds, or triangles of bread fried in butter make excellent bases.

4) Have your butter soft before you start; take it out of the refrigerator well ahead of time. To make it easier to spread, beat it with a little hot water (proportions: 2 tablespoons water for 1/4 lb. butter). This will result in a soft spreadable cream with which you can easily mix mustard, crushed hard-boiled egg yolks, anchovy or tomato paste, chopped shrimp, etc.

5) Sometimes mayonnaise can be substituted for butter (for fish, shell-fish, eggs, vegetables, salads, etc.). If you make your own mayonnaise,

SUGGESTIONS FOR COLD

BASIC SPREAD	TOPPING OR FILLING	GARNISH
Butter	Roquefort cheese, chopped black olives (1)	Tomato sliver
Butter	Roquefort cheese, Cognac (1)	Almond slivers
Butter	Heavy cream, chopped almonds, chopped parsley, grated Parmesan (1)	Almond slivers
Butter	Heavy cream, grated Swiss cheese (1) Salami slice	Lemon or pickle sliver
Mustard butter (5)	Pickled beef	Apple butter
Mustard butter	Raw smoked ham	Pickled cauliflower
Horseradish butter	Smoked tongue, chicken (2)	Truffle sliver
Pimento butter	Smoked tongue	Pimento sliver
Butter	Raw smoked ham	Asparagus tips
Butter	Ham, mustard, smoked salmon, lemon juice (3)	Chopped egg, parsley
Butter	Chopped crisp bacon	Oyster
Butter	Caviar	Pimento sliver
Horseradish butter	Fish eggs (4)	Smoked salmon sliver
Horseradish butter	Herring fillet slivers	Apple sliver
Mayonnaise	Cooked fillet of sole mashed with lemon juice	Mussel

(1) Mashed together.
(2) In alternate slices.
(3) In vertical layers.

beat in a spoonful of boiling water at the very end; this will keep the mayonnaise from separating. If you have meat or fish gelatin, melt a little and add it to your mayonnaise *just* before spreading—fish gelatin for fish canapés, meat gelatin for meat or vegetables. (Commercial gelatin—which can be used for either—is easy to use but be careful not to use too much). Once you have added the gelatin, spread the mayonnaise *immediately* before it stiffens.

6) A thin flat brush will simplify the spreading of softened butter or mayonnaise for a large number of canapés or sandwiches.

7) Closed sandwiches made with untoasted bread should be pressed if made ahead of time. Pile them on a board, cover with a slightly damp tea-towel and weight them down with a second board (or tray). This will keep them flat and prevent that tired, warped look.

8) Open-faced canapés cannot be pressed. Line them up on flat trays and cover tightly with sheets of cellophane.

9) If you have a steady hand and the decorations of your canapés are fairly solid and do not risk falling off, glaze them lightly by passing a brush dipped in liquid gelatin over each one. Lay them absolutely flat to cool and dry. Once the glaze has hardened, arrange them on platters. The gelatin gives them a pretty professional touch.

CANAPES AND SANDWICHES

BASIC SPREAD	TOPPING OR FILLING	GARNISH
Curry butter	Shrimps	Green pepper sliver
Mint butter	Smoked salmon	None
Horseradish butter	Tuna fish	Chopped capers
Anchovy butter	Chopped egg, beets, parsley (1)	Anchovy fillets
Sardine butter	Raw onion, cucumber (2)	Paprika
Mayonnaise	Cucumber, egg (3)	Cocktail onion
Butter	Thin slice of truffle (4)	Chopped egg yolk
Lemon butter	Cream cheese, chopped watercress, walnuts, salt, pepper, lemon juice (1)	Smoked tongue, egg, beet (2)
Mayonnaise	Thinly sliced raw mushrooms, salt, lemon juice	Chopped parsley
Mustard butter	Chopped celery, capers, mayonnaise (1)	Ham sliver
Chive and tarragon butter	Mashed artichoke hearts (4)	Chicken sliver
Ham butter	Cucumber, radish (3)	Olive
Mayonnaise	Chopped Boston lettuce and mayonnaise (1)	Maraschino cherry
Sweet butter	Fine quality jam or jelly	Almond slivers
Butter	Finely crushed hazelnuts, sugar	Watercress leaf
Honey butter	Chopped dates and nuts (1)	Date sliver

(4) Marinated beforehand in oil and lemon juice (at least 1 hour).
(5) Any of these butters are made by mixing softened butter with the powdered or chopped substance or the juice which gives the butter its name.

INDEX

This book was prepared by the following RÉALITÉS staff

PIERRE LEVALLOIS, Art Editor
Margit Rowell, Editorial Assistant
Marie de Comeiras, Layout Assistant
Shakuntala Le Tourneur, Decoration

Researchers and Translators
Alexander Watt, Flora Feigenspan, Liesl Graz and Helen Mason
GARITH WINDSOR, Editorial Advisor

This book was printed in France by Les Imprimeries de Bobigny
on special heliographic paper manufactured by Montevrain,
and on Alfalux coated paper manufactured by Lux.   Binding
by Prache, Auger, de Franclieu et Cie.   July 1st 1962

Photographs by Luc Ionesco and
J. Fronval (51-63-67-93-99-111-121-127-213), B. Kugler (39-
66-75-139-155-191), L. Iselin (157-169-179), A. Courteville
(131-193), P. Almasy (57), E. Boubat (239), M. Desjardins
(15), A. Guillemot (27), C. Kalischer (227), P.-L. Millet (26),
G. Pétremand (175).

We would also like to thank Valentine de Miré (63-111),
Madame Jean Dugrenot, (23-29) Marie de Peretti (29) and the
following firms for their help with the photographs: A la Ville
du Puy, Au Pays Breton, Baccarat, Comoglio, Christofle,
Damiot, Richard Ginori, Puiforcat, Sanson.